WEB DEVELOPER.COM®

GUIDE TO

PRODUCING LIVE

WEBCASTS

J E A N N I E   N O V A K
P E T E   M A R K I E W I C Z

WILEY COMPUTER PUBLISHING

JOHN WILEY & SONS, INC.

New York • Chichester • Weinheim • Brisbane • Singapore • Toronto

Publisher: Robert Ipsen
Editor: Cary Sullivan
Assistant Editor: Kathryn A. Malm
Managing Editor: Marnie Wielage
Electronic Products, Associate Editor: Mike Sosa
Text Design & Composition: Pronto Design & Production, Inc.

Designations used by companies to distinguish their products are often claimed as trademarks. In all instances where John Wiley & Sons, Inc., is aware of a claim, the product names appear in initial capital or ALL CAPITAL LETTERS. Readers, however, should contact the appropriate companies for more complete information regarding trademarks and registration.

This book is printed on acid-free paper. ∞

This publication is designed to provide accurate and authoritative information in regard to the subject matter covered. It is sold with the understanding that the publisher is not engaged in rendering professional services. If professional advice or other expert assistance is required, the services of a competent professional person should be sought.

Internet World, Web Week, Web Developer, Internet Shopper, and Mecklermedia are the exclusive trademarks of Mecklermedia Corporation and are used with permission.

Library of Congress Cataloging-in-Publication Data:
Novak, Jeannie, 1966–
     Web developer.com : guide to producing live webcasts / Jeannie Novak,
     Pete Markiewicz.
          p.   cm.
     Includes index.
     ISBN 0-471-29409-8 (paper:alk.paper)
     1. Webcasting.   I. Markiewicz, Peter George, 1956– .
     II. Title.
     TK5105.887.N69   1998
     070.5'797--dc21
                                                                      98-34422
                                                                      CIP

Printed in the United States of America.

10 9 8 7 6 5 4 3 2 1

CONTENTS

INTRODUCTION

This book is designed to give developers, broadcasters, designers, and decision makers a complete introduction to Internet broadcasting, or webcasting—one of the most promising (and hyped) areas of today's Internet boom. Despite the fact that real-time sound and even video have been available on the Internet since early 1994, recent advances in hardware and software have thrust webcasting into the limelight. Webcasting is being taken seriously both on the Internet and in traditional broadcast circles, and many believe that it forms the vanguard of the long-rumored convergence of telephone, computer, and television into one digital medium. What are the real prospects of webcasting living up to these expectations? How can web developers, content providers, multimedia authors, traditional broadcasters, and Internet providers separate fantasy from reality and develop an effective webcast strategy? This book will provide answers to these questions.

How This Book Is Organized

The contents of this book may be conveniently divided into two sections. The first half of the book (Chapters 1–6) is designed to provide a comprehensive overview of the medium. This discussion considers hardware, software, technologies, and team design required for webcast productions. After a brief review of the state of webcasting in Chapter 1, "The Rise of a New Industry," Chapter 2, "Developing a Webcast Strategy," goes on to discuss the theory behind webcast production and introduces the core technologies used to implement a webcast. Chapter 3, "Webcast Equipment and Authoring Environments," introduces the technical side of the industry by discussing the equipment needed to capture and encode webcast content. The analog environment of microphones, cameras, mixers, amplifiers, and effects processors must be understood in order to develop digital webcast content. Chapter 3 is also the section where traditional broadcasters can see how their area of expertise interacts with Internet technology. Chapter 4, "Webcast Servers and Connectivity," continues the technical discussion by detailing how streaming media content is delivered through the Internet, and introduces the services provided by webcast-specific Internet providers (webcast ISPs). The chapter also considers the required server hardware, software, and tools for developers who want to run their webcast delivery in-house instead of outsourcing production. Chapter 5, "Planning, Licensing, and Management," considers the day-to-day aspects of real-world webcast production, including implementing project schedules, managing relations with venue operators, working with performers, and copyright/licensing issues. Rounding out the first part of the book, Chapter 6, "Webcast Promotion, Commerce, and Analysis," provides a guide to promoting webcasts in traditional media and on the Internet, utilizing e-commerce technology to make webcasts a paying proposition. Chapter 6 concludes by describing archive and backup strategies that preserve the completed webcast for further access by the Internet audience.

The second half of the book moves to specific areas of the webcasting world: datacasts, wordcasts, audiocasts, animacasts, and videocasts (Chapters 7–10). Chapter 7, "Datacasts and Wordcasts," introduces the concept of a datacast, which is a broadcast stream of nonaudio/video information rendered as on-screen multimedia. This chapter also considers the related text-only webcast, or wordcast (which is very useful in low-bandwidth situations), and it provides the first of several case studies featuring actual webcast sites. These studies show the reader how particular media strategies were developed and implemented successfully by a variety of groups. Chapter 8, "Audiocasts," moves into audio-only webcasts, or audiocasts, which currently form the bulk of Internet broadcasting. Recent advances in encoding and delivery of Internet audio have made it practical to provide near-broadcast-quality voice and music online, and the case studies illustrate how practical audiocasts may be created and distributed. Chapter 9, "Videocasts and Animacasts," considers the potential and reality of Internet videocast technology. A key point of this chapter is a description of the very real differences between television and webcast media, which should help the reader avoid the hype and develop useful implementations of this technology for their projects. Chapter 10, "The Future of the Webcasting Industry," concludes by looking at the trends shaping the future of the webcasting industry, providing a framework developers may use to develop their own long-term strategy.

Who Should Read This Book

The information contained in this book should benefit several types of readers. Internet service providers (ISPs) and web developers will discover a condensed guide to the software and hardware they will need to conduct webcasts for their clients. Since this audience often has little experience with traditional broadcast media, the discussion of webcast program development (Chapters 5 and 6) and traditional broadcast capture software (Chapter 3) should prove particularly useful. Interfacing with these systems is an important component of all webcasts when live events are planned.

On the other side, traditional broadcast producers, directors, and engineers familiar with this world will find the information necessary to adapt their unique skills to webcasts. Chapters 2 and 4 and the case studies will provide the most new information to this group. Broadcasters should be prepared to unlearn as well as learn production techniques as they read these chapters. The third group that will benefit from this book comprises executive-level decision makers. This group may want to skim the earlier, more technical chapters and proceed directly to the specific case studies described in Chapters 7–9. Comparing the case study strategies with their own may help these readers evaluate just how practical their own webcast plans are.

Tools You Will Need

In order to maximize the value of this book, it is important for readers to see and hear webcasts for themselves. We suggest visiting the major webcast software sites for RealNetworks (www.real.com) and Microsoft NetShow (www.microsoft.com/netshow) and downloading the free media players. Readers with older systems should also consider upgrading their systems to handle webcasts. Receiving most webcasts will require a Pentium or PowerMac computer with at least 16 megs of RAM and 1 or more gigabytes of hard disk space. It is also a good idea to have external speakers to hear just how good (or bad) webcast music can sound.

What's on the Web Site

You may access online information related to the book by logging on to our support site at kspace.com/webcasting. This site contains a link to the companion web site for this book at www.wiley.com/compbooks, which features all the links from the manuscript, as well as additional listings for outstanding webcast sites. The links leading to the case study sites will be the most valuable for those who want to see real-world applications of the technology. Hardware and software specialists may use the other links to access current technology and check the progress of professional organizations that are promoting industry-wide standards. The success of radio and television broadcasts is due in no small part to agreed-upon media standards, and consolidation around a universal standard will speed webcast adoption by the Internet audience.

Conclusion

The webcast industry is growing at a rapid and exciting pace, and we hope this book will provide the information you need to begin working in this fast-growing and challenging area of Internet communication. In many ways, the webcasting industry is today where the Internet was as a whole in 1994—undergoing rapid expansion with plenty of opportunities for developers to participate in creating the next mass medium. Good luck with your own webcast productions!

PART ONE

OVERVIEW OF WEBCAST PRODUCTION

THE RISE OF
A NEW INDUSTRY

T
he weekly television series, *Millennium* (www.foxworld.com/millnium/), featured a new variation on an old theme: the witness of a murder by people powerless to prevent it. The twist was that the witnesses saw the murder scene online—transmitted to them via webcast.

After an uncertain and frequently overhyped start, *webcasts*—or Internet-based *broadcasts*—are emerging as the hottest growth area of the virtual world. Webcasts are attracting sizable audiences, and market research is already showing a measurable impact on web surfing and online commerce. The integration of web content with broadcast television by WebTV (www.webtv.net) signals the ongoing migration of traditional broadcast to a new model that embraces the Internet.

The purpose of this book is to introduce the reader to the complete process of creating and executing a successful webcast within the limits of content, budget, and technology. It will be valuable to web developers seeking to expand their online work into *streaming* media development; content providers looking for a way to deliver audio, video, or multimedia via the Internet; and engineers, producers, and other broadcast professionals planning to apply their expertise to this new medium.

Definition of Webcasting

Due to the growing media attention surrounding Internet-based broadcast, the term *webcast* is frequently applied in a confusing fashion. In the recent past, standard web sites were erroneously promoted to media companies as comparable to television, which is in fact a radically different medium; it is one-way, noninteractive, and does not require active participation from its audience. More recently, mass email and web sites utilizing *Active Server Pages (ASP)* and *dynamic HTML (DHTML)* have been compared to broadcasting. For the purposes of this book, the use of the term "webcast" will be limited to Internet content matching the following criteria:

Streaming data. Webcasts send a constant flow of information, known as a *media stream,* to their audience with only occasional pauses. This constant flow distinguishes a webcast from standard web browsing, in which small amounts of content (web pages) are repeatedly selected and downloaded by the end user. While streaming audio and video are common formats for webcasts, they are not all-inclusive. Alternate webcast formats include *wordcasts* of streaming text in a banner ad or chat window, *datacasts* relaying ambient temperature records of a putative bat house, and streaming multimedia showing animated features to the audience. Technologies and industry standards, such as Microsoft's *Active Streaming Format (ASF),* are being developed to integrate all these streaming formats into a unified whole.

Unique time and place. While webcasts may be archived on the Internet for *on-demand* viewing, they may also be presented live. Examples include play-by-play sporting events, concerts, and corporate board meetings. This imposes constraints of time and place not normally found on the web, which is more similar to a print publication than a live show. Unlike traditional radio and television broadcasts, webcasts may be live without supporting CD-quality sound or the "full-motion full-screen" video we see with television broadcasts. Many Internet webcasts use slow technologies (such as web-based cameras that send a single frame to the Internet on a scale of minutes to hours).

Interactivity. A broadcast stream does not become a webcast simply by being digitized and sent through the Internet. By using Internet protocol, all webcasts acquire the potential for two-way communication unparalleled in traditional mass media. As an example, webcasts using Perceptual Robotics, Inc. (www.perceptualrobotics.com) video cameras allow the audience to point and control shots taken by cameras. Other webcasts may encode information linking to informational web pages or discussions between the audience and webcast participants. Figure 1.1 uses a plot of transmission speed versus interactivity to illustrate the difference between webcasting, other Internet protocols, and traditional broadcasting.

Distinct from push technology. In 1997, the terms "webcasting" and "push" were often used interchangeably, but they have since become separate Internet technologies. Push refers to a variety of strategies used to collect content from the Internet and automatically deliver it to the end-user's hard disk. Content collection follows specific filtering guidelines to form a push channel, and users are presumed to prefer browsing pushed content to searching for it on the general Internet. Webcasts are different from push in supporting delivery of a single media stream rather than automatically delivering a subset of total Internet content.

Advantages of Webcasting

The value of webcasting (like the Internet itself) has often been questioned. As an example, consider the webcast network created by Broadcast.com (formerly AudioNet [www.broadcast.com]), whose primary content consists of repurposed radio broadcasts gleaned from the same distribution networks used by conventional media. Why should site visitors bother to use expensive computer technology to receive a signal readily available through $10 radios? The success of Broadcast.com and other services highlights the unique features of the Internet that make it an attractive alternative to traditional broadcast:

Low cost. As a "network of equals," the Internet allows webcasters to develop and deliver their content using computers similar to high-end consumer hardware. The low cost of this equipment allows almost anyone to become involved in webcasting. IP *multicast* networks allow a single webcast stream to be replicated for delivery to tens of thousands of potential viewers for several thousand dollars a month. Low costs allow small and independent broadcasters to repurpose

Figure 1.1 Comparison of webcasting, other Internet protocols, and traditional broadcasting.

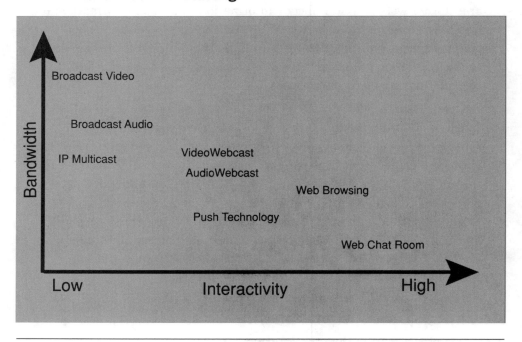

content for a fraction of their current broadcast budgets, making it possible for them to compete effectively with large media companies.

Niche audience. The Internet enables the unique capability to reach small audiences with wide geographic dispersion. For this reason, it is possible to design webcasts targeted at tiny audiences that are ignored by conventional broadcast.

Media diversity. Webcasts are steadily moving toward the integration of text, graphics, audio, video, and online chat with audio/video signals. Within the webcast itself, new technology allows hyperlinks from characters or regions within the video image to link back to web pages. Email, chat, and online commerce add interactive features unavailable in current mass media.

On-demand. The digital nature of the Internet and the power of the audience's computers make it simple to create archives of webcast content. Visitors to a webcast may store the information on their hard disks or copy it to new media such as *CD-RW* drives (www.verbatimcorp .com/cdrwspe.htm) for later use. Content providers may create large media databases indexing their old webcasts for access—and new search engine software allows site visitors to conduct searches based on audio and video attributes, as well as text-based descriptions. By providing constant access to broadcast-style information, on-demand webcasts challenge the very notion of time slots so important in traditional broadcast. For example, it is unlikely that the Internet will ever have a must-carry rule (in which broadcasters are required to carry signals from multiple sources) like that found in network and cable television.

Audience growth. A recent study by European consultants at Nua (www.nua.ie/surveys/how_many_online/) estimates that at the start of 1998, the number of Internet users worldwide reached 100.5 million, with the number expected to double by 2001. FIND/SVP (etrg.findsvp .com/timeline/trends.html) estimates that 75 million Americans will use the Internet in 1998. The web is pulling audiences away from traditional media. A new study by Price Waterhouse (www.pw.com) indicates that Internet use has displaced television viewing in many households. As many as one-third of this group will have the means and interest to receive webcasts at bandwidths higher than the current 56K modem standard by 2001. In parallel with this remarkable growth, webcast technology is being upgraded to support an ever-larger number of users. The first webcasts in 1994 played to audiences that numbered in the dozens. Currently, a single media server supports hundreds of audio or videocast streams, and multicast technology widens this reach to tens of thousands of individuals.

Entry level. Unlike other media that are usually controlled by established media conglomerates, the Internet is wide open. The movers and shakers of tomorrow's media may be seen creating today's webcasts, and groups of all sizes may use webcasts to get in on the "ground floor" of the dominant medium for twenty-first century communication.

Limitations of Webcasting

Despite the promise of webcasting, it is still a long way from providing the immersive audio/video experience enabled by traditional broadcast. In particular, traditional broadcasters seeking to expand their content into the new medium need to know the limitations of webcasting, which include:

Quality. The low data-transmission speeds characteristic of today's Internet impose severe limitations on the quality of the webcast experience. While a direct broadcast satellite (DBS) dish may receive data in the 2Mbps range, a modem is limited to 0.05Mbps. These speeds may provide tolerable audio quality (comparable to FM radio), but restrict video to a mere 1.5" × 2.5" screen. Video runs in the 5–15 frames per second range, and motion often contains artifacts—rendering an action scene (e.g., a basketball game) almost unrecognizable.

Small audiences. Unlike radio and television, webcasts require a dynamic connection between the computer providing the content, or *media server*, and the end-user's equipment. This places major limitations on the number of users able to view a webcast. Current computer technology limits the audience to about 1,000 per webcast media server—puny by the standards of other media. While strategies that replicate content across a large number of media servers (collectively called *multicast*) may increase audiences, most older computers can't handle webcast data; and many webcast formats require the user to download a custom software player. These factors all conspire to restrict webcasting to *narrowcast* audiences of a few thousand.

Multiple standards. Webcasting is a new medium, with the resulting large number of incompatible hardware and software standards competing for dominance. Major commitments to one standard are difficult because hardware and software are in a state of rapid flux.

No formulas for success. The Internet is so different from other media that formats that work well in broadcast (e.g., sitcoms) may utterly fail to capture an audience. Webcasters planning to work in the medium must be willing to take risks to develop new and untested content forms in order to determine what will work best.

History of Webcasting

The history of webcasting is confined to the narrow band of time dating from the rise of the commercial Internet in 1993 to the present. Running in "Internet time," webcasting has repeated the stages passed through by other media at such a dizzying pace that it is often difficult to distinguish between current and obsolete technology among the haze of press releases and industry deals.

Pre-Internet. In the early 1990s, major media groups updated interactive broadcast concepts originally developed in the 1980s into the "information superhighway." The chief driver for the new medium was expected to be on-demand delivery of feature films. Phone and cable companies began rapid development of the digital set-top boxes customers would need to access the "500 channel" universe. Despite high hopes, these efforts have largely ended in failure. A symbol of this change occurred in December 1997, when Time Warner (www .timewarner.com) shut down its Full Service Network, an interactive TV trial in Orlando, Florida. Despite some renewed interest, most groups have modified their plans away from interactive TV to the Internet/webcast paradigm.

MBONE. The first true webcasts ran during 1994 over the experimental *MBONE* network (see Figure 1.2). This protocol is a form of *IP multicasting,* which has the ability to replicate webcast content to thousands of servers, providing increased access to content without overloading network connections. Access to these events (which included music concerts and full-length feature films) was confined to users with high-end Sun (www.sun.com) workstations at their disposal. MBONE's multicasting technology allowed the primary media server to distribute its signal to other repeater servers on the network. This approach made efficient use of bandwidth and has since become a major component of commercial webcasting.

Figure 1.2 The MBONE Information Web (www.mbone.com).

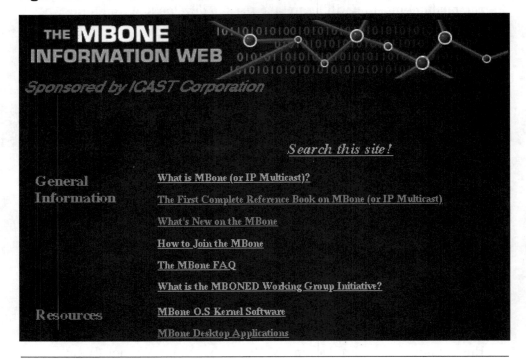

MBONE was a noncommercial testbed for Internet broadcast and is currently being supplanted by a variety of protocols. While MBONE developed concepts for large-scale webcasts, smaller-scale shows were available through White Pine Software's CU-SeeMe (www.wpine .com). Many MBONE concepts have been transferred to the IP Multicast Initiative (www.ipmulticast.com), and MBONE-style multicasts are becoming increasingly common on the Internet.

Streaming audio. The first contact most Internet users had with webcasting came in 1995 when Progressive Networks (renamed RealNetworks at www.real.com) released its RealAudio server and client programs. Unlike earlier Internet audio, RealAudio started playing as soon as the user chose to hear it and continued until the end of the webcast. Initially confined to low-quality audio delivered by

14.4 modems, RealAudio won a wide audience by offering its end-user software for free over the Internet. Its spread was also enhanced by broad cross-platform support of Mac, Windows, and UNIX systems. To promote the nascent webcast market, RealNetworks also created web sites dedicated to webcasting such as Timecast (www.timecast .com). Today, RealNetworks' RealAudio is the dominant streaming audio webcast technology, and other companies have adopted that firm's business strategy to promote their own expansion.

Webcams. In 1995, Netscape added HTML tag extensions to its browser that supported automatic web page updates. A second update allowed developers to write *CGI (Common Gateway Interface)* scripts that sent a sequential series of images to a web page. Adapting this technology to overcome the limitations of slow Internet speeds, video and multimedia enthusiasts created ambient "slow" television consisting of single-frame updates transmitted on a scale of seconds to hours. Cameras providing this content were mounted on beach fronts, ski slopes, and circus tents, and soon became known as *webcams* or *spycams*. Despite the slow frame rates, webcams now constitute a popular area of ambient webcast, be it the conference room occupants of JPL's Mars Observer project (see Figure 1.3) or the street corner of the Elbo Room (see Figure 1.4). As end-user connectivity improves, the screen refresh rates of these webcams are increasing, and older methods are being supplanted by commercial webcast servers.

Streaming video. Xingtech Streamworks (www.xingtech.com) was the first to demonstrate a working Internet-based video system for 28.8 modem speeds. Based on the *MPEG (Motion Pictures Expert Group)* compression system developed for digital broadcast and CD-ROM systems, it provided a jerky "talking head" image somewhat larger than a postage stamp. The availability of this Internet video system induced other developers to create alternate compression schemes using *wavelet* (www.harc.edu/HARCC.html) technology. Wavelet compression uses fundamentally different coding algorithms, or codecs, to support high-quality video through low-bitrate Internet connections. Streaming video solutions were quickly developed by RealNetworks

Figure 1.3 Mars Observer Conference Room (mars.jpl.nasa.gov/mgs/realtime/mgsroom.html).

(through RealVideo, companion software to RealAudio), VDO (www.vdo.net), Vivoactive (now part of RealNetworks), and Vextreme (now part of Microsoft's NetShow webcast system). By late 1997, Internet video supported bandwidths between 28.8 and 512Kbps, and the images were often accompanied by a streaming audio soundtrack.

Streaming animation and multimedia. Macromedia's *Shockwave* (www.macromedia.com) initially brought the complex multimedia characteristic of the CD-ROM world to the web. Early versions of Shockwave were nonstreaming and required the user to download large files before viewing; several groups worked to convert multimedia from static to dynamic streaming formats. With the release of Macromedia's

Figure 1.4 The Elbo Room (www.justsurfit.com/elboroom/cam.shtml).

Flash and mBED's Interactor (www.mbed.com), authoring platforms for real-time delivery of animation during webcasts have become a reality. Flash and Interactor allow multimedia-style animation and interactive controls to be linked with broadcast-style audio and video. Streaming animation protocols have been integrated into webcast audio and video systems, and the release of RealPlayer G2 in 1998 by RealNetworks provided end users with a player capable of delivering audio, video, and multimedia webcasts with equal ease. Figure 1.5 shows an example of Flash-based animation delivered as a webcast on the RealNetworks site, illustrating that streaming animation has joined streaming audio and video as a component of webcasting.

Figure 1.5 Flash-based animation delivered as a webcast on RealNetworks (www.real.com).

Multicasting. Despite the presence of MBONE, the initial commercial webcast systems used *unicast* technology (see Chapter 2, "Developing a Webcast Strategy"), which allows the delivery of multiple webcast streams from a single media server. Conventional computers cannot support more than approximately 1,000 users, so unicast technology poses serious problems when scaled for large audiences. In 1997, many servers began to support MBONE-like multicast protocols, and groups such as RealNetworks, Uunet (www.uu.net), MCI (www.mci.com), and America Online (www.aol.com) developed rental networks based on these standards. A global multicast standard is currently being developed by the IP Multicast Initiative (www.ipmulticast.com).

Standards consolidation. With the entry of Microsoft into the webcast market in 1997, dozens of incompatible standards developed in 1995 and 1996 underwent rapid consolidation. After its widely publicized buyout of WebTV Networks (www.webtv.net), Microsoft purchased video maker VXtreme (www.microsoft.com/netshow/vxtreme) and licensed both RealAudio/RealVideo and VDO (www.vdo.net) protocols for its proprietary Active Streaming Format (ASF). This format provides a method of synchronizing multiple audio, video, and multimedia streams into an integrated webcast presentation. Embodied in the Netshow (www.microsoft.com/netshow) system, ASF is being promoted as a universal standard for delivering webcasts. Competition for ASF has emerged from the World Wide Web Consortium (W3C) *Synchronized Multimedia Integration Language (SMIL)*. SMIL (www.w3.org/ TR/WD-smil) provides a text-based tag markup format for synchronized streaming multimedia, freeing developers from proprietary formats and enabling multiple vendors to supply software tools. Other groups are consolidating around open-standards players and servers developed with the *Java* programming language. By using this increasingly popular standard, webcasts may be delivered to any end user without requiring download and installation of a software plug-in.

Who Should Produce Webcasts?

A recent press release on the RealNetworks site (www.real.com) indicated that web sites enhanced with RealAudio/RealVideo had a 38 percent improvement in traffic over sites not featuring this technology. This study confirms the informal consensus that end users increasingly evaluate web sites based on their ability to deliver advanced media. While all web developers may find value in developing webcasts, certain groups—ranging from independent performers webcasting from a local club to marketers interested in adding webcasting to their advertising and promotion efforts—are likely to receive special benefit in the near term. Traditional broadcasters may also receive benefits from repurposing their content for the Internet. Some groups that may benefit from webcasts include:

Independent performers, musicians, producers, and filmmakers. As with any new medium, companies providing webcast technology and services are actively seeking content. This creates a major opportunity for independent content developers often denied access to traditional broadcast media. Many webcast sites such as *VDOIndies* (www.vdoindies.com) accept and post audio and video from independents at no charge. Taking advantage of sites like this is an economical way for independents to join the webcasting revolution.

Marketing professionals. The ability to reach the Internet's high-end demographic enhances advertising and promotional campaigns. A key area is banner advertising, which is quickly moving from static images to displaying audio and video components. Advertising may also be directly embedded in the webcast stream itself.

Traditional film, television, and radio industries. Classic, rare, and hard-to-find television programs and films may be repurposed for webcasting and attract a fan audience. Examples of general use include promotional trailers at MovieLink (www.777film.com), interviews at Broadcast.com (www.broadcast.com), and live events centering around Oscar night (www.oscar.com).

Venue operators. The ability to stream a live broadcast can do wonders to extend a regional venue's audience into a global demographic. Examples of venues that have relied on webcasting for this purpose include the Troubadour (www.troubadour.com) and the Electronic Cafe International (www.ecafe.com).

Sound engineers and camera operators. As webcasters enter the realm of broadcast-style production, they need help from professionals who have experience in this area. Sound engineers are necessary to ensure that a live performance reaches the computer hardware sending it to the Internet, and camera operators can provide broadcast-style zooms, cuts, and pans during live events.

Internet service providers. Certain Internet service providers (ISPs) that make a special effort to support the requirements for webcasts stand to become the media giants of the next century. Opportunity exists at the level of delivery, live studios for webcast production, and even original content development.

As the quality of webcasts rises, the arts and entertainment industry will have an increasing stake in the Internet, both as an alternative method for delivering content to a worldwide audience and in licensing issues concerned with sending content over this new channel. For this reason, entertainment and commercial organizations also need to keep informed of this rapidly growing field.

Examples of Webcasting

For a market in its infancy, Internet webcasting has already produced an astonishing array of services. The following highlights some interesting webcasts available on the Internet today. Webcasting site archives are available from RealNetworks' Timecast (www.timecast.com) and via general search engines such as Yahoo! (www.yahoo.com) and AltaVista (www.altavista.com).

Ambient webcasts. Webcams are usually used in *ambient webcasts,* which consist of an unattended webcam pointed at a scene from which it relays images automatically at a frame rate ranging from seconds to hours. This low-bandwidth format is used on tens of thousands of sites scattered over the world. Sites such as Yahoo Deutschland's ConnecTV (www.contactv.2nd.net/) provide searchable databases of web cameras pointed at unlikely targets. NASA (www.nasa.gov) has been especially active in using this basic webcast technology. Web sites such as the Spacezone (www.spacezone.com/ nasavid/85vid.htm) and Lunar Prospector (www.lunar.arc.nasa.gov) feature cameras following the activity of Mission control or engineers assembling next-generation spacecraft. The United Space Alliance Space Shuttle Tracking Monitor, shown in Figure 1.6, provides multimedia-based webcasts coupled with feeds from NASA television. Visitors to the site may load Java applets that dynamically display the orbital positions of the Shuttle, the Mir spacestation, and other satellites. A good directory of sites using webcams may be found at EarthCam (www.earthcam.com).

Figure 1.6 Java applet on the United Space Alliance site (www.unitedspacealliance.com/live/) showing shuttle position in real time.

Internet radio. Thousands of radio stations now repurpose their content for the Internet; subsequently, their audiences have grown so significantly that they require attention by licensing and performance rights organizations. Early pioneers such as Radio HK (Figure 1.7) have been joined by new arrivals including GRIT Internet Broadcasting (www.grit.net), L.A. Live (www.lalive.com), and CBS Sportsline Radio (ps2.sportsline.com/u/radio/live/). The MIT list of radio stations (wmbr.mit.edu/stations/list.html) recently began listing "bitcasters" among its archives. With its less demanding bandwidth and hardware requirements, Internet radio is currently the brightest spot in the webcast scene and may provide the first large-scale commercial success for this new medium.

Figure 1.7 Radio HK (www.radiohk.com/radio/).

Traditional television and film. Until recently, television producers saw the web solely as an advertising and promotion medium, and focused their efforts mainly on increasing web traffic. With the appearance of WebTV and other Internet-television hybrids, however, many groups are exploring a much closer association. The People's Court (www.peoplescourt.com) provides live video streams of courtroom cases and runs an interactive poll with web users asking who should win the case. The tallies are integrated into the show tape, which airs weeks later on traditional broadcast. Elsewhere, trailers promoting network television are stored on-demand in UltimateTV's (www.ultimatetv.com) Promo Lounge, shown in Figure 1.8.

Music promotion. Sites such as the authors' Kspace Independent Internet Artists (www.kspace.com) have provided streaming audio

Figure 1.8 UltimateTV's Promo Lounge (www.ultimatetv.com).

clips for independent artists since the advent of RealAudio. Enabling end users to immediately hear music has effectively translated to sales and promotion. As streaming video became practical, groups such as SonicNet (www.sonicnet.com) implemented an ad-supported site that premieres new music videos (see Figure 1.9). The service currently downloads more than 1,000 videos daily from the site, challenging the MTV broadcast model with on-demand webcasts.

Sports. The highly focused interest of spectator sports audiences makes them especially attractive to webcasters. During 1996 and 1997, AudioNet (now Broadcast.com) conducted webcasts of more than 2,500 men's and women's NCAA games during the NCAA basketball season. Groups including InterneTV (www.itv.net) provide pay-per-view webcasts of live sporting events. Not to be outdone, traditional broadcasters including Army Sports Radio (www.usma.army.mil/ Football), Sports Byline USA (www.sportsbyline.com), and Outdoor Life Cable Network (Figure 1.10) have moved to online webcasts.

Original content. A few bold developers are moving beyond repurposed content and developing their own webcasts. These groups are frequently Internet service providers (ISPs) that use it to enhance their prestige. An example of an original webcast may be seen at InterneTV's Austin. Shown in Figure 1.11, this online soap consists entirely of RealVideo, VDO, and Vivoactive clips arranged and "framed" with web-based content. Other original webcasts include Tech Talk (www.ttalk.com) and Musical Starstreams (www.starstreams.com).

Webcast calendars. The time-dependent nature of live webcasting has introduced a need to tune in at the right time. To answer this

Figure 1.9 SonicNet's Streamland (www.streamland.com).

Figure 1.10 Outdoor Life Cable Network (www.greatoutdoors.com).

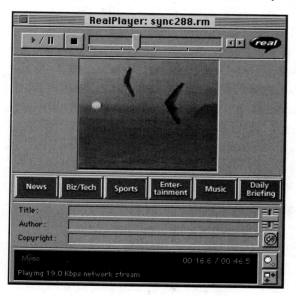

need, companies such as RealNetworks have created services such as the Timecast web site, shown in Figure 1.12, which lists thousands of audiocast and videocast providers, along with dates and times for events.

Media aggregators. Some groups, such as Broadcast.com, have moved beyond listing content to providing complete webcast services to individuals and companies (see Figure 1.13). These media aggregators list live and recorded webcast content. Broadcast.com currently delivers more than 200 live and on-demand webcasts, including some 175 radio and television stations, play-by-plays of thousands of college and professional sporting events, live music including concerts and club performances, and on-demand audiocasts for more than 1,600 full-length CDs.

On-demand media archives. Perhaps the most exciting aspect of live webcasts is their integration into the on-demand browsing model

Figure 1.11 InterneTV's Austin (www.intertv.com/austin/).

that is so successful on the web. Unlike media aggregators, these archives exclusively store recorded content. With media storage becoming cheaper by the month, it is increasingly practical for web sites to host large webcast archives. A pioneer in this area is LA-based VideoDome (Figure 1.14), whose site lists promotional and infomercial webcasts among its offerings. Freed from the restrictions of broadcast time slots, media archives may offer the public little-known content and information of interest to unique niche audiences.

Figure 1.12 RealNetworks' Timecast (www.timecast.com).

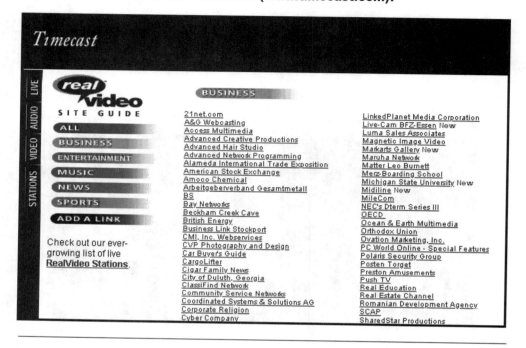

Figure 1.13 AudioNet's CD Jukebox (www.audionet.com).

Figure 1.14 VideoDome (www.videodome.com).

Next . . .

Webcasting may not be for everyone; search engine or stockbroker web sites, for example, may draw little benefit from real-time Internet broadcasting in its current form. But for groups with a compelling reason to use streaming content that are able to construct the infrastructure and management needed to support a project, webcasting may provide a major benefit. In the next chapter, the basics of developing the webcast production team are discussed, along with a strategy for identifying and developing appropriate content.

PART TWO

THE PRODUCTION PROCESS

DEVELOPING A WEBCAST STRATEGY

D ue to the high profile of webcast initiatives, many groups feel a need to get involved in webcast production. As with any medium, the real value of such an effort varies widely depending on planning, content, and features of the intended audience. A common mistake is to focus on the glamour of the technology while neglecting the critical elements of production design, content development, and—most important—team development. Lack of attention to these areas has led to many disappointing webcasts. To prevent this problem, the first thing aspiring webcasters must do is remove their propeller hats and realize that they have left the programmer-Internet guru world for the content business!

Throughout the rest of this book, the individual or team responsible for staging a webcast will be referred to as the *producer*. Similar to a producer in the traditional broadcast industry, the webcast producer is responsible for organizing content and technology and must develop a strategy that puts all these elements in place by the time the actual webcast occurs. It is necessary for the producer to develop a plan containing a timeline that covers all aspects of the project and justifies the funds being spent. Hardware and software concerns are only the beginning; real-world issues such as camera placement and performer salaries are also part of a successful webcast.

This chapter considers the first stage of webcast production: the development of a clear webcast strategy. Attention to concept development will help focus the webcast and ensure that it is appropriate for the target audience. Developing an overall strategy takes several steps. First and most important, the developer must put together a webcast production team with the skills and experience necessary to handle all aspects of the production. The basic concept must be evaluated in terms of current Internet realities and modified as necessary. Once an appropriate concept is defined, it is necessary to elaborate on the original webcast concept in terms of its target audience. After content and audience are defined, an appropriate quality of transmission and webcast delivery format must be selected. The basic strategy is completed by choosing the default hardware/software platforms that will be used in actual development.

The Webcast Production Team

The first step in planning a webcast is to define and assign the various jobs of the production team. Figure 2.1 illustrates positions on the team in the form of an organizational flowchart. Depending on the content, webcasters have developed a variety of team organizations drawn from broadcast, multimedia, and print worlds. The following provides one possible breakdown of job positions for a typical webcast:

Producer. This individual is the head of the team and is responsible for coordinating the activities of all other individuals.

Content developer. Often incorporated into the producer position, this individual provides production skills and management for the

Figure 2.1 Diagram of the webcast production team.

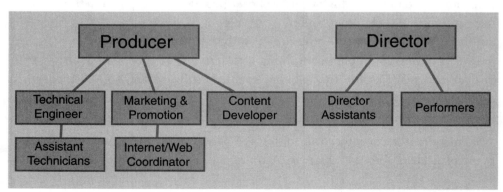

material included in the webcast. Possible duties of the content developer include scriptwriting and the selection of content, presentation formats, and software platforms.

Director. The director coordinates the movement and presentation of people and objects in front of the camera, including props, performers, and announcers. The director monitors the webcast to ensure that the content is being presented effectively during the event. The director also coordinates individuals responsible for scenery and costumes, and directs the cuts and pans between audio and video input.

Performers. This group includes individuals actually seen or heard during the webcast, including actors, musicians, news announcers, and hosts.

Technical engineer. This individual is responsible for ensuring that all the complex hardware and software needed to support the webcast operates correctly. The technical engineer should have a wide range of knowledge from analog devices such as lights, cameras, and microphones to computers, interface boards, and network connections. Strong "people skills" will also be necessary to deal with other groups supporting the webcast, particularly the ISP providing the connection to the rest of the Internet. This individual should have experience in real-time monitoring and troubleshooting. More than one live webcast has been ruined by an unexpected last-minute incompatibility between programs, or failure to check that the ISP is actually receiving digital information.

Assistant technicians. Working with the technical engineer, these individuals are responsible for monitoring individual components of the webcast infrastructure. Examples include camera and lighting operators, sound mixers, and software experts.

Marketing director. This individual is responsible for promoting the webcast and its content online and offline. Duties include posting to search engines, securing an audience of reviewers, and creating press releases for traditional media. The marketing director may also analyze statistics of visitor traffic for a webcast and correlate them with demographics or purchasing patterns.

Effective and Ineffective Webcast Content Features

In the development phase of a webcast project, the webcast team will need to consider whether the envisioned content will make good use of the Internet medium. The following lists some features that make for effective webcast content, along with examples:

- Local/regional events are more effective than nationally televised events, since anyone can see the national events—on a much larger screen!

- Works-in-progress, outtakes, or "director's cut" film excerpts are more effective than a broadcast of a complete film in theatrical release, since the shorter excerpts are less bandwidth intensive and are rarely seen.

- If exhibiting a full-length film is a requirement, showing a rare, recently discovered film (e.g., from the silent era) or a television show that is no longer in syndication is more effective than showing a current film or video. This is something your audience will not be able to see anywhere but on the Internet.

Internet/web coordinator. By its very name, a webcast attests to its close association with the hypertext browsing world of the web. The Internet/web coordinator creates and maintains any associated web sites and is responsible for archiving webcasts for on-demand viewing. Other duties include overseeing the multimedia components of the webcast and posting related information to the web site.

Other strategies for organizing the production team may be readily devised. For small-scale webcasts, it may be sufficient to have a team consisting of one producer and one engineer. Larger groups from the broadcast industry may elect to add webcast responsibilities to the existing job descriptions of their production team. Solo webcast development, however, is not a viable option except for ambient unattended webcasts.

- Infomercials are more effective than 30-second commercial spots, since more information is provided about products. This takes advantage of the information-gathering orientation of the Internet audience.

- Ambient scenery with an exercise training voiceover is more effective than a standard video workout because the latter demands full-length, moving shots of people, which are difficult to see in a small webcast window.

- Pay-per-view live events (such as sports events or concerts) are more effective than pay-per-view feature films because of the interactive nature of live events.

- Content containing censored or controversial material is more effective than uncensored content, since the Internet is an uncensored, decentralized medium.

- Architectural walk-throughs (such as museum or gallery tours) are more effective than viewing stand-alone images of famous works of art, since anyone can see the latter in an art book. A walk-through creates a sense of place that can only be experienced otherwise by visiting that particular museum or gallery.

| NOTE | **DECLINE OF THE WEBMASTER**

During the first few years of the commercial Internet explosion, a so-called webmaster often had complete responsibility for creating and managing Internet content. Most developers now reject this as impractical. In fact, the 1997 Annual Webmaster Survey conducted by *WebWeek Magazine* (www.webweek.com) indicated that many developers rejected the use of the "webmaster" term to force recognition that Internet projects are a team effort.

Identifying Webcasting Content Goals

Until recently, running a webcast was practically an end in itself; simply staging the event generated publicity and recognition. As webcasts become more common and groups experienced in traditional broadcasting enter the area, content will become the primary determinant of a webcast's success. The following questions might be considered by the webcast production team to help analyze their intended content before beginning the project. Content appropriate for webcasts versus content appropriate for traditional media (e.g., television, film, video) is shown in the sidebar on pages 32–33.

Is the webcast for entertainment, education, or commerce?
Informational webcasts are likely to mix streaming audio and video with animation and web-based information. Educational audiences often possess less than cutting-edge equipment, whereas producers coordinating entertainment-oriented projects may feel the need to utilize the latest technology. Commerce-oriented webcasts need to develop methods of analyzing the return on the initial investment.

Is the webcast designed to expand the reach of traditional broadcast content? Radio broadcasts repurposed for the Internet have become real success stories, since even tiny broadcast stations gain instant access to a global network of listeners. In contrast, watching a mass media sitcom through current web video would be far less interesting than watching the same show on regular TV.

Is the webcast designed to encourage audience interaction?
Systems such as WebTV that integrate traditional television with the Internet provide a special opportunity to augment broadcast content with audience discussion and feedback. Television shows such as *Babylon 5* (www.babylon5.com) already benefit from fan communities on the web, Usenet, and chat rooms; and the juxtaposition of webcasts with these services on the same computer promises even greater benefit. In considering the webcast plan, define the varieties of interaction desired: Is it in a living room, cocktail party, town meeting, or boardroom conference? Defining the space will help to identify the desired audience interactivity necessary for success.

How large an audience? With a practical maximum audience in the thousands, webcasts are not mass entertainment. Projects funded through television-style advertising may be difficult or impossible to implement on today's Internet. In contrast, narrowcasts of specific streaming content exploit the Internet's power to reach small audiences with wide geographic dispersion. Depending on the content, it may be economically viable to webcast to hundreds, dozens, or even a single viewer.

Will the webcast complement or compete with traditional media broadcasts? At present, the quality of Internet video is so different from television that the audience for one has little influence on the other. However, Internet-based radio may soon pose a direct challenge to traditional broadcast. If you're looking for music from Brazil, why wait for a local station to play the music when you can tune in directly into a Brazilian Internet radio station? Determine where the specific content fits into the competitive landscape and plan accordingly.

What production value level is necessary? The low resolution of webcasts—as well as the free-wheeling nature of the Internet itself—reduces the necessity for expensive costumes, scenery, and special effects. However, professional control of lighting, camera placement, and sound quality may have major effects on the final output.

Is the content available elsewhere? If the webcast provides content unavailable elsewhere, the marketing director should construct a publicity plan emphasizing its uniqueness. On the other hand, if the webcast offers content repurposed from mass media, additional features (such as audience interaction, prizes, giveaways) may be necessary to create interest.

A good way to develop a feel for existing webcast content is to go online and examine archives at sites including The Web Times Network (www.webtimes .com/main.html), Timecast (www.timecast.com), The Media Channel (www.mediachannel.com), and Broadcast.Com (www.broadcast.com). You may want to attend webcasts listed by these services and determine which most effectively use the medium.

Audience Size and Composition

Since webcasts play to small crowds, it is extremely important to define the demographics and *psychographics* (i.e., interests and desires) of the audience.

Examine the proposed content and create a profile of Internet users likely to be interested in receiving it. This profile should be compared to current Internet statistics archives at sites such as CyberAtlas (www.cyberatlas.com). Using this information, estimate what proportion of the target audience will be able to receive the webcast. Here are some general rules for evaluating the potential audience for a webcast:

Audience interests. Most Internet users associate webcasts with new or hard-to-find information. Webcasts that repurpose information are likely to be of less interest than those with new material developed specifically for the Internet.

Audience location. Webcasts are often available to employees at work, a location largely denied to other media. The intimacy of an on-screen webcast makes it easier to integrate into the workday (as opposed to watching a television in the office), but a public environment may be inappropriate for receiving controversial or censored content.

Audience sophistication. Webcasts aimed at "newbie" audiences on services such America Online and WebTV should avoid requiring users to download and install software. New users may also require education in the features and limitations of webcasts.

Audience software. Despite industry consolidation, several standards currently exist for webcasting, each with its own custom media player. Java-based players avoid problems with plug-ins but may run slowly. And due to the extreme instability of Java on the Mac, none of the commercial Java-based webcast players function on the Mac platform.

Audience hardware. Site visitors with 486 Windows and Quadra-level Macs simply don't have the processing power for high-resolution audio or any video streaming product. Webcasts targeting these users should stay away from video and instead concentrate on audio content that will withstand low-quality reproduction. Despite widespread attempts to develop fast Internet connectivity through cable modems, ADSL, and other technologies, the majority of the at-home Internet audience will be surfing at 56K or slower for the foreseeable future.

Webcast Formats

The next phase in webcast development is to choose among the possible methods available to digitize and deliver content. This stage involves: a) understanding the basics of webcast delivery; b) choosing a software platform to encode and deliver the webcast; and c) selecting a combination of audio, video, and multimedia bandwidth limits that are both appropriate to the content and capable of being supported by the intended audience's Internet connections. Media transport modes will be discussed first, since they form most basic aspect of webcast formats.

Media Transport Modes

Media transport modes define how data packets are sent between source and receiver. Transport protocols currently used for webcasts include *Transmission Control Protocol (TCP), User Datagram Protocol (UDP), Real-Time Protocol (RTP)* (a UDP variant), *HyperText Transfer Protocol (HTTP),* and Vosaic's proprietary *VDP* (www.vosaic.com). TCP was originally designed for text and data transmission, and it places a premium on error correction. As a result, its automatic repeated requests for "dropped" packets may cause a jerky flow of audio and video. By contrast, UDP will drop some data in order to maintain the constancy of the media stream. TCP and HTTP pass transparently through corporate *firewalls,* which reject UDP and RTP signals. However, TCP and HTTP are slower than UDP. Depending on the audience, you may elect to support a larger audience using HTTP at the expense of smooth delivery.

Media Delivery Strategies

The flexible, interactive nature of the Internet allows webcasts to utilize a wider variety of technologies and strategies than those found in traditional broadcast environments. These media delivery strategies, defined in this section, are one-to-many, many-to-many, and many-to-one. Each strategy has several advantages and disadvantages and is appropriate for specific types of webcast content and budgets. Figure 2.2 illustrates these varying strategies.

One-to-Many

The one-to-many standard closely resembles traditional broadcast in that one content provider sends a number of identical information streams to individual

Figure 2.2 Media delivery strategies.

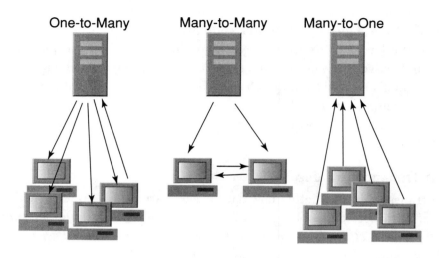

One-to-Many   Many-to-Many   Many-to-One

end users. In this system, a single computer or *media server* manages all the web-cast streams. Within the one-to-many model, several subcategories may be distinguished:

HTTP streaming. In this simple strategy, webcast data is delivered using the web's existing HTTP communications protocol. While not originally designed for webcasting, *HTTP streaming* works reasonably well for audiences in the dozens to the hundreds. Control of webcast delivery is entirely the responsibility of the player software, which cannot provide feedback to fine-tune the web. HTTP streaming is also an option used by specialized media servers.

Unicast media servers. Unicast systems consist of a client player and a specialized media server capable of dynamic control of a communication protocol and dynamic adjustment of the webcast to accommodate hardware and available bandwidth. High-end worksta-tions running unicast servers may supply up to 1,000 streams at 28.8 modem speeds. Custom servers are also better at load balancing when a large number of simultaneous webcast connections are being maintained. Most companies distribute free evaluation versions of their client/server system on the Internet.

Multicast networks. As shown in Figure 2.3, multicast signals overcome the unicast scaling bottleneck by delivering broadcast streams to other media servers, which in turn deliver it to many end users. The decentralized content delivery ensures that bandwidth requirements along the network remain low. On the emerging commercial IP multicast networks run by America Online (www.aol.com), Uunet (www.uu.net/lang.en/products/uucast.shtml), and RealNetworks/MCI (www.real.com/rbn/), a few hours of multicast time typically cost a few thousand dollars, and 24-hour webcast delivery is available for less than $10,000 per month. Multicasting expands reach and audience size at the expense of interactivity and user feedback. Currently,

Figure 2.3 Unicast servers and multicast networks.

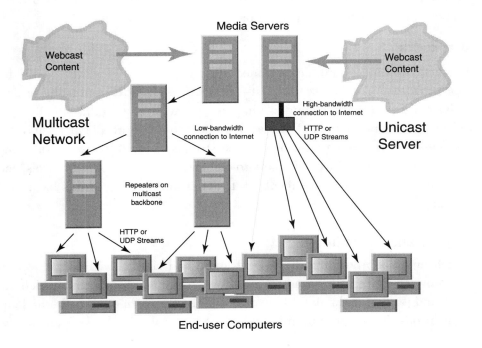

all multicast systems function only in live mode and do not implement on-demand viewing. Standard Internet routers cannot carry multicasts unless specifically enabled for it. The complexity and geographic dispersion of multicast hardware make it impossible for small content providers to own their own multicast network.

Many-to-Many

One of the unique features of webcasting is the ability of the audience to talk back to the webcast performers and with each other. This is a departure from television-style one-way communication to models emulating the auditorium, soapbox, and cocktail party. Many-to-many webcasts consist of a unidirectional media stream with crosstalk and backtalk text streams delivered via chat rooms and email. Webcast media servers allowing many-to-many communication overlap with conferencing systems such as CU-SeeMe (www.cuseeme.com) and Microsoft NetMeeting (www.microsoft.com/netmeeting). Some vendors have even developed personal media servers to support small-scale audio/video backtalk. To be successful, most many-to-many webcasts combine several technologies and require sophisticated production management.

Many-to-One

The many-to-one communication mode (the opposite of what we usually think of as broadcast) does not really exist—unless the torrent of mail being returned with a common (angry) theme to a hapless spammer qualifies as a many-to-one webcast. True many-to-one webcasts would require multiple participants to integrate media into a real-time webcast stream directed to a small or individual audience. Some form of many-to-one may emerge from protocols being developed to send audience feedback through multicast networks back to the primary content server.

Players and Metafiles

Web browsers do not directly support audio and video. To initiate a webcast, the browser passes the selected hyperlink to another program, which then loads and processes the data. Players may take the form of stand-alone helper applications, Netscape plug-ins, or ActiveX controls. A few companies download the player directly as a Java applet. For systems such as RealAudio that require complex interactions between client and server, selecting a hyperlink actually downloads a text-based *metafile*. Depending on the *MIME (Multipurpose Internet Mail Extension)* type passed to the web browser, a helper or integrated plug-in player is loaded. As you can see in Figure 2.4, the player reads the metafile, which contains instructions for the player program to contact the media server and may specify additional parameters for managing the webcast. Metafiles are created by the content provider and are vendor specific.

Media Encoding Strategies

All webcasts employ some form of compression/decompression, or codec, scheme to deliver information at sustainable data rates. Prior to the rise of the Internet, digital audio/video encoding frequently utilized the MPEG (www.powerweb.de/mpeg) standard. MPEG-based systems function poorly at modem speeds, but at higher bandwidth they offer near perfect compression

Figure 2.4 Interaction of media servers, players, and metafiles via the web.

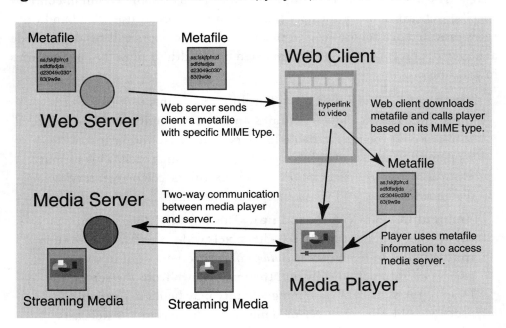

for full-motion, full-screen video, as well as compatibility with **CD-ROM** and *Digital Versatile (or Video) Disc (DVD)* media. To support the low bit rates (20–50Kbps) characteristic of consumer modems, most streaming media software uses specialized algorithms created specifically for the Internet. Many systems use wavelet (www.harc.edu/HARCC.html) compression algorithms, and a few systems such as RealPlayer G2 are experimenting with the fractal (inls.ucsd.edu/y/Fractals/) compression scheme pioneered by Iterated Systems (www.iterated.com). Fractals allow extremely high compression ratios but also require fast hardware for decoding at the user end. Various types of webcast content respond differently to compression, and you will need to generate samples and test the results to determine optimum encoding for the webcast.

Webcast Delivery Formats

Available Internet bandwidth results in trade-offs for webcast delivery. In cases where multiple media types compete for the same bandwidth (e.g., video with soundtrack), it is necessary to divide bandwidth among the streams in a way that works best with the content. The following lists some common content-specific webcast delivery formats that are in widespread use. The bandwidth rates provided are theoretical; in practice, the developers will need to encode at about 70 percent of the maximum listed bandwidth to allow for irregularities in transmission.

Text stream (14.4K and up). This format streams text-only word-casts and datacasts, and it contains an interface similar or identical to Internet chat rooms. Available to users with 14.4K and faster modems, it has a limited interface but a very wide reach. This format ensures maximum participation and is useful for celebrity interviews, distance learning, and virtual corporate meetings.

Ambient webcam (14.4K and up). This format delivers a static picture without sound, usually 100–300 pixels wide. The frame rate runs from minutes to hours, and *metatag* information encoded in a web page is used to periodically pull the image down from the server. Despite the slow data rate, image quality may be high. Available to users with 14.4K and faster modems, it is appropriate for webcasts where image rather than motion is of prime concern.

Voice-quality audio (14.4K). This format encodes monoaudio with greatly restricted dynamics and a 3.5–4.0kHz frequency response similar to the telephone. This format is useful for news/talk radio and audiobooks, and it may provide acceptable music quality for certain types of rock music.

AM radio-quality audio (28.8K). One of the most common formats used to encode music and voice, this audio format has a better dynamic range and a 4.0–4.5kHz frequency response. It is often supplied along with higher-quality audio to support users with slow modems or bad connections, and it is particularly effective for spoken word and music emphasizing vocals.

Small screen slide shows (28.8K). This format consists of silent video with relatively high-quality images less than 200 pixels in width sent at frame rates of 0.2–0.5 per second. This video format is useful for photography collections, nature/travel video, and summary thumbnails of regular video collections.

Talking head videos (28.8K–56K). This common format, shown in Figure 2.5, combines a low-quality (> 4kHz) audio with a small video screen refresh at 1–10 frames per second. Typical content involves close-ups of people speaking into the camera. As long as the speaker refrains from large movements, the apparent quality may be quite high. This format is useful for videoconference-style webcasts and news reports. Subtle facial expressions, on-screen animation, and distance shots are not effective within this format. High-motion sequences (e.g., a fast-moving basketball game) will either freeze suddenly or reduce in quality so that individual elements are nearly unrecognizable.

Quarter-screen animation (28.8K–56K). This format involves animation within a 300×200 pixel screen and an apparent frame rate near 10 per second. The audio track is comparable to AM radio. Properly designed, streaming animation webcasts in this range appear to have very high quality, exceeding broadcast video, and can support larger screen sizes. Figure 2.6 illustrates quarter-screen animation versus streaming video using the same bandwidth.

Figure 2.5 The talking head webcast delivery format.

Slide shows with voice or music (28.8K–56K). This format includes audio tracks with a frequency response of 4.0kHz range and highly compressed video at frame rates in the range of 0.2–1.0 per second. This is a realistic alternative to full motion for music, and is excellent for reproducing ambient video featuring slow pans through natural environments.

FM radio-quality audio (56K–80K). This format includes audio with a dynamic response of up to 8kHz, with or without stereo channels. It works well with most types of music, including instrumentals and vocals backed with acoustic instruments.

Broadcast-quality audio (80K–112K). This audio format utilizes stereo channels with up to 16kHz frequency response, and it compares favorably to FM stereo radio. It is useful for previews from new

Figure 2.6 Quarter-screen animation versus video format.

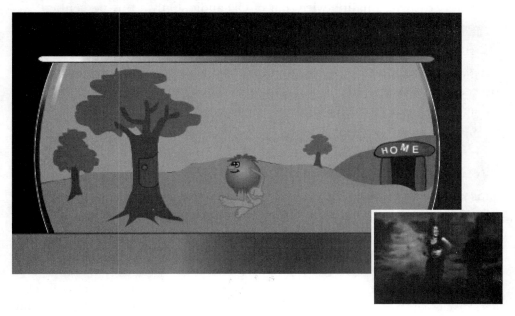

record albums and to accommodate demanding music styles including solo piano and symphonic works. Available to users with dual *ISDN (Integrated Services Digital Network)* connections.

High-quality small screen video (80K–512K). This video format refreshes the screen 10–20 frames per second with improved color balance and sharp images. It is most often used for film trailers. The audio track with 4–6kHz response effectively reproduces all types of music.

Near-CD-quality audio (80K–512K). This audio format contains audio CD tracks compressed at a 10:1 ratio with at least 16–20kHz frequency response. This falls short of true CD audio (44kHz), but most people cannot tell the difference. It is often used to deliver pay-per-listen music.

Full-motion, full-screen video (512K–2,000K). This format uses 10–30 frames per second for screens opened to 640 × 480 pixels or greater. It is directly comparable to digital video used in satellite broadcast, and it could be used to deliver audio in the proposed DVD standards with quality twice that of CD audio. Only a tiny percentage of Internet users can receive webcasts at this bandwidth.

While some of these formats superficially resemble broadcast audio and video, keep in mind that there are real limitations in the Internet delivery process. In designing the webcast, be sure that content received at the lower range of bandwidth is still useful to the audience, and make allowances for the differences between broadcast and data networks.

Webcast Media Platforms

This section describes the most common streaming media players and servers used on the Internet, concentrating on key vendors and software standards. All of these groups provide specialized clients and servers, and most also supply a specialized media server for their product. A summary of the similarities and differences between these platforms is listed in Table 2.1. Authoring environments—including encoders, servers, players, and synchronization utilities—are discussed further in Chapter 3, "Webcast Equipment and Authoring Environments."

RealNetworks

RealNetworks (www.real.com) is currently the oldest and best-supported environment for streaming Internet media. Not only have more than 24 million copies of the RealMedia player been downloaded, but its brand-name recognition is much higher than other formats. In January 1998, RealNetworks announced that streaming media files on the Internet jumped from 100,000 in September 1997 to 280,000 in mid-January and that 85 percent of the files were in RealAudio or RealVideo format. At least 100,000 RealServer media servers were in operation at that time. RealNetworks software supports encoders and players across Macintosh, UNIX, and Windows NT/95 platforms. In 1998, RealNetworks introduced RealPlayer G2, shown in Figure 2.7, which supports integrated audio, video, and multimedia streaming. Audio is compressed using the *DolbyNet* protocol developed jointly by RealNetworks and Dolby Labs (www.dolby.com), and video uses several low bit-rate algorithms developed by RealNetworks with other vendors.

Table 2.1 Comparative Summary of Common Webcast Media Platforms

Company	Player Platform	Authoring Platform	Authoring Software	Server Platform	IP Multicast	Live Encoding	Input Files
Real-Networks	Mac, UNIX, Windows NT/95	Mac, Windows, UNIX	Stand-alone, Premiere, SoundEdit 16	UNIX, Windows NT	Yes	Yes	AIFF, WAV, AVI, MOV
Liquid Audio	Mac, Windows	Mac, Windows	Stand-alone, ProTools, NetShow	UNIX, Windows NT	No	Yes	AIFF, WAV
VDO	Mac, Windows	Mac, Windows	Stand-alone	UNIX, Windows NT	Yes	Yes	AVI, MOV
Vosaic	Mac, UNIX, Windows NT/95	Windows	Stand-alone	UNIX, Windows NT	No	Yes	AVI, MPEG
Quick-Time 3.0	Mac, Windows, UNIX	Mac, Windows, UNIX	Most multimedia programs	Any web server (HTTP)	No	Yes (via third-party programs)	AIFF, WAV, AVI, MOV
Flash (Macromedia)	Mac, Windows	Mac, Windows	Flash, Director, Authorware	HTTP, RealMedia	Yes (via RealPlayer)	N/A	Flash, Director, Authorware
StreamWorks (Xing)	Mac, Windows	Mac, Windows	Stand-alone, Premiere	UNIX, Windows NT	Yes	Yes	AVI, WAV
NetShow	Mac, UNIX, Windows NT/95	Mac, Windows	Stand-alone, Premiere	Windows NT	Yes	No	AVI, MOV

*All servers support at least 1,000 streams on a 200mHz Pentium running Windows NT or Intel-based UNIX.
MOV = QuickTime; AV = Video for Windows; AIFF = Audio Interchange File Format; WAV = Audio for Windows

This pioneering player/server combination is the most popular webcast delivery system on the Internet. The widely distributed player supports streaming audio, video, and animation via the recently added RealFlash option. A more feature-rich version of the player (including tunable channel models and searching) is available to consumers for $29.95. A basic 60-stream version of the RealServer is currently free for download for Windows NT and UNIX platforms. The server supports a wide range of communication protocols including HTTP/TCP and UDP. The commercial version of the server (~$4,000) bundles more advanced encoding/management tools and adds IP multicast to the server software. A separate file must be created for each bandwidth supported by the webcast producer.

The RealMedia 5.0 system also supports pay-per-view commerce tied to webcasting events. The RealPlayer implements user authentication in two modes: In the hidden mode, name and password authentication is stored on the end-user's

Figure 2.7 RealPlayer 5.0.

system and delivered automatically when the user logs in to a protected area of the web site. This relatively low-security approach is most suitable for general membership-oriented webcasts. For commerce, private meetings, or distance learning systems requiring greater security, a dialog box prompts the user for a name/password pair. RealNetworks also offers promotional support for webcasters by operating popular archives and event calendars, including Timecast (www.timecast.com) and RealPlanet (www.realplanet.com). RealNetworks recently began working with Audible, Inc. (www.audible.com) to allow the download of RealPlayer content into handheld devices for later playback.

Liquid Audio

Liquid Audio (www.liquidaudio.com) provides a streaming media system optimized for music webcasts and closely tied to electronic commerce. The Liquid Audio software uses Dolby Digital's AC-3 codec (originally developed for multitrack theater music) for very high-quality audio. The Liquid MusicPlayer, shown in Figure 2.8, is highly optimized for purchase of recorded music in pay-per-download and hard-copy CD formats, but it should also be readily adaptable to live pay-per-view webcasts as well.

Figure 2.8 The Liquid MusicPlayer.

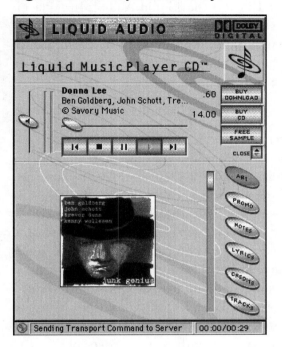

The Liquid Audio webcast/commerce system opens a webcast in a preview mode, where 28.8 modem users are able to hear streaming audio delivered at a quality comparable to FM mono radio. If users decide to order the product, the Liquid MusicServer requests payment information (in the form of credit card numbers or cybercash) from the user and authorizes the transaction via a third-party Internet commerce system such as VeriFone vPOS (www.verifone.com) or CyberCash (www.cybercash.com). Once the transaction is complete, the server encrypts and downloads a CD-quality Liquid Audio track at 10:1 compression over the original file. The Liquid MusicPlayer decodes the track, which may be stored on the user's hard disk or copied to *CD-R* or CD-RW media. The Liquid Audio system also logs transactions for reports to copyright organizations and has built-in multimedia specifically for music. The Liquid MusicPlayer gives access to album graphics, liner notes, and lyrics.

Currently, the chief barrier to widespread use of Liquid Audio is the requirement that users download and install the Liquid Audio MusicPlayer. Experience indicates that player installation is difficult for many users, and this may delay the spread of Liquid Audio's technology. As of early 1998, Liquid Audio distributed its player for free but did not provide evaluation copies of its server for download through the web.

VDO

VDO (www.vdo.net) offers a capture, encoding, and delivery system optimized for realistic video. The VDO player runs on Mac and Windows systems, and has been integrated into Microsoft's Internet Explorer 4.0. Unlike other platforms, the VDO encoder supports multiple bandwidths with a single media file, simplifying media management on the server. Like the RealNetworks product, VDO's encoder is available as a stand-alone or Adobe Premiere plug-in for Mac and Windows computers. The subjective rating of VDO video quality is quite high, both in its ability to reproduce sharp images and to portray realistic motion. At ISDN speeds, playback in small windows compares favorably to video streamed off a local hard disk or CD-ROM. The VDO server supports multiple transmission protocols and can switch from UDP to HTTP for webcasting behind firewalls. This quality factor is one reason that many video-specific services, including the Internet Television Network (www.intv.net) and VideoDome (www.videodome.com), have adopted VDO for their streaming media standard.

As consumer bandwidth increases, VDO's higher image quality may help it compete with RealPlayer. In 1998, VDO renewed its interest in the general consumer market. Players for Mac and Windows platforms are free, and a basic server for Windows NT and Solaris is also available for download. Figure 2.9 shows a VDO player running in isolation, though most webcasters embed the player components into a custom web page.

In 1998, VDO announced an interesting extension to its system called VDOMail. This Windows-specific software allows end users to record video and audio messages and include them as part of an email message. The audio/video file may be sent directly to the mail recipient or uploaded to a VDO server. In the latter case, the video may be webcast in real time to the recipients when they open the email message. This offers the potential for a webcast promoter

Figure 2.9 The VDO player.

to invite audience members via email and include a portal to the webcast directly in the message body. The server upload option also allows senders to address audio/video messages to large mailing lists without repeatedly resending the video files.

Xingtech StreamWorks

Despite the common use of MPEG compression for CD-ROMs, DVDs, and digital satellite broadcast, Xingtech's StreamWorks (www.xingtech.com) is unusual in its support of streaming MPEG media. Unlike other formats optimized for the low bit rates characteristic of slow modem connections, standard MPEG cannot be streamed except at the upper range of current Internet speeds (between 512K and 2Mbps). At these speeds, the StreamWorks player, shown in Figure 2.10, provides high-quality audio and full-screen, full-motion video. StreamWorks players for Macintosh, Windows, and X-Windows platforms are available as free downloads.

MPEG normally requires dedicated hardware for real-time compression, but Xing has addressed this issue with its release of the MPEGLive! encoder. In recent tests, real-time encoding and Internet delivery of full-screen, full-motion video was demonstrated on an Intel/MMX PC without dedicated video hardware. This may help Xing position itself for high-speed Internet access when it becomes available to the general public, and it will allow independent webcasters to compete in forthcoming digital broadcast standards. Currently, StreamWorks is a good choice for high-bandwidth intranets requiring high-quality video.

Figure 2.10 The StreamWorks player.

Vosaic Mediaserver

Vosaic (www.vosaic.com) also uses MPEG audio and video compression standards to deliver webcast content. Standards supported include MPEG-1, MPEG-2, H.263 (www.nta.no/brukere/DVC/), and GSM (Global System for Mobile Communications) audio (itre.ncsu.edu/gsm/). The support for H.263 allows Vosaic to interface with videoconferencing software such as Microsoft NetMeeting (www.microsoft.com/netmeeting). The emphasis on MPEG provides good support for high-bandwidth streaming and compatibility with existing digital broadcast, but may result in reduced image quality at low bit rates. The Vosaic Mediaserver downloads a Java-based player to the end user, bypassing the installation of custom plug-in player software.

Vosaic sells two versions of its server. At the low end, TVStation and RadioStation servers are available at modest cost. Professionals may purchase the high-end Vosaic Mediaserver and license usage on a per-stream basis. While the use of Java allows webcasting without specialized players, current encoding tools are not as well developed as in other platforms.

Apple QuickTime 3.0

Most developers encounter Apple's QuickTime (quicktime.apple.com) during the production of audio and video for CD-ROM environments. Beginning with the 2.0 version, Apple provided an intermediate jump-start format between download-and-play and true media streaming. QuickTime video with the jump-start option enables the display of each frame to the end user as it is received; and those with very high connection speeds (e.g., 30,000 bytes/second) experience true video streaming. In 1998, Apple released QuickTime 3.0, which provides native support for low bit-rate dynamic media streaming and for encoding a single video at multiple bit rates. New audio and video compression algorithms also provide better quality at lower bit rates than were possible with earlier versions. QuickTime also has native support for video created with VDO and AVI.

As a potential delivery platform for streaming media, QuickTime has advantages and disadvantages. On the one hand, the maturity of the QuickTime video platform and compatibility with authoring environments, including Macromedia Director and SoundEdit 16 (www.macromedia.com) and Adobe Premiere (www.adobe.com), ensure a following among developers. On the other hand, the dramatic fall of Apple's market share between 1995 and 1997 meant that only a tiny fraction of consumer systems had QuickTime installed by default. QuickTime may be most appropriate for developing webcasts integrated with static content delivered on CD-ROM or DVD. QuickTime was recently chosen by the International Organization for Standardization (ISO) as the starting point for the new MPEG-4 standard (www.iso.org) designed to provide multimedia delivery over a variety of networks and devices.

Microsoft NetShow

NetShow (www.microsoft.com/netshow) uses Microsoft's Active Streaming Format (ASF) to provide a container for synchronized audio, video, Java applets, and multimedia similar to QuickTime. It currently includes Internet webcast protocols supporting RealNetworks, Liquid Audio, VDO, VoxWare (extremely high-compression voice audio), and Xing MPEG. Microsoft has also announced that its Media Player based on NetShow will be a standard feature of Windows 98. The NetShow platform uses a server integrated with Microsoft Site Server that is specific to and optimized solely for Windows NT. Like RealPlayer, it supports IP multicast and streams in UDP and TCP/IP. Its tight integration with Windows NT allows the production team's web administrators to use standard NT tools and applications for monitoring the webcast.

VRML 98

A public format developed by Tony Parisi and Mark Pesce in 1994, *Virtual Reality Modeling Language, VRML* (vrml.sgi.com/moving-worlds/), has gone through a series of booms and busts as a 3D modeling alternative to video. A streaming media standard has been incorporated into the proposed VRML 98 spec, which may make it useful for webcasts. One of the most interesting features of VRML is its definition of audio space: Sound in VRML worlds increases or decreases in intensity as users approach or retreat from objects. This feature, used directly or incorporated into standard video webcasts, may help to increase the ambient feel of future webcasts. As of early 1998, no tools existed to implement streaming VRML worlds.

Streaming Media Platform Selection Process

Selecting hardware and software is a critical process in the development of any webcast. Despite the complexity, a few basic rules may be applied to make sure the platform is a match for the content. First, consider the intended audience. If the webcast is being delivered over a highly standardized intranet, integration of the webcast with existing software is important. Most webcasters may decide that an end-to-end Microsoft solution works best in this case—particularly if everyone on the intranet may be required to install Microsoft software. On the other hand, webcasts aimed at the educational market will have to support the diverse array of hardware and software maintained by teachers and students. In this case, RealNetworks audio and video are clearly superior to Microsoft Netshow. Traditional broadcasters may elect to use MPEG (even if current quality is low) for its compatibility with the existing content. Multimedia developers may be drawn to Macromedia's Shockwave platform but may do better to work directly with streaming media enabled by Apple's QuickTime 3.0.

Macromedia Flash

Flash (www.macromedia.com) provides the most popular delivery platform for streaming Internet animation. Far easier to learn than Macromedia's Director product, it shares a common multitrack timeline metaphor for assembling animation with embedded audio and video. Simple hyperlinks to URLs and other Flash animation pages are supported, but there is no incorporated scripting language comparable to Director's Lingo. One of the most powerful features in favor of Flash is its integration into the newest generation of RealPlayer G2. This allows the design of large-screen basic animation to accompany streaming audio. In operation, Flash animation running as a stand-alone application or within RealPlayer performs credibly over 28.8 modem connections. Macromedia's new Universal Media Initiative also allows Flash files to play back via a downloaded Java applet, as well as through the Shockwave plug-in.

Choosing a Platform

With a large diversity of software options available for webcasts, developers will have to decide whether to adopt one or more media standards. Some groups focus on a single player/server combination and simply point the audience to a second site with the required player or provide a local copy for download. Others provide webcast content in as many formats as possible to ensure the largest potential audience. Table 2.2 compares the relative usage of the major streaming standards. The table shows that RealNetworks has the highest representation, followed by various MPEG solutions and VDO. A comparison to the .WAV audio format shows that webcast-style media is quickly supplanting download-and-play formats. *New Media* magazine also runs a discussion group on its web site comparing the various streaming media standards (newmedia.com/threads/stream/index.html).

In some cases, developers may opt for less common platforms in order to optimize delivery of their content. Filmmakers interested in promoting their films and videos might use VDO because of its high visual quality. Liquid Audio is a good choice for webcasters looking for a one-stop solution to webcasting and commerce. Due to its support for H.263 standards, Vosaic may be useful in environments where videoconference software is being used. MPEG platforms

Table 2.2 Streaming Standards as Reported by Hotbot (www.hotbot.com)	
RealMedia Audio/Video (.ram, .rm, .rpm)	169,364
WAV Audio (.wav)	129,988
QuickTime Video (.mov)	74,760
MPEG Audio/Video (.mpeg, .mpg)	39,213
AIFF Audio (.aiff, .aif)	28,143
AVI (.avi)	24,179
Flash (.spl, .swf)	9,455
VDO (.vdo)	2,725
NetShow (.asf, .asx)	2,169

may not be the ideal choice for webcasts over the public Internet, but may be a good solution for training and distance learning performed over an intranet or campus network.

Next . . .

Based on this general introduction to the concept development and methodology for webcasting, webcasters should have a strategy mapped out and be considering how to put together the pieces to create a webcast production studio. In the next chapter, the production studio is considered, including how to select equipment for capturing audio and video, encoding raw analog or digital streams into web-compatible formats, and assembling the encoded media into a complete webcast presentation.

WEBCAST EQUIPMENT AND AUTHORING ENVIRONMENTS

3

After the webcast production team has been organized and the core streaming media platforms have been selected, it is necessary to assemble the various components essential to a successful webcast. These components may be divided into two main categories: the webcast production studio, which includes systems used to record the content, convert it to a suitable digital format, and embed it in a larger multimedia presentation; and the delivery system, which includes connections between the webcast site and Internet provider, servers for Internet delivery, and relevant features of end-user hardware and connections. This chapter considers the elements that go into a successful production studio; delivery systems are discussed at greater length in Chapter 4, "Webcast Servers and Connectivity."

The size and complexity of the production studio varies depending on whether the content is original material developed in-house, a *simulcast* of material also being carried by traditional broadcast, or *repurposed* material taken from recorded archives. If the content is all original, the webcasters will need to understand all aspects of real-world production. Successful projects will require the integration of the skills of recording engineers, directors, writers, and other traditional broadcast positions into the webcast group. In other cases, the webcast will piggyback an existing broadcast and thus be able to take advantage of a preexisting production team. In this situation, the webcast producers will focus their efforts on effectively adapting hardware and software in the existing production studio or venue for their own purposes. Finally, if content is repurposed

Table 3.1 Webcast Production Studios

Company	URL
Webcast1	www.webcast1.com
InterneTV	www.internetv.com
ITV.net	www.itv.net
Mediadome	www.mediadome.com
Internet Global Communications	www.justsurfit.com
Virtual Netcast Corp.	www.lalive.com
Criterion Productions	www.criterioninfo.net/aboutus/intersvcs.html
Gardy-McGarth	www.gardy-mcgrath.com
The Internet Broadcast Center	www.internetbroadcast.com
Pseudo Online Network	www.pseudo.com
JAMtv	www.jamtv.com
VStream Inc.	www.vstream.com

from recorded or authored material, the producers will want to add value by embedding streaming content in a larger multimedia presentation.

In many cases, the webcasters may decide to focus exclusively on their content and promotion and outsource the actual production work. Table 3.1 shows companies that have begun to specialize in this area. Webcasters considering using these services should ask for quotes based on their planned production and try to estimate the costs involved in doing it themselves. Outsourcing to a studio is particularly attractive for one-time webcast events sponsored by traditional broadcasters and other groups working outside the Internet.

Webcast Audio

The greatest progress to date in webcasting has been made in delivering real-time audio webcasts, or *audiocasts*. Beginning with the introduction of RealAudio by RealNetworks (formerly Progressive Networks at www.real.com), audio webcasts have formed a significant part of the Internet experience. The main reason for this is the relatively low bandwidth required to deliver audio in real time. With efficient compression, voice-quality sound may be webcast with 8Kbps bandwidth or less, comparable to the speed of a 14.4 modem; and music approaching FM-quality stereo broadcasts may be delivered by 56K modems or ISDN Internet connections. Webcast audio has a larger set of tools available, and audio content (e.g., music, sportcasts) is popular with the Internet audience.

In the following section, various aspects of audio relevant to webcasting are considered, including the characteristics of audio as a medium, devices used to capture and process audio, and differences between working with prerecorded and live audio signals.

Features of Audio Capture

Since Internet audio can approach the quality of other broadcast media, most webcast producers should pay special attention to this aspect of their production. Control of sound is the responsibility of the Internet/web specialist and the audio engineer (a type of technical engineer discussed in Chapter 2, "Developing a Webcast Strategy." Both will need to consider the key features of audio. Webcasters who are familiar with digital information processing will need to learn about the characteristics of *analog* audio signals, whose basic parameters are discussed in more detail later in this section.

> **Frequency range.** This is the scale defining the highest and lowest *pitches* sampled by the capture system. Pitch is measured in *Hertz (Hz)*, or cycles per second. The human ear is sensitive to sound starting at about 30Hz and ending at about 15kHz. Complete sampling of this range requires support for near-CD-quality sound, or about 44–48kHz. Most audio webcasts deliver sound with a much lower frequency range of 4–8kHz, comparable to a good telephone connection or AM radio. This range may be used to deliver high-quality voice-only webcasts, but cannot reproduce broadcast audio. The new RealSystem G2 standard from RealNetworks promises to double the frequency response, which would bring the sound to near-broadcast quality.

Dynamic range. This defines the highest and lowest volume (or *amplitude*) for sound passed by the webcast. It is directly related to the noise level of the sampled sound and is expressed in *decibels,* a logarithmic unit based on the minimum sound the human ear can hear. CD-quality audio can encode a dynamic range up to 90db. While the decibel measurement is usually associated exclusively with sound, it is also often used by audio engineers to describe the strength of an audio signal's voltage, current, or power.

Timbre. All sounds possess a characteristic collection of primary and *harmonic* frequencies that act as "fingerprints," identifying them to a listener. Some instruments (e.g., woodwinds) have a complex timbre and require more bandwidth to encode than others (e.g., bass guitar). The human voice, while possessing individualistic and complex timbre, may be adequately represented for speech recognition with a small set of frequencies. This explains why voice-only webcasts tolerate low bandwidth better than music webcasts.

Density. This feature is specific to audio delivery over the Internet. It refers to the ratio of sound versus silence during a given period of sampling time. Low sound density (e.g., slow-tempo picked guitar) contains many silences that may be encoded with lower bandwidth. Sophisticated servers and players may use these low-bandwidth windows to download part of the next (high-bandwidth) sound. High-density sound (e.g., an orchestral crescendo) contains fewer silences and requires a higher average bandwidth for Internet delivery.

During the development of the webcast, the audio engineer must identify the features of the audio and determine the sound quality needed to deliver it. This also includes the characteristics of the intended audience, which may expect different quality levels based on their prior experience with the content. For example, audience members listening to a webcast from a live concert may tolerate low quality better than those sampling music excerpts provided to sell a CD online. The features of the sound itself may also affect the webcast production. For example, due to the higher sampling rate needed to capture high-frequency audio, bass-heavy music may be easier to webcast. Paradoxically, sound approaching random noise (e.g., static or "industrial" music) has a greater dynamic and frequency range, and it will be harder to encode than a classical recital on a relatively pure-toned instrument such as a flute. For the same reason a voice-only newscast may be difficult to webcast if there is a significant component of random background noise.

Components of the Audio Capturing System

Production groups that formed on the Internet frequently forget that audio is an analog phenomenon, and that most high-quality sound capture and recording uses a mixture of analog and digital devices. Analog events are recorded in a continuous, nonsegmented stream, whereas digital events are recorded in discrete steps. Analog processors manipulate sound by varying voltage, current, or other features of the electronic signal received by the microphone. In contrast, digital systems convert the audio into binary code and store it in 8-bit, 16-bit, or other quality formats. Connecting these two worlds forms one of the major jobs of the webcast audio engineer.

Webcasts featuring audio, particularly live audio, often require integrating several pieces of analog and digital equipment. Typically, a final audio signal is captured digitally onto the encoding computer after passing through several stages of analog processing. This section presents an overview of the main components of modern analog audio systems. The general information provided here may be sufficient for developing simple webcasts, but producers planning original content and live webcasting should invest in books such as *The Acoustic Musician's Guide to Sound Reinforcement* by Mike Sokol (Jerome Headlands Press, 1998; kspace.com/jhp) or plan on bringing in a professional audio engineer at the consultant or team level.

Microphones

Live audio is captured using *microphones*, a broad class of transducing devices that convert sound energy into electrical current and/or digital data. This subsection discusses various types of microphones in greater detail in terms of their components. Based on these features, appropriate use of different microphone types during webcasts is also illustrated. A schematic of various microphone types discussed in the text is shown in Figure 3.1, and a list of microphone companies is provided in Table 3.2.

Figure 3.1 Microphones.

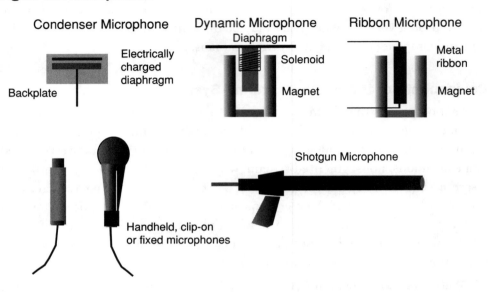

Pickup Mechanism

All microphones have a *diaphragm* or *membrane* that vibrates in response to sound waves, and use various means to convert this vibration into electrical energy. The hundreds of commercial microphones fall into three broad classes: *condenser,*

Table 3.2 Microphone Manufacturers

Company	URL	Type of Microphone
RythMic	www.rythmic.com/	Musical instrument
Electro-Voice	www.electrovoice.com	General purpose
SD Systems	www.sdsystems.com/	Musical instrument
Telex Computer Audio	www.computeraudio.telex.com/	Computer
Shure Brothers	www.shure.com/computer.html	General and wireless
Sennheiser	www.sennheiser.com/	General purpose
Neumann|USA	www.neumannusa.com/	Studio

dynamic, and *ribbon.* They are distinguished by the *pickup mechanism,* a mechanical device that converts sound into electrical energy. They are also characterized by the amount of distortion they introduce into the signal, their ability to respond to sudden audio changes or transients, and by the background noise they introduce into the signal. The following provides a brief description of each major class of microphone:

Dynamic microphones. This type uses a flat plate, or diaphragm, that transforms sound waves into motion. The diaphragm is connected to an electric coil called a solenoid that surrounds a permanent magnet. Movement of the solenoid generates an alternating electric current. Dynamic microphones are unidirectional, relatively large, and suitable for handheld voice recording and fixed recording of musical instruments. Large dynamic microphones can handle high-volume sound without excessive distortion or damage to working parts. The membrane used in a dynamic microphone is attached to a metal voice coil that is surrounded by a magnet; it is also supplied with power to induce an electrical charge. Vibrations of the voice coil induce a low-resistance electric current that can be transferred over many feet of wire without external amplification or distortion. Since dynamic microphone signals may be transported over long cable lengths, these microphones are good choices for live events where mixing and amplifying equipment are at a distance from the performance stage.

Condenser microphone. This type works by forming an electrical potential between a vibrating membrane and a back plate. Sound vibrations change the voltage on the back plate, resulting in a small current. The output from a condenser microphone must be amplified extensively in order to be useful, and an internal amplifier is usually included in the microphone assembly. The *electret* microphone is a variation of this design, which has a permanent charge on its back plate, eliminating the need for a separate power supply. Electrets may be made very small and have a unidirectional response, and are popular for clip-on microphones for clothing and on the bodies of musical instruments.

Ribbon microphone. The ribbon microphone uses a thin metal strip that vibrates directly without a separate membrane. As the ribbon moves, it cuts across magnetic lines of force and generates a small electric field—which in turn induces an output current. Due to the shape of the ribbon, the microphone has a *bidirectional* response with maxium sensitivity at 180-degree intervals. Ribbon microphones are most commonly used to record voice rather than musical instruments. Compared to other microphones, ribbon microphones tend to be larger and more sensitive to wind noise and damage by high-volume sound.

Directional Response

Some microphones are *omnidirectional* and receive signals equally well from all portions of the surrounding area. They are useful for recording ambient sounds in a recording space, but they often pick up unintended noise from the audience or backstage areas. Unidirectional or *cardioid* microphones are highly directional and only pick up sound in a narrow space. Both dynamic and condenser microphones may be made directional. Ribbon microphones are frequently bidirectional in their response. While more selective than omnidirectional systems, they also pick up noise 180 degrees from their preferred direction. For extremely selective recording, microphones are sometimes placed in tubes. These *shotgun* microphones are *ultradirectional* and are useful in noisy environments, such as an interview conducted in a crowd.

Connection to Amplifier

Microphones are commonly connected to amplifiers and other audio equipment that process their raw output using shielded cable. Most audio equipment connects to cables through XLR or RCA plug connectors, shown in Figure 3.2; and computer interfaces frequently use mini-plug connectors. If inadequate shielding is present in the cable or at connections, buzzes and hums will result as the cable picks up radio frequency signals from nearby computers or audio equipment. For greater flexibility, wireless microphones use small built-in radio transmitters to communicate with a receiver.

Cables connecting microphones to other equipment are also distinguished by their shielding. Shielding is necessary since all electrical equipment generates electromagnetic waves, which can in turn generate small currents in cable wire. This current appears as static, interference, or "crosstalk" between components. Another sign of poor shielding is loss of high frequencies relative to low ones in the audio signal. In general, webcasters should purchase professional-quality cable sold for the home theater market, which has improved shielding. Suppliers of this kind of equipment include Delco Wire and Cable, Ltd. (www.delcowire.com) and Canare Cable (www.canare.com/cablemainframe.html).

Frequency Response

Microphones vary widely in their response to high and low frequencies. Most manufacturers try to flatten response, but distortions invariably appear, particularly for off-center sounds recorded by highly directional microphones. Webcasters interested in recording high-frequency sounds might use condenser microphones, while large dynamic microphones are more effective at picking up low bass notes produced by percussion instruments.

Size

Condenser microphones may be very small, and are frequently used as unobtrusive clip-ons during interviews. Dynamic and ribbon microphones are generally larger, and are most suitable for recording sound from a wide area.

Filters and Stands

Since microphones are sensitive to air movements as well as sound, most contain a filter placed over the membrane. This is the familiar foam ball that gives

Figure 3.2 Cable connectors used by audio and video systems.

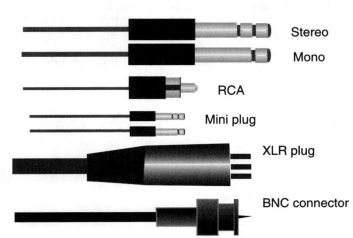

microphones a characteristic shape. The filter creates a zone of "dead air" around the pickup, which reduces noise. Ground vibrations transmitted to the microphone body may also cause recording problems. These vibrations may be reduced by using an appropriately designed microphone stand or by putting the microphones into special shock mounts.

Electrical Shielding

The coiled wires found in most microphones are sensitive to electrical interference from alternating current in lights and other devices. In addition, most computers operate at speeds that produce radio frequency interference. For this reason, microphones used in webcasts must have adequate shielding.

Since the features of microphones vary so widely, it will be necessary for the webcast production team to select one or more types for use during recording. Choosing the correct microphone for a webcast is highly dependent upon the content. For many applications involving recording a single speaker in the webcast production studio, the basic microphone provided with most computer sound cards will be sufficient for capture. Groups planning more complex events, particularly on-location webcasts, are likely to need several microphone types to accommodate all situations. In all cases, the webcasters should check the kind of cable connectors required and purchase new cable if necessary. Suggested uses of the microphone types discussed are listed in Table 3.3.

Table 3.3 Suggested Uses of Various Microphone Types

Microphone Type	Suggested Use
Condensor	Musical instrument (especially high-frequency)
Electret (condensor type)	Interview (small clip-on systems; one per participant)
Dynamic	Musical instrument (especially low-frequency percussion)
Ribbon	Voice
Shotgun (any type)	Interview (in noisy crowd)

Effects Processors

Effects processors are types of hardware that alter the raw audio signal. They may partly compensate for problems with the pickup mechanism at the microphone level or they may be used to deliberately distort the audio for dramatic effect. The use of effects processors is very widespread, and webcasters planning on live recording should familiarize themselves with their form and use. Effects may also be introduced into recorded sound; but in this case, the webcasters will frequently wait until after the sound has been digitized. Here are some of the common forms of effects processors that webcasters are likely to come in contact with:

Echo. Adds a diminished copy of the sound trailing the main signal at a specified interval.

Reverb. Adds multiple weak echoes to the sound, mimicking the numerous reflections of sound waves that occur in enclosed spaces such as auditoriums. Large amounts of reverb may make the music sound like it was performed in a large open space, while music with no reverb may sound flat and synthetic.

Graphic equalizers. Enhance one set of frequencies relative to another (e.g., accenting the midrange frequencies found in the human voice relative to low- and high-pitched instrument sounds).

Expanders. Take faint signals and amplify them relative to the sound as a whole. For example, an expander might be used to selectively amplify the softer sound of acoustic instruments relative to electric ones playing at the same time.

Limiters. Compress sound with a large frequency or dynamic range so that it fits into the narrower levels accepted by the recording equipment such as tape recorders.

Noise reduction processors. May be used to remove background sounds and transient audio clicks and pops in the signal.

Professional musicians also use more sophisticated distortion and harmonic processors. In general, these will contribute little to the sound quality of a webcast, which frequently is already distorted by the extreme compression necessary to deliver it through the Internet. Purchase of advanced effects processors should not be necessary for webcasts. The developers should also remember that many analog effects processors are duplicated in the digital realm by audio editing software. In many cases, it may be more efficient to sample the sound without processing and perform manipulations after the signal has been captured and digitized.

Mixing Boards and Multitrack Systems

Once a microphone has picked up a signal, it is normally routed through several additional stages before reaching its final destination. Depending on the number of microphones used to record the webcast signal, these steps may range from simple to complex. The sound processing component that integrates everything is the *mixing board*, which accepts signals from several sources and combines them into one or two outputs. Mixing boards are the central switchboards of an audio system. Complex audio events may require dozens of microphone inputs to be delivered and adjusted into the mixing board. A common use of mixing is to *normalize* audio, or set the maximum dynamic or loudness of the signal. For example, a signal from a speaker might be normalized along with remote microphones used by audience members so that the former does not drown out the latter.

Mixing board output may be directed to speakers, recorders, or analog or digital line feeds. Additional mixing board outputs allow the sound engineer to monitor output via headphones or graphic displays. In choosing a mixing board, webcasters should consider the number of input and output channels, whether submixes are practical, and if any additional signal conditioning or processing is provided by the board. The Mackie (www.mackie.com) line of mixers is very popular among musicians, and recent products such as the HUL (Human User Interface) have included close integration with Digidesign ProTools (www.digidesign.com) sound editing software, shown in Figure 3.3. Webcasters will probably want to look at the lower-priced ($1,000–$2,000) mixers designed for home recording rather than higher-end systems for broadcast studios and performance spaces.

If simplicity is a major concern, webcasters might want to consider an integrated system like the Telos ZephyrExpress (www.zephyr.com), shown in

Figure 3.3 The Mackie (www.mackie.com) Human User Interface mixer.

Figure 3.4. This compact, integrated system combines an audio mixer and monitor with an ISDN connector that may be used to send sound over regular phone lines to a remote site for capture to computer. Because it can deliver broadcast-quality signals over the phone system, webcast producers can keep their digital equipment in a central studio while supporting live events.

To connect microphones, electric instruments, and sound processors to the mix, it is sometimes necessary to use a simpler switchboardlike device called a *patch bay*. While not essential, a patch bay organizes an otherwise confusing mass of cables and allows routing different combinations of signals among different components. Small-scale webcasts may not need a patchbay, since the mixing board itself provides some organization of input and output.

Handling multiple inputs is essential for all but the simplest webcasts; and in most cases, webcasters will have to purchase their own mixing boards. Mixing is an art, and a production team that anticipates complex recording

Figure 3.4 Telos (www.zephyr.com) ZephyrExpress.

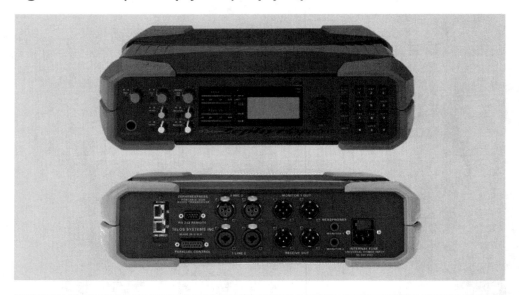

environments should make sure their audio engineer has been trained to use these traditional systems. Even in simulcast productions where the producers get audio from an existing *mixdown*, it is usually helpful to have an engineer on-site. Webcasters who are interested in all-digital solutions but who haven't purchased sound equipment might consider Yamaha's new DSP Factory (www.yamaha.com); it replicates a high-end digital recording and mixing console for less than $1,000 and provides 16 tracks of CD-quality audio and 254 mixer channels, along with analog/digital conversion and effects processing. With reduced costs and direct integration into the webcast environment, it is a superior solution for many production groups. Remember, however, that digital format is no substitute for expertise; producers will still need trained support for audio capture and mixing.

Speakers and Monitors

Virtually all audio systems send output to speakers. Speakers provide a monitoring capacity for sound recording, and in live performance provide amplified audio directly to the audience. In order to effectively re-create the original sound, the audio signal is split among multiple speakers optimized for different dynamic and frequency ranges. Knowledge of this practice is important when webcasters play a peripheral role in an audio event and must position their microphones to pick up sound from speakers. Care must be taken to position the usually small computer microphone so that it picks up the full range of audio.

Monitors are speakers or headphones that deliver the mixed audio to the performers rather than to the audience. Without a monitor, the performers would hear only sound reflected off the walls of the performance space, which is delayed by a fraction of a second. This delayed echo makes it difficult for performers to hear themselves. While not a major problem for speeches and discussions, echo can make it impossible for musicians to keep time while performing. The monitor solves this problem by providing a second audio signal without any delay for the performers. In studio recordings, monitors are usually headphones; however, in live concerts, a specialized pair of monitor speakers are often positioned on-stage for the performer's use. Sound engineers need considerable experience to learn how to adjust monitors to re-create a sound for the use of the performers that approximates what the audience hears.

Analog/Digital Converters

Processed audio from most current microphones/amplifier systems is output in analog form, which must be resampled and digitized. With the widespread use of multimedia, sound capture has become nearly ubiquitous, and hardware that enables sound capture on most computers is easy to find. Examples of companies that provide sound cards to the industry include Creative Labs (www.creaf.com), Digital Audio (www.digitalaudio.com), and Digidesign (www.digidesign.com). These cards easily capture audio at CD-quality levels. Inexpensive Windows sound cards from Creative Labs capable of recording and playing CD-quality audio typically run less than $50, and Macintosh systems have built-in circuits providing this function. In contrast, high-end sound cards from Digidesign that accept multiple audio inputs may cost thousands of dollars. Some recently introduced microphones and sound equipment convert information for transfer through the *Universal Serial Bus, USB* (www.teleport.com/~usb/usbfaq.htm), of Windows-based CDs. Webcast producers should ensure that any software they plan to use supports their sound cards.

Macintosh systems have built-in sound circuitry and normally do not require additional sound cards, unless the converter is combined with the mixer/effect processors to create a mini recording studio.

Recorded Audio Capture

Rather than getting their signal from an array of microphones, mixers, and processors, webcasters using recorded input will attach their computer and webcast encoding software to a playback device providing prerecorded audio. Recordings of live performances are typically derived from analog tape, while samples taken from finished audio products, such as a CD, are in digital format. For this reason, it is important to support capture and conversion from both formats. Here are some more specific features of recorded audio most likely to be encountered by the producers:

> **Analog tape recordings.** Cassette systems record continuous analog output onto tape. Referred to as reel-to-reel, this type of system may be encountered in many recording studios. Audio from these systems can be sent directly to the analog input found on most computer sound cards. The same outputs can be used to record audio-only information from a videotape. Analog tape has the advantage of ubiquity, and tape recordings are usually very easy to create. A webcaster receiving a cassette or other tape can be virtually certain that a system will play it back correctly when it is connected to the computer's sound card. Analog tape's main disadvantage is fidelity: Smaller tape decks usually record low-quality sound comparable to phone connections.

> **DAT recordings.** Popular in the music industry, *digital audio tape (DAT)* systems use 4mm tapes similar to backup drives on computers. They record sound as digital information in a format similar to audio CDs, but they are distinct from the digital format used on computer storage media. Professional DAT drives typically have analog and digital outputs. For capture of low- and medium-quality audio, the analog outputs may be directly connected to a capture card on the computer. While attractive in its simplicity, the scheme passes the sound through two analog/digital conversions, one when it exits the DAT drive and another when it enters the computer's audio port; this

double conversion results in a loss of fidelity. To avoid this, sound can be output in its digital format to cards such as Lucid Technology's NB series (www.lucidtechnology.com/pci24.htm) for Macs, and Townshend's DAT-Link (www.tc.com) for UNIX. Silicon Graphics' Indy and Indigo2 (www.sgi.com) computers record digital audio files directly from CD and DAT sources over their built-in SCSI bus. DAT transfer is preferred when working with professionally produced music, particularly where the goal is to retain maximum fidelity in the final webcast. Since DAT use is not widespread, the tape decks and capture cards tend to be more expensive than other systems. While the quality of DAT is very high, the increased expense makes them unnecessary for voice-only webcasts.

Audio CD/CD-R/CD-RW recordings. All forms of compact discs encode digital sound in a format similar to DAT recorders. CD and CD-ROM drives may output analog or digital output to the computer, depending upon the configuration of the software. For example, the CD player application on many computers uses standard analog output from the drive. A direct digital read of audio CD data requires a specialized program capable of accessing its storage format. Common audio editing programs such as Digidesign's Pro Tools (www.digidesign.com) and Macromedia's SoundEdit 16 and DECK II (www.macromedia.com) have built-in audio loaders. Standalone programs such as Asante's Toast (www.asante.com) also provide this function. CDs have less utility for voice-only webcasts, where a smaller and less expensive tape deck may be a more effective solution.

Webcast Video

If audio forms the most practical application of webcasting, video is the most attention grabbing. Fueled by expectations for all-digital television, many groups see video as the "killer app" of webcasting, capable of delivering an experience that will create the first Internet mass audience. Video also presents a much greater challenge to the webcaster and to the computer industry as a whole. Until recently, the extremely high bandwidth needed to digitize and capture video to computers made it a novelty, but recent consumer equipment is now approaching the speed and capacity levels necessary to deliver true digital video (DV). Webcasters using this equipment to move into the video realm will encounter a range of noncomputer devices even more complex than the audio systems discussed previously. This section addresses those aspects of video important to webcast video engineers, including basic properties of video signals, cameras, recording formats, and image processors.

Features of Video Capture

Video systems record single or multiple images at a characteristic frame rate, creating an illusion of movement. Once the expensive property of broadcast studios, low-cost video cameras have become common components of computer systems. In this subsection, features of video specific to webcasting are considered in greater detail. Traditional film (e.g., 35mm and 70mm formats) is not covered here since most production teams will transfer it to video prior to digital capture.

The many features defining video include resolution, contrast, frame rate, screen size, focus, and color balance. These have been combined to comprise a set of video standards that must be supported by webcasters recording and playing back analog video. The following evaluates the basic features of video in more detail, particularly where they are significant for webcast video production.

Resolution. In the broadest definition, *resolution* refers to the clarity or sharpness of a video signal; a high-resolution image is much sharper than a low-resolution image. For analog video systems, resolution corresponds to the number of video *scan lines*, which cross the screen horizontally, and by the spatial response to color or pattern changes within the scan line. Resolution is directly related to the required *capture area* needed for video software, which is defined as the number of pixels used to encode the information in the analog signal. This quality is roughly comparable to a 1,000 × 1,000 computer monitor with thousands to millions of colors. The 1/2" VHS format commonly used in VCRs has significantly lower quality, and is comparable to a VGA computer monitor (640 × 480 screen).

█TIP█ VIDEO SAMPLING RATES AND CAPTURE AREAS

Despite the temptation to compare scan lines directly to pixels, video signals require higher sampling to prevent loss of detail. In general, sampling of an NTSC screen without any loss of resolution requires a capture area of 1,000 × 1,000 pixels in size. Failure to sample at these higher rates will lead to significant degradation of the image. The situation is comparable to audio samples, where CD-quality digital signals are recorded at twice the highest frequency discernable to the human ear. Note, however, that except in special situations where extremely high-bandwidth video is contemplated, it is safe to sample with lower capture areas. For example, sampling a VHS signal at 320 × 240 pixels will provide maximum quality in typical webcast video windows smaller than 200 × 200.

Contrast. This method for measuring the quality of video images takes the brightest and darkest points in a scene and determines the difference between them. This parameter, also known as *luminance,* specifies the number of greys that exist between black and white. High-contrast images appear sharp, with clearly defined edges, while low-contrast images appear dimmed, as if they were seen through smoke. Thousandfold brightness ranges are easily encoded in standard analog video. Digitized video records contrast as the number of discrete shades that can be encoded by computer video capture software and varies from 256- to 1,000-fold differences.

Frame rate. The *frame rate* video feature measures the number of individual images presented in a given time to produce the illusion of motion, and is normally measured in frames per second. This feature controls how accurately motion is represented within the video image. The faster the frame rate, the better the image, particularly for rapid movements. In television, frame rates of 30 or 25 are used—significantly slower than the 24 frames/second common for film. Many video signals are also *interlaced* to reduce jerkyness. In this mode, half the total number of screen lines are sent in each cycle, with even and odd lines alternating, giving an actual frame rate double the typically quoted value. The technique results in less screen flicker at low frame rates. Most webcasts run at rates comparable to early silent film, at 7–15 frames/second. In most webcast video formats, the frame rate is actually dynamic and changes in response to the amount of motion being represented. For example, while a performer is walking, several frames per second might be sent, but this rate may drop to one per second or less if the performer is seated or motionless.

Color. Traditional analog video color is measured as *chrominance*, involving the hue and saturation, but not the brightness. The hue of the image corresponds to the color; saturation refers to the intensity of the color. Images with low saturation appear "greyed out" or pastel. Despite the lower bandwidth of black-and-white video, virtually all webcasters elect to use color signals. Analog video may encode a nearly infinite range of colors, but video digitized for webcasts typically ranges between 256 and a few thousand colors. More subtle shades are approximated by *dithering*, a process defined as creating a pattern of dots with two colors that approximates a third continuous shade. The result is a gradation of color, with one color gradually blending into another.

Focus and field of view. All cameras use a lens to focus light from the subject. Single lenses have fixed focus, which means that objects must be at a set distance to be in focus. This range of distance is the depth of field. The location of this area is determined by the degree of curvature of the lens, or *focal length*, measured in feet. For example, an f1-2 lens has a focal length of two feet, making it suitable for close-ups. The depth of field is small, usually only a few inches on either side of this value. Camcorder lenses generally range from f1-2 to f1-5, which makes them optimal for relative close-ups. Filming more distant scenes often requires adding a telephoto lens with a much longer focal length. Telephotos typically have a focal length in the f1-10–20 range, and contain a large depth of field beginning several feet away from the camera and continuing out to infinity. A consequence of long focal lengths is a reduced field of view. This means that telephoto shots only show a small area relative to lenses with shorter focal lengths. Small viewing areas also reduce the amount of light available to form the video image. Simple video cameras often use a single lens that provides good focus from 1–2 feet to infinity. More sophisticated cameras use multi-element lenses that zoom to different focal lengths. In a high-end video system, the lens assembly may be the most expensive component and frequently costs several thousand dollars.

Format. A video *format* consists of a specific frame rate and resolution used as standards for recording and displaying information. Common formats are necessary to ensure that video recorded on one system can be played on another. In the United States, the *National Television Systems Committee* (NTSC) is the most common analog video format. The NTSC video format uses 525 scan lines (480 visible) at a rate of 30 frames per second. The European video format, *Phase Alternate Line (PAL)* uses 625 horizontal scan lines (585 visible) at a rate of 25 frames per second. PAL is uncommon in the United States, but widely used in Europe and Asia. A format similar to PAL called *Sequential Color and Memory (SECAM)* is used in France. For all these formats, the frame rate is actually double, and each frame displays either the even or odd lines of the image in an interlaced mode. Video destined for satellite broadcast and digital videodisc (DVD) systems is normally encoded to digital format using the MPEG (www.crs4.it/HTML/LUIGI/MPEG/mpegfaq.html) format. This standard significantly compresses the video signal with little loss of picture quality. It is also used by the webcast encoders provided by StreamWorks (www.streamworks.com) and Motorola Truestream (www.mot.com). More information on video formats is available at AMRS World Standards (www.alkenmrs.com/video/wwstandards1.html).

Synchronization. Video recorders usually record audio, and the two signals are written to different parts of the tape, or tracks. Synchronization refers to the correct alignment of sound and video tracks. If synchronization is off, the movement of a speaker's lips may not match their spoken words; or an explosion may be heard before or after it appears on screen. Analog video and audio are synchronized using *time codes*, numerical markers written to the storage media in the audio and video tracks. This makes it possible to associate a particular video frame with a corresponding instant of sound. This method ensures that physical changes (e.g., tapes stretching with repeated play) will not affect synchronization. The high-end code for synchronization was created by the *Society of Motion Picture and Television Engineers (SMPTE)*, and it is widely used in the video industry. High-end video recorders allow time codes to be written separately and to be created when different video signals are combined. Some digitization systems can read SMPTE, allowing them to import multiple audio and video tracks already presynchronized in the analog world. Once captured to digital format, video editing software also allows audio and video tracks to be resychronized if necessary.

The greater complexity of video relative to audio production means that webcasters will need extensive knowledge of the medium in order to use it correctly. Groups developing original content will either require formal training in video production or will have to outsource the work to professional production companies. Even if the video is prerecorded, knowledge of the parameters used to create it will be helpful during the capture process to the webcaster's computer. Additional information on video services, manuals, and workshops is available from the Bay Area Video Coalition (www.bavc.org) and the Video University (www.videouniversity.com/).

Components of the Video Capturing System

Live video is captured using a video camera, which consists of a system for focusing an image onto a light *transducer,* and a second system that converts the light into electrical signals. The majority of video cameras use some form of *charge-coupled devices (CCDs)* to sample the image presented by the lens. CCDs are specialized integrated circuits that bear many similarities to RAM, except that each memory cell is light-sensitive. Circuitry in the camera periodically "dumps" light-induced electrical charges in the array to an output channel, which converts it to standard video. Output may be converted to one of the standard analog video signals or reformatted for direct digital storage. Most cameras have multiple outlets allowing the video image to be sent to a computer or other equipment for further processing.

Commercial video cameras vary widely in price depending on their features. At the high end, systems in the $20,000-plus range are used in professional broadcast and filmmaking. These systems are overkill for current webcast production studios that cannot take full advantage of the high resolution they supply. At the low end, systems for under $100 are adequate for capturing small-screen video or full-screen still images. Older cameras are still quite useful, and webcasters on a budget should check online classifieds like those at Biksco Media Services (www.biksco.com/used/).

Since Internet video quality is still quite low compared to standard broadcast, high-end systems are not as necessary as they are for webcast audio. Many webcasts may be able to use simple video cameras designed specifically for computer systems. As the quality of webcast video improves, more complex productions will need the help of professional camera operators and video engineers. Despite this, it is still important for everyone involved in producing the video to understand the basic features of video hardware. Below is a discussion of some of the common equipment used in videocasts and their functions.

Camcorders

Camcorders are CCD Video Cameras that convert the digital signal of the CCD to a standard analog video signal written to tape. There are three common types of camcorder systems: Low-end consumer camcorders record using the popular but relatively low-quality VHS format; some consumer cameras use a slightly higher-quality system called Hi-8; and most broadcast video productions use Sony's Beta format. Most video cards and A/V Macintoshes support VHS and Hi-8 by default. Capture of broadcast-quality video requires specialized cards and computers capable of handling extremely high (2–5 megabit/second) bandwidth. Recently, new all-digital camcorders using the digital video (DV) standard have become common.

During transfer from the CCD, most camcorders do a digital-to-analog conversion of the video signal for output to devices such as VCRs. To send the resulting signal directly to a computer, it is necessary to do a second conversion back to digital format. Several groups have developed small, inexpensive converters for this purpose; they usually output to the parallel ports or Universal Serial Bus (USB) interfaces of Windows-based PCs. Originally restricted to grabbing single frames, new versions now support the capture of video at varying speeds. The Snappy converter, shown in Figure 3.5, is a good example of this type of system. Still frames may be digitized at up to $1,100 \times 1,100$ pixels, which recovers virtually all the information latent in an NTSC-style video signal. A similarly priced and featured option is offered by the Connectix QuickClip (www.connectix.com), which supports video capture at 320×240 pixels at 15 frames per second. Still images may be saved at 738- $\times$ 480-pixel resolution. With these systems, the audio track must be saved separately using a standard sound capture card. Comparable plug-in video capture boards capable of real-time capture of 640×480 signals and CD-quality audio are widely available and typically cost a few hundred dollars. Examples include ATI Tech's All-in-Wonder (www.atitech.com), Data Translation's Broadway (www.b-way.com), and Intel's Smart Video Recorder (www.intel.com). Standard Macintosh systems cannot use camcorder video adapters, but all A/V Macintoshes have built-in support for combined (e.g., 320- $\times$ 240-pixel) video and audio capture from camcorders or videotape players. Other devices similar

Figure 3.5 The Snappy video converter (www.play.com/pages/snappy/ index.html).

Webcast Camcorders

Here are some important features of the ideal camcorder for a webcast:

Resolution. At least 400 lines (Hi-8, Super-VHS, or Beta recording format).

3-CCD chips. Provide greater definition and color clarity.

Microlens technology. Low-light sensitivity, particularly for live events.

Digital Signal Processing (DSP). Allows storing and instant recall of common camcorder settings.

Image stabilization technology (EIS, OIS, DIS). Automatically adjusts for small camera movements.

Variable shutter speed. Needed to film computer monitors to avoid flicker while filming the monitor with a camcorder.

Compatible with standard alkaline batteries. NiCad-rechargable batteries may be difficult to find on location. Plug-in A/C outlets and car cord chargers are also useful.

Protective lens coatings. These reduce UV fogging and protect against scratches.

Macro lens. Allows quick-focus shifts between near and far objects.

The following features are not as necessary, and should not be considered as a factor in a purchasing decision:

Resolution. 700 lines and above. This increase will not contribute to the final webcast signal.

Infared wireless connections. Allow the camcorder signal to be sent to a recorder without cables; but generally too pricey for webcasters on a budget.

Color LCD viewfinders. Usually too fuzzy to focus well.

Digital zoom. Enlarges the image electronically, which typically is not necessary during a webcast.

Multiple detachable lens assemblies. Webcast video is usually not sophisticated enough to require different lens combinations.

to the Snappy include FutureTel Video Sphinx Pro (www.futuretel.com), Videonics' Python (www.videonics.com), Dazzle Media's Dazzle (www.dazzlemultimedia.com), and AVerMedia's MPEG Wizard (www.aver.com).

Webcams

As the name implies, a *webcam* is a small, specialized CCD video camera specifically designed to output its signal to a computer. Unlike camcorders, webcams use the computer's processor to process the video signal, resulting in great reductions in size and cost. Both Macintosh and Windows versions frequently use a standard serial port or USB for output. Since the host computer processes the signal, the available frame rates and screen sizes are a function of its clock speed and memory. Many webcams also support web-friendly features, including timers for frame grabs, and utilities for automated image conversion and uploading to web sites. This makes it relatively easy to support ambient webcasts.

Popular examples of webcams include Connectix Corp.'s QuickCam, shown in Figure 3.6, that sells for around $200. This simple, fixed-focused color camera uses the computer's serial port to capture still images or moving video; there is no audio input. A somewhat more sophisticated system is provided by Vista Imaging Corp.'s ViCAM (www.vistaimaging.com) and Kodak's DVC 300 Digital Video Camera (www.kodak.com). Operating in video mode, the DVC captures 320×240 pixel color images at 5–7 frames per second. The camera also samples audio in a format compatible for *Video for Windows (AVI)*, a digital format used exclusively on Windows computers. Simple webcams can imitate variable focal lengths by sampling only part of the overall image projected on the charge-coupled device (CCD), which is used to convert light into an electric signal in the camcorder. Using such a system, the DVC 300 also supports variable settings, including telephoto (20 degrees), normal, (30 degrees) and wide angle (42 degrees).

Digital Video Cameras

While less common than traditional analog video, digital video (DV) (www.megavizyon.com/dvback.htm) is steadily gaining ground. Backed by manufacturers such as Sony, Philips, Thomson, Hitachi, and Panasonic, DV

Figure 3.6 Connectix Corp.'s QuickCam (www.connectix.com).

camcorders use a 5:1 digital compression algorithm to store broadcast-level video to tape. Depending on the image content, the encoder dynamically decides whether to compress picture fields separately or to combine two fields into a single compression block. As such, DV coding is thought of as something between motion-JPEG and MPEG. The professional version (*DVCpro*) has double the tape speed of the proposed analog camcorder replacement (*DVCcam*). The two standards are incompatible and use different types of magnetic tape.

Example DV systems include Cannon's XL-1 and Optura lines (www.canondv .com). Due to the recent introduction of these systems, webcasters may elect to wait until later in 1999 to replace their current camcorder with a DV model. The extremely high quality of DVCpro will be unnecessary for webcasts until the broadband Internet becomes a reality after 2005. A good place to keep track of DV developments may be found on the Digital Camera Resource Page (www.dcresource.com/) and Raley Communications Digital VideoResource (www.raley.com/ index2.htm).

High-speed digital video transfer will be enabled on PCs and other electronic systems during 1999 via the Firewire (www.ti.com/sc/docs/msp/1394/1394.htm) format, which replaces the standard computer serial port with a channel allowing 100–400 megabit/second transfers. Since these systems are new, relatively expensive, and provide video quality far exceeding current webcast standards, they are probably not worth the increased price unless streaming video is also being used for other purposes. In the latter case, Firewire will allow independent filmmakers to edit and produce broadcast-quality film on a single computer workstation.

TIP CAMCORDER CABLES

Like microphones, camcorders require cables to output their signal for further processing. Video signals travel at much higher frequencies than audio, so they are much more prone to frequency loss. This means that audio cables cannot be used to carry video, as they are generally inadequately shielded. Poorly shielded cables may lose signals if they become bent, are on top of each other, or are too close to power cords. The lowest-quality cable is RF (radio frequency) coax. Using a BNC plug, as shown in Figure 3.2, this cable is used to carry signals from television antennas and VHS decks. Due to its poor resolution, it is not recommended. A composite cable carrying an RCA or BNC plug is a much better choice. Even higher quality is available using S-video cable, which splits the color and brightness of the signal into two separate cables. While not found on VHS systems, it is usually an option for Hi-8 and Super-VHS camcorders. High-quality cables are available through companies such as Monster Cable (www.monstercable.com).

Current webcasts do not take advantage of the increased resolution of high-end video, so the decision to purchase a particular camera should be based on other features. Ask the following questions before purchasing: Does the camera have variable focus? Does it come with a stand allowing smooth scans or zooms over the performance space? If the camera connects directly to the computer, does its software support standard computer formats such as AVI and QuickTime? In most cases, simplicity of setup and operation will be more important to webcast producers than theoretical resolution.

Video Processing Equipment

Parallel to the mixers and effects processors found in audio, video systems may include additional processor modules that combine and/or modify the video signal from one or more cameras. Most of these devices are analog in nature and are rapidly being supplanted by comparable digital processing using video editors such as Avid Cinema (www.avidcinema.com), Adobe Premiere (www.adobe.com), and Radius Edit DV (www.radius.com/Products/0517.html). The following lists these devices for the sake of completeness, though it is unlikely that webcasters will need to purchase them for their production studio:

Caption equipment. One of the most common devices found in the video studio, *caption equipment* overlays letters and words on a video signal. This equipment is not very useful to webcasters, particularly those who use streaming multimedia software (described later in this chapter), which can create captions outside the video image.

Patch bay. Typically with fewer inputs than their audio counterparts, video *patch bays* often allow rapid switching between 2–3 cameras during the event.

Proc amp. The *proc amp* converts video signals and improves picture contrast and color. A related device, sometimes called a *video detailer,* sharpens images at the expense of increasing noise or speckles in the image.

Time base corrector. The *time base corrector* system adjusts the analog video signal (usually using the SMTPE standard describe earlier) to reduce the amount of flickering in the image.

The cost of all of these processors can easily run into the tens of thousands of dollars. Most webcasters will want to save their money and invest instead in one of the computer-based video capture and editing systems described in the next section.

Recorded Video Capture

Many webcasters will work with prerecorded video encoded with a variety of formats and resolutions. Basic computer standards such as QuickTime were covered in Chapter 2, "Developing a Webcast Strategy." This subsection expands on that discussion to include the digital and analog noncomputer formats and media that webcasters are likely to encounter in their work. A more comprehensive summary of the various formats may be found at web sites such as the Video Encoding Formats site (www.hut.fi/~iisakkil/videoformats.html). In the following subsection, the wide variety of media used to store video are discussed in greater detail. Since many of these media require specialized players to recover the signal, the discussion also considers the relative importance of each standard for the webcaster.

> **Tape.** Several formats exist for recording video on tape, the most common of which are shown in Table 3.4. Extremely high-quality three-quarter-inch formats used exclusively in professional broadcast have not been included. Most consumer systems use the relatively low-quality half-inch VHS format. Hi-8 and Super-VHS provide somewhat higher quality, and most professional video producers use the high-definition three-quarter-inch Betacam video format for postproduction. Since these tape formats are incompatible, webcast producers will need a different playback device for each type they plan to support. Most filmmakers consider VHS unsuitable for serious work, and webcasters should consider the Hi-8 format as offering the best price/performance for their projects. Macintosh A/V systems have Hi-8 and Super-VHS support built in by default, and most Windows video cards support Hi-8 input as well. If Hi-8 is used, it will also be necessary to get a VCR capable of playing back the signal—though it is also possible in most cases to use the camera itself as the playback device. Like digital video, Betacam provides extra resolution that most webcasters will not use, and the beta-compatible hardware costs significantly more than other formats. If webcasters will be accepting video from a variety of sources, it may be necessary to purchase multiple decks to manage them.

Table 3.4 Common Videotape Formats

Format	Description
VHS (1/2" cassette)	Uses three formats: SP (standard play), LP (long play), and EP (extended play).
Super VHS (S-VHS; 1/2" cassette)	Uses special tape to record 70 percent sharper than standard VHS.
Betacam (1/2" cassette)	High-quality professional; increased tape width and recording speeds give higher resolution than any other format.
8mm	Records two hours in standard play and four hours in extended play; high-quality sound, but video quality is as low as VHS.
Hi-8 (8mm tape)	High-quality 8mm (400–500 lines resolution); backward compatible with 8mm format; high-quality sound.

Videodisc

The *videodisc*, or *laserdisc*, is a high-quality, read-only analog format that is popular among videophiles for quality recordings of classic films (www.cs.tut.fi/%7Eleopold/ Ld/FAQ/index.html). Videodiscs provide much higher image quality than conventional VHS tape players and are popular with video hobbyists. However, the greater expense and more limited video selections available in this media have prevented it from becoming a popular consumer format, and it appears destined to be replaced by DVDs, discussed in the next subsection. Though videodisc players have standard video outlets, it is unlikely that most webcasters will need to support this format as DVD gains ground in the marketplace. During the current era of low quality webcasts, videotape formats provide sufficient quality; and when high-quality webcasts appear, the DVD format is likely to be ubiquitous.

Digital Videodisc

Digital videodisc (www.videodiscovery.com/vdyweb/dvd/dvdfaq.html) is a relatively new format that encodes video signals at a resolution approaching broadcast quality, and it shares similar MPEG-2 encoding technology. DVD uses a 5" disc comparable to an audio CD to store near-studio-quality video and better-than-CD audio. In overall quality, DVD is vastly superior to videotape and generally is better than laserdisc output. Unlike the audio CD and DAT formats, which were developed prior to the microcomputer revolution, DVD is designed to be easily read by computers. This, combined with its high quality and capacity, will make the DVD format a major component of future webcast production studios.

Webcasters may elect to support the DVD standard in two ways: If computer equipment is already available, producers may purchase a DVD-ROM, which is a DVD player that doubles as a disk drive for a computer. Note: Only the more expensive DVD-ROMs have the MPEG-2 chip necessary for video playback and capture. Alternately, producers may elect to purchase a consumer system, which is a good choice when funds are limited, since the cost of stripped-down DVD decks has fallen to a few hundred dollars. DVD is a format all webcasters should plan to support, due to its high quality, compact medium, and direct support for digital transfer.

Video CD

The *video CD (VCD)* is an older format using 5" CD-ROM-style disc technology that also compresses and displays videos compressed using the MPEG-1 standard. Popular in Asia, the VCD market in the United States is limited and few players or titles exist. Due to its simpler compression format, VCD is adequate for low-action video, but produces unacceptable pixelation (grainy images) with high-action video. Certain DVD players can also read VCDs; and some MPEG-1-based Internet-video software, such as StreamWorks (www.streamworks.com), can digitize VCD video. VCD is not the ideal format for webcast conversion; the motion degradation inherent in the format will compound similar motion problems found in most streaming video compression codecs.

Satellite/Direct Broadcast

Video signals may also be sampled from a satellite, cable, or network television broadcast. In this case, an antenna and television receiver are used to capture the analog video signal, which is digitized using commercial video cards. New forms of satellite are compressed using the MPEG-2 standard (www.satnet .com/mlesat/Article7.html). Depending on the type of signal (e.g., movies, sports), the data rate may be anywhere from 1 to 4 megabits/second for conventional television, about 8 megabits/second for studio broadcast, and more than 14 megabits/second for proposed high-definition television standards. Clearly, webcasts will be throwing away most of this information for some time to come!

Most webcasters will find the majority of their material recorded in VHS, Hi-8, or Beta format. In most cases, adequate capture for webcast requires little more than a VHS player and an inexpensive video card. Webcast groups receiving material from broadcasters may need to explain these limitations, since most will send beta format by default. Instead of resolution, the webcasters might explore optimizing frame rate or color balance for a smaller screen size.

Media Capture and Authoring Hardware

The computer used to capture and digitize audio, video, or other media should emphasize speed and capacity. Table 3.4 shows a typical configuration for capturing broadcast-quality audio and medium-quality video (e.g., 320 × 240) in real time for Windows and Macintosh systems. Table 3.5 describes typical configurations for Windows and Macintosh suitable for audio and video capture, along with estimated costs for each component of the system.

Table 3.5 Windows and Macintosh Capture Systems

	Macintosh	Windows	Est. Cost
Computer	G series A/V	300mHz Pentium II	$ 3,000
RAM	64-96 megs	64-96 megs	$ 300
Hard Disk	4-9 gigabyte drive	4-9 gigabyte drive	$ 500
CD-ROM	24×	24×	$ 100
Video Capture	built-in	hardware card	$ 300
Backup	4-9 gigabyte tape	4-9 gigabyte tape	$ 500
Monitor	17"	17"	$ 500
Operating System	8.0 or greater	Windows NT	$ 200
		TOTAL	
			$ 5,100

As webcast speeds and resolutions improve, much more powerful capture computers will be necessary, particularly with respect to storage capacity. An MPEG-2 broadcast stream will need at least 200K/second of storage. A minute of video will occupy 12 megabytes/minute, indicating that hundreds of gigabytes will be necessary to store large media archives. The recently proposed MPEG-4 broadcast format will require even larger storage requirements. Webcasters should plan to purchase increasing disk storage in the next few years, beginning with about 10 gigabytes in 1999 and working up to a terabyte (1,000 gigabytes) by 2005. Requirements for RAM memory will likely soar into the multigigabyte range in the same period.

| TIP | **OUTSOURCED ENCODING**

Encoding.com, created by Martin Tobias, provides services for creating and storing on-demand streaming media services. The service is designed to fill the gap between standard video capture/editing and the specific requirements of web-formatted video. The range for conversion is $45–$130/minute of footage. The service also encodes MPEG-2 for digital video and offers some support for live broadcast events as well. Due to the complexity of production, up to 40 parameters are set through discussion between the client and Encoding.com, including color palette, codec, frame rate, frame size, and perceived quality. Encoding.com accepts all major formats including Hi-8, VHS, and MiniDV, Betacam, and Digital D1. Once compression is complete, the staff optimizes the quality of the master using Terran Interactive's Media Cleaner Pro (www.terran-int.com) or Equilibrium's DeBabelizer (www.equilibrium.com). The company also sends engineers on location for $150/hour.

Authoring Software Environments

After the raw audio or video signal is captured and converted to a streaming media format, it must be formatted for delivery. For basic sites, a simple HTML page with a hyperlink to streaming media may be all that is necessary. Webcasters may also embed streaming media in a combined multimedia presentation and add interactive components. In the case of video, interactivity may be encoded in the image itself.

There are several authoring environments that combine capture with additional tools that are useful for webcast development. These include video frame grabbers, streaming media encoders, traditional multimedia authoring platforms, and new Internet-centric multimedia editors. The following subsections describe these tools in greater detail and considers their relevance for webcast production.

Advanced Video Frame Grabbers

Most video systems provide software with the basic utilities for still and moving video capture. For more features, including direct Internet upload and support for multiple file types, producers may install programs such as Webcam32 (www.kolban.com/webcam32), shown in Figure 3.7. This $25 Windows program

Figure 3.7 Webcam32 (www.kolban.com/webcam32).

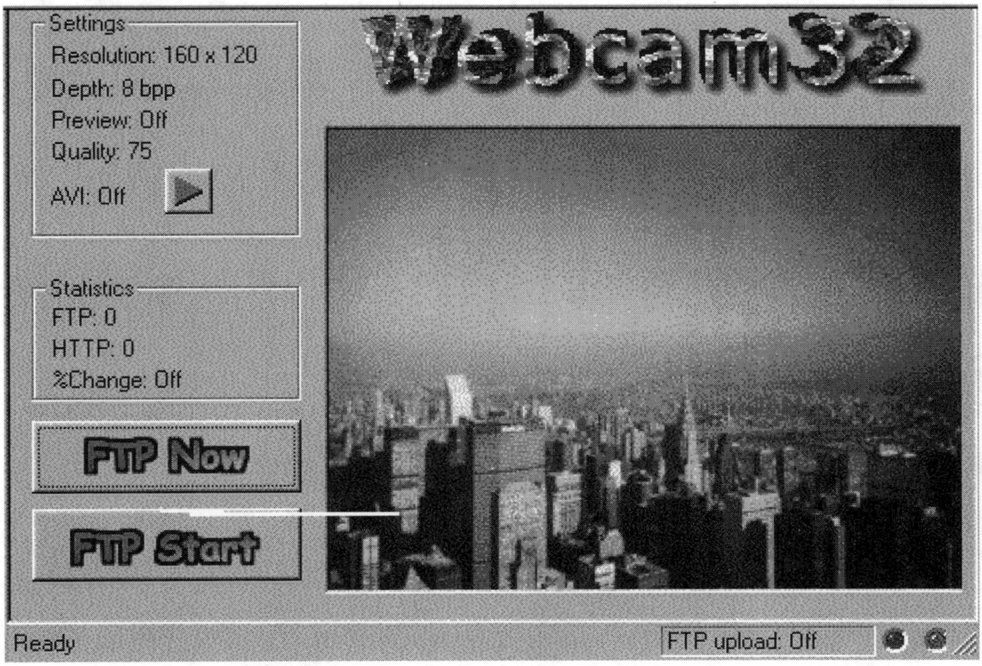

converts captured video directly into AVI video, JPEG images, or BMP images, and automatically uploads it to a web server. The system can also be set to take pictures only when there is movement in its field of view, or to operate during specific hours of the day. Webcam32 also functions as an HTTP web server, allowing a very simple setup for ambient webcast pages. It may also run as a Common Gateway Interface (CGI) (www.hoohoo.ncsa.uiuc.edu/cgi/) program, automatically processing the image and delivering it to a standard web server.

Streaming Media Encoders

As discussed in Chapter 2, "Developing a Webcast Strategy," the major streaming media vendors all provide free basic software encoders that may be used to capture and compress recorded and live video signals. RealSystem's (www.real.com) Live encoder, the basic version of which is shown in Figure 3.8, and VDOLive (www.vdo.net) are good examples of these systems. At present, virtually all live encoders are optimized for 28.8 or ISDN modem delivery. This means that webcasters should plan for significant quality differences between recorded and live webcasts. If extremely high quality is desired, the production team may elect to

Figure 3.8 The RealAudio Live! encoder.

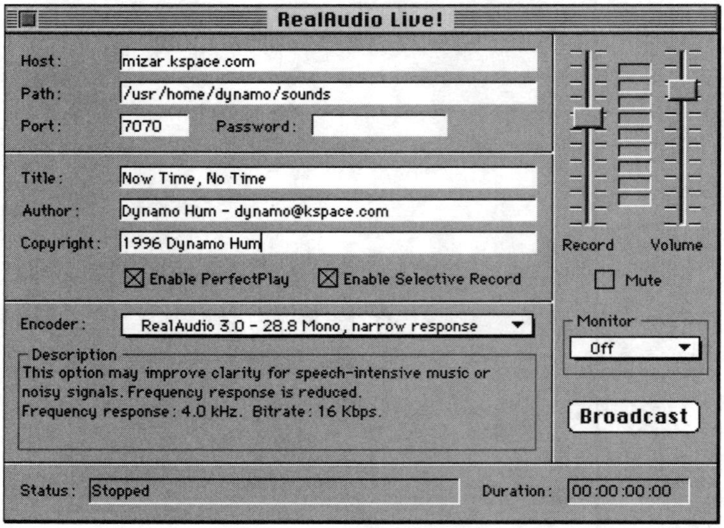

sample live audio with a webcast encoder and use a second computer to capture CD-quality audio using standard audio capture software. If the production team decides to capture software from StreamWorks (www.streamworks.com) or Vivo (www.vivo.com), the encoder must be purchased. Groups working extensively with MPEG-compressed video might consider StreamWorks since it uses MPEG video for its own conversion. Recently, StreamWorks successfully demonstrated real-time processing of standard broadcast using midrange Pentium computers.

Traditional Multimedia Authoring Platforms

The major streaming audio and video vendors have developed plug-ins that may be used with audio authoring systems such as Macromedia's SoundEdit 16 and DECK II, and Digidesign's Pro Tools. Similar streaming video plug-ins are available for Adobe Premiere (www.adobe.com), which is frequently used to edit and compress standard QuickTime movies. These systems allow filmmakers to continue implementing video editing software used in multimedia development to create their streaming video files. With the addition of plug-ins from RealNetworks, VDO, or Vivo, Premiere may also output webcast format video. Macromedia (www.macromedia.com) has also developed its own streaming media standard, which is included in Macromedia Director. This makes it theoretically possible to deliver webcast-style content in the standard Director environment, extending the utility of traditional CD-ROM packages.

Webcast-Specific Authoring

Development packages for webcast-specific authoring assume that the Internet, rather than the CD-ROM, is the preferred delivery system for multimedia. They resemble traditional authoring packages in that they offer support for synchronization of audio, video, animation, titles, interactive controls, and a CD-ROM-style interface. They also support common Internet data formats and are optimized for the low bandwidth characteristic of consumer modems. Like traditional systems, they define a synchronization protocol that allows seamless combination of audio, video, animation, and user actions into an overall production. With Shockwave, Macromedia started a trend of converting standard multimedia delivered on CD-ROM into the Internet environment. This trend was continued by companies such as Microsoft, GEO, and mBED. The following describes some of the capabilities and features of these programs.

Shockwave

Originally designed as a downloadable format for movies made in Director, Shockwave (www.macromedia.com) now supports streaming animation and audio, which makes it an excellent tool for webcasting. Shockwave movies may be authored in Macromedia Flash, Director, or Authorware, making an easy transition for existing multimedia developers. Each of these tools creates Shockwave that is optimized for a different purpose: real-time animation (Flash), CD-ROM style interfaces (Director), and presentations/distance learning applications (Authorware). The main drawback is that site visitors must download the relatively large Shockwave player. Shockwave offers a comprehensive set of media tools drawn from its Director heritage, and it is a compelling option for high-end webcast production studios using audio and animation. Streaming video developers who are not interested in elaborate multimedia or do not have experience on the platforms that support Shockwave authoring might want to consider another system.

NetShow

NetShow (www.microsoft.com/netshow) is an integrated streaming media authoring environment using Microsoft's "container" for streaming multimedia. Called Active Streaming Format (ASF), it is destined to replace the older AVI format. NetShow is currently being touted as a complete authoring and delivery environment. It currently includes Internet webcast protocols from RealNetworks, VXtreme, Liquid Audio, VDO, VoxWare (extremely high-compression voice audio), and Xing MPEG. NetShow takes all these formats as input and integrates them into a single ASF file. Audio may be synchronized to Java applets, ActiveX controls, and JavaScript embedded in web pages. NetShow is also compatible with other Microsoft presentation programs such as PowerPoint.

The server (provided free with Microsoft Site Server) is specific to and optimized solely for Windows NT. Like RealPlayer, it supports IP multicast, and streams in UDP and TCP/IP. Its tight integration with Windows NT allows the production team's Web administrators to use standard NT tools and applications for monitoring the webcast. The player incorporates a channel-type design for webcast access and is available for Mac and Windows platforms.

NetShow provides a comprehensive and robust platform for development and delivery; however, its Windows-centric orientation may be difficult, particularly for groups with backgrounds in Macintosh multimedia production or who plan to stream from an ISP that uses UNIX systems.

GEO Emblaze

Emblaze Creator (www.emblaze.com) allows web programmers and designers to author Internet-oriented webcasts that include streaming animation, audio, video, and interactive multimedia content without plug-ins or expensive server software. Unlike other systems, the end user does not need to download a custom player. Instead, small Java applets (approximately 8K for audio and 50K for video) are downloaded from the web server to the user's computer. The applet dynamically requests, decodes, and decompresses the streaming multimedia files. Emblaze requires Java-enabled web browsers such as Netscape Navigator 3.0+ or Microsoft Explorer 3.0+ on Windows or UNIX. The sound quality is comparable to many plug-in-based systems, with 11kHz/16-bit sample rate for audio (slightly below CD or broadcast quality) and 10 frames/second for streaming video through 28.8-56K modems. The Creator environment is in direct competition with Microsoft's NetShow, but the Java-based delivery may help Emblaze carve a niche among a new audience.

mBED Interactor

The mBED Interactor (www.mbed.com) creates interactive animation along with streaming audio for delivery over the web. A variety of formats are supported, including GIF and JPEG image formats, WAV and RealAudio and RealVideo. Interactor also supports 8-bit alpha-channel masks, which facilitate mixing several animated objects with transparency and *antialiasing*. Animated objects may move along straight lines or curves, effectively duplicating the "sprite" animation found in Director and other CD-ROM authoring environments. Each medium may be associated with a hyperlink to another mBED application or web page. Completed multimedia applications may be converted to dynamic HTML, Java applets, or full-featured "mBEDlets," which require a custom player plug-in. Developers familiar with CD-ROM authoring will find many common features in the mBED interface, but its main appeal is its focus on Internet and Java-based delivery of content.

Flash

Flash (www.macromedia.com) is rapidly gaining ground as a choice streaming media authoring environment. Many sites, such as the House of Blues (www.hob.com), have replaced their HTML home pages with interactive Flash animation, and other groups have produced promotional webcasts integrating streaming audio and video clips with character or other animation. Playing Flash currently requires that the user download a plug-in, but Java-based versions are being developed. Unlike NetShow and Emblaze, Flash authoring is supported on Macintosh platforms, easing the migration of existing multimedia developers. Produced by Macromedia, its authoring environment employs a time/multitrack metaphor similar to Director.

Flash does have some limitations as an authoring environment. Current versions do not support an internal scripting language, and the image editing tools fall short of dedicated software. It remains to be seen whether Flash will evolve to replace standard web content or will simply augment it.

| NOTE | **TELEVISION PRODUCTION SOFTWARE** |

Webcasters familiar with the CD-ROM world may find themselves considering using high-end video production studios optimized for television as an alternative to streaming multimedia programs. As an example, the $5,000 Trinity software package from Play Inc. (www.play.com) provides a variety of built-in television editing features including switchers, transitions, linear/nonlinear editing, and character generators. Despite these advantages, the systems are not the best choice for webcasts. Currently, their feature list is overkill for webcasting, and the lack of integrated streaming video further reduces their appeal. They may, however, form an interesting addition for webcasters who are also involved in film/television production and produce parallel versions of their content. To address these problems, Play, Inc. is actively developing a separate product called LBTV (low-bandwidth television) specifically for Internet television-style production.

Java

The Java (www.javasoft.com) object-oriented programming language is useful for webcasters who want to deliver audio and video without proprietary players or plug-ins. It is also appropriate in wordcasts/datacasts for which commercial player software does not exist. Java applets are stored on a web server; upon user request, the program is downloaded and executed by the web browser. The design of Java favors cross-platform compatibility. Despite various problems, it still remains the only system that is not locked to a particular operating system or software configuration.

Currently, Java is most often used to create custom streaming multimedia players for datacasts. Examples include telemetry from remote machines and text-only tickers delivering streaming wordcasts. Some companies, such as Vosaic (www.vosaic.com) and Graham Technologies (www.gts.com), have experimented with streaming audio players built entirely in Java. To date, the greatest problem is the relatively slow speed of Java applets. Downloading and triggering a streaming media applet may take several minutes, an unacceptable lag time for most visitors. Compatibility issues also pose major problems for developers. Incompatibility between Microsoft's Java implementation with the standard originally developed by Sun Microsystems (www.sun.com) has made it difficult to implement advanced applets. Many Macintosh systems have a buggy version of the Java interpreter that crashes when it encounters certain applets. As processing speeds and compatibility improve, Java may become the method of choice for implementing datacasts (see Chapter 7, "Datacasts and Wordcasts").

SMIL

The proprietary authoring systems described here face competition from an open-standards format called the Synchronized Multimedia Integration Language (SMIL). Developed by the World Wide Web Consortium (www.w3c.org), SMIL (www.w3.org/TR/WD-smil) is an early application of the *eXtensible Markup Language (XML)*. SMIL is a text-based, tag-markup format allowing simple creation of streaming multimedia using an ordinary text editor, thus freeing developers from proprietary formats. The markup tags define a series of media objects encoded into timelines running simultaneously or in sequence. Like JavaScript, SMIL execution is a client-side, rather than server-side, process. The attributes of each media object may be configured to control the events that trigger starting or stopping a media stream, allowing user interaction. Another feature is that SMIL does not define the media elements themselves, which allows for the integration of existing streaming technologies. If the standard becomes popular, it is likely that SMIL interpreters will be built into Web browsers and media players.

Beatnik

Beatnik (www.headspace.com) is not designed as a true webcast medium, but its interactive features may help integrate streaming media with standard Web content. Its chief purpose is to integrate standard Web surfing with audio cues. Sounds may be cued to *mouseovers*, paging, selection of controls, and times. Added to streaming audio and video, Beatnik provides the trappings of the virtual theater to audiocast and videocast.

Web authoring environments are currently in a state of very rapid flux; therefore, producers should select a product based on its perceived long-term placement. If the webcast will reach a wide audience, systems that do not require plug-ins to be downloaded may be the best choice. In corporate intranets, it may be convenient to standardize on a single platform such as NetShow and leverage the existing installed base of Windows NT systems. Webcasts designed to augment material originally developed for CD-ROM may use the Shockwave system to their advantage.

Adding Interactivity to Hyperlinked Video

The tendency of the Internet audience to jump from one place to another puts the television remote to shame, and webcasts are no exception. In order to introduce interactivity into streaming video, new tools have been developed that link portions of an image stream or objects within the video to other areas of the web. The following lists some of the recently developed tools for this purpose:

Ephyx V-Active. This package, selling for $695, allows the creation of *hotspots* within AVI, QuickTime, and MPEG files, as well as RealVideo and NetShow. It uses image-tracking technology to define and follow a clickable hotspot as it moves within the scene. When site visitors select the hotspot, a link is made to a web page, media object, or programmable behavior.

Digital Renaissance Temporal Annotation Generator (TAG).
The Temporal Annotation Generator (TAG) authoring environment supports numerous file formats. The product consists of a $150 encoder and a $500 server with a media database. Playing the integrated media application over the Internet requires a plug-in.

in:sync Kohesion (www.in-sync.com). This video editing package for Windows NT/95 combines mixing multiple audio and video tracks with direct RealVideo output. The software supports time-event and hotspot hyperlinks for video output to Progressive Networks' RealVideo. The platform also supports real-time audio mixing and video streaming. Different points of the completed video may refer to different URLs, and local areas of an image may act as clickable hotspots within the video; link to other video; or specify jumps to standard web pages. *Alpha channels* are supported, allowing sophisticated matting and antialiasing effects. The program does not support SMPTE.

QuickTime 3.0 (quicktime.apple.com). The newest version of QuickTime allows frame-by-frame linking to other video or pages on the web. Figure 3.9 shows an example of this form of addressing, in which clicking on an individual's picture brings up an associated web site on-screen. While potentially very powerful, tools taking advantage of the full features of QuickTime 3.0 are still being developed. It is likely that most streaming multimedia vendors will include QuickTime 3.0 compatibility in their next generation of software.

Putting It All Together: Sample Production Studios

If you've made it through all these descriptions of streaming media, you may feel a bit confused about which direction to take. To clarify matters for you, following is a list of some possible production studios that might be used by webcast producers. A diagram of the possible layout of each system is shown in Figure 3.10.

Figure 3.9 QuickTime 3.0 frame-by-frame linking.

Developers will need to determine whether the webcast authoring will take place in the analog or digital world. Groups experienced in traditional broadcasting may find that sound equalization, mixing, titles, transitions, and edits are best performed using analog cameras, microphones, and mixers. Groups more familiar with computer systems may elect to digitize "raw" media and do their editing within a webcast-friendly multimedia authoring program.

Ambient system. For uploads from webcams, the production studio might consist of a low-cost Connectix digital camera connected to the serial port of a standard computer. Camera software or third-party products such as Webcam32 may be combined with a modem or ISDN connection to send single-frame updates to the web site.

Audio/video archives. A standard multimedia production computer such as a PowerMac G3 or Pentium /Windows NT is suitable for this

Figure 3.10 Sample production studios.

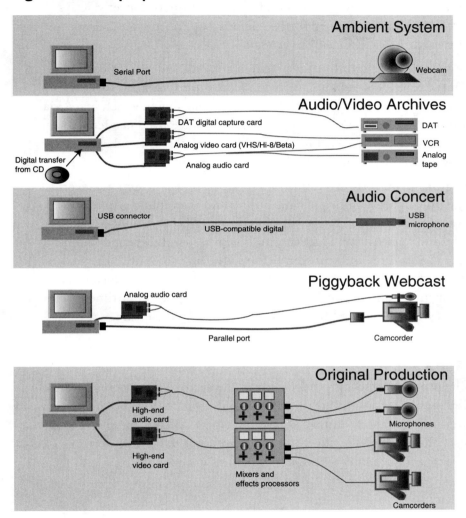

midrange webcast solution. Authoring uses standard multimedia programs such as Premiere and Pro Tools, combined with encoders using freeware streaming media. Encoded webcasts may be uploaded with slower modem-based FTP connections since the site functions as an on-demand archive.

Audio concert. For this system, a condenser microphone with a USB connection is tied directly to a midrange Pentium or PowerMac system. The audio is encoded for live delivery at 28.8 modem speeds and is forwarded to a webcast server via an ISDN line.

Piggyback webcast. In this system, a single standard camcorder is adapted for video and audio delivery from a performance space. A digitizer such as Snappy is used to convert the signal, which is fed via USB to a midrange Pentium computer. Freeware live encoders from selected vendors are used to convert the video stream and send it to the webcast server via an ISDN or faster connection.

Original production. In this high-end studio environment, several personnel operate multiple camcorders and microphones according to a written script. Professional audio/video engineers manage placement and operation of cameras, microphones, and mixing equipment. After digitization and transfer to the authoring computer, the various audio/video segments are assembled using a webcast authoring system such as NetShow or Emblaze. The resulting web/multimedia application is uploaded to a server for on-demand viewing.

Next . . .

After the production team has defined the physical and authoring layers of the webcast, they must determine how they will deliver their webcast content over the Internet. The next chapter considers aspects of server upload and management, the response of the Internet to webcast data, and features of consumer connections and equipment relevant to webcasts.

WEBCAST SERVERS AND CONNECTIVITY

After selecting the components necessary to capture and encode media for the webcast, the next step is to plan a strategy for delivering the resulting information to the Internet audience. This is a multistep process that begins with uploading webcast data from the production studio to the Internet service provider (ISP). Information delivered from the webcast is then processed by the hardware and software of a media server, which provides on-demand access to audio, video, or multimedia streams. The process ends with the webcast data traveling over the Internet to the end-user's hardware and software. Elements of these delivery systems are depicted schematically in Figure 4.1. This chapter describes these systems and associated strategies for selecting the best mix of hardware and software to support webcast delivery.

Uploading from the Production Studio to the ISP

Uploading from the production studio (or scene of the webcast) to the ISP is the initial link in the webcast chain. This is often the most difficult area for the production team to develop, as it requires a reliable high-bandwidth connection from the webcast location, which is often distant from the ISP. An Internet "dial tone" (the notion of connecting to the Internet automatically from a phone) is still a distant dream, so webcasters must currently rely on a medley of upload solutions, including dial-up modems, the Integrated Services Digital

Figure 4.1 Elements of webcast delivery systems.

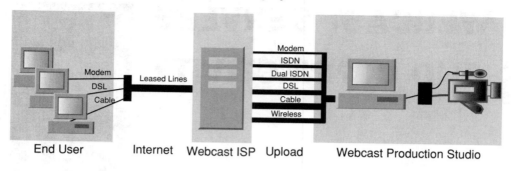

Network (ISDN), and digital subscriber lines (DSLs), developed for consumers and business services. Due to the lack of standardization in connection hardware and software, however, webcasters should expect to develop a unique connectivity solution for each webcast venue/production studio. If phone lines are being used for upload, the webcaster will need to determine whether faster options like ISDN or DSL are available, and arrange for their installation and testing. If these options are unavailable, it will be necessary to use one or more analog modem connections, or in favorable instances, high-speed *leased lines*. For on-demand webcasts, slower connections are appropriate—provided that sufficient time is allocated for uploading to the media server. If the webcast is being delivered live, bandwidth will directly determine which webcast formats should be used. (For more information on webcast formats, see Chapter 3, "Webcast Equipment and Authoring Environments.")

Let's take a look at the most common types of access available to the webcaster. Figure 4.2 illustrates a comparison of these connectivity types to the webcast delivery formats discussed in Chapter 2, "Developing a Webcast Strategy." Note that the most common method for connecting to the Internet—a single analog modem—is sufficient only for the low end of webcast production. For text-only wordcasts, ambient webcams, and datacasts (also discussed in Chapter 3), modems provide enough bandwidth to support a live webcast. In contrast, broadcast-quality audiocasts, videocasts, and streaming multimedia require faster options.

Figure 4.2 Connectivity types versus common webcast delivery formats.

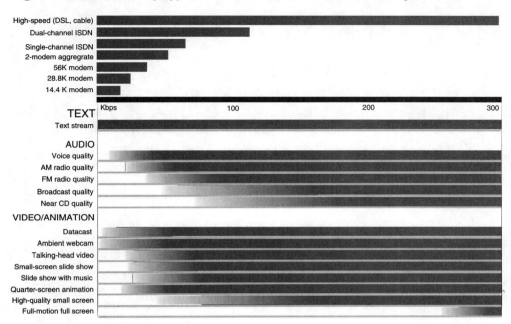

Modem Connections

Now that the incompatibility between the two 56K modem standards—x2, led by 3Com Corp. (www.3com.com) and K56flex, led by Rockwell (www.rockwell.com) and Lucent Technologies (www.lucent.com)—has been resolved by agreement between the manufacturers to support both standards, fast adoption of the 56K modem standard is expected. This is good news for end users using dial-up Internet accounts; but webcasters should remember that streaming media uploads via 56K modems will be restricted to a maximum of 33Kbps, which reduces the level of confident data upload (allowing buffering for transient slow-downs) back to 28.8, or about 30Kbps. For this reason, modems are not useful for real-time audio and video delivery from a webcast. However, they may be quite effective at streaming text-only wordcasts or a slow-frame webcam image series.

Recently, some vendors have announced "dual modem" solutions that combine data from several modems into a single stream for greatly improved

Case Study: Audio Upload and Encoding by Liveconcerts.com

URL: www.liveconcerts.com
Contact: Eric S. Magnuson ericm@real.com

Liveconcerts.com provides access to performances by a variety of musicians and entertainers from clubs throughout the United States. Operated as a joint effort by RealNetworks (www.real.com) and the House of Blues (www.hob.com), it simultaneously promotes entertainment unavailable elsewhere, while demonstrating the state of the art for streaming audio and video.

The general strategy for audiocasts uses line conditioning to deliver near-CD quality analog audio to the Liveconcerts.com studio, where it is digitized and streamed across the Internet. A schematic of the systems used to deliver audiocasts is depicted in Figure 4.3. At the club, audio is recorded and mixed by in-house engineers supplied by House of Blues. The audio signal destined for webcasting is taken from the standard mix and sent to a Telos Zephyr (www.zephyr.com) connected to an ISDN line. This system converts the analog audio to a non-Internet stream of digital data suitable for sending via ISDN. By avoiding an Internet connection, transmission quality is significantly improved. At the studio, the ISDN line output

throughput. These systems may make it practical for webcasters to send live data from unimproved locations with *Plain Old Telephone Service (POTS)* connections provided that several phone lines are reserved. For example, the Diamond Shotgun system (www.diamondmm.com) combines two analog modems into a single channel running at 56 or 64Kbps. Combining the signals of several modems connected to the Internet provides a bandwidth increase which enables music-quality audiocasts.

Non-Internet Connections

In some cases it may be easier for webcasters to "upload" a non-Internet audio or video stream from a remote site and encode it at another location. In this is converted to an analog signal by a second Zephyr which routes it to two dual P-Pro 200s. These systems redigitize and encode the audio stream in real time using the RealNetworks Live Encoder. The audiocast stream is output in 20K and 34K bandwidth levels, corresponding to average connection speeds available through 28.8 and 56K modems. On the rare occasions when audio is encoded at the performance space, the RealNetworks team uses a single processor P-Pro 200 running Linux, which has the capacity to encode three streams simultaneously. With this approach, the output is webcast-ready, and is sent over an Internet connection to the media server.

Figure 4.3 Diagram of upload and encoding system used by liveconcerts.com.

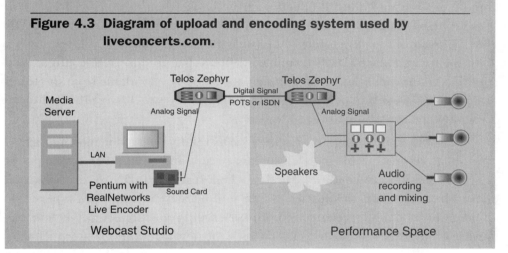

case, webcasters will need *line conditioning* equipment used by traditional broadcasters to send information from remote locations to the central office. Common examples where conditioned lines are used include audiocasts from clubs and phone interviews. To condition the line, two modemlike devices are installed at each end of a phone line or ISDN connection. These devices send and receive digital data using special non-Internet codecs optimized for audio delivery. The resulting audio signal is generally of higher quality than that which would be transmitted over the same line by two analog modems. A good example of line-conditioning hardware is provided by the Telos Zephyr (www.telos.com). This integrated system combines a simple audio mixing board with a conditioned CD-quality signal sent through a phone line.

ISDN Connections

Developed by the phone companies during the late 1970s, ISDN connectivity combines two 64Kbps data/voice channels for up to 128Kbps of bandwidth for a webcast. Under ideal conditions, this is sufficient for small-screen (e.g., 200 × 200 pixel) video running at several frames a second. Though not a common consumer option in the United States, ISDN has been installed by venues supporting live webcasts, such as the Troubadour (www.troubworld.com) music club in Los Angeles. Single-computer modems are available from vendors including Motorola Bitsurfer Pro (www.mot.com/MIMS/ISG/Products/bitsurfr_pro/) and the 3Com/US Robotics Sportster 128K (www.3com.com/client/pcd/products/prod-modem.html#isdn). Products such as the Fallaron Netopia ISDN modem (www.fallaron.com) allow several computers to be connected to a single ISDN line. Companies such as Teles AG (www.electronic-frontier.co.uk/teles/index.html) have announced ISDN terminal adapters that promise auto-configuration of ISDN connections. More information about ISDN is available from the ISDN Infocenter (www.isdn.ocn.com/), which features an "ISDN 101" tutorial (www.isdn.ocn.com/isdn101/).

One of the remaining drawbacks of ISDN relative to analog modems is that the phone company must install a custom circuit, and constant electrical power must be supplied to condition the line. This restricts ISDN to locations that have already set up the service. After setup, ISDN is generally superior to modem or modem aggregates in both speed and reliability. Nevertheless, the future of ISDN is still uncertain. And with the development of faster technologies that do not require line conditioning, ISDN may never achieve widespread availability.

DSL Connections

Digital subscriber lines (DSLs) are becoming increasingly popular technologies for providing medium-speed (0.1–10Mbps) connections capable of operating through ordinary phone lines. Unlike modems and ISDN, DSL technologies bypass most of the *Public Switched Telephone Network (PSTN)*—the system currently used for phone communication—thereby avoiding busy signals and long connection delays. Since a DSL does not tie up phone switches, it can be left on 24 hours per day at a relatively low cost ($40–$150/month). This means it is practical to use DSLs to host web sites and ambient webcasts. Like 56K modems, DSL connections are generally asymmetric; while download speeds may run at several megabits per second, upload speeds are generally comparable to dual ISDN. On the other hand, DSL is usually limited to phone lines running two miles or less between the site and provider, making it impractical for almost half of U.S. households.

Examples of recent DSL products include Nortel's (www.nortel.com) DSL modem, a $200 solution providing 1Mbps downstream and 128Kbps upstream. Similar solutions are being developed by Rockwell (www.nb.rockwell.com), 3Com (www.3com.com), and other modem makers. Commercial DSL service is available from groups including Convad Communications Co. (www.convad.com), which recently rolled out DSL support in California through Concentric Network Corp., Slip.Net, Verio Northern California, and Whole Earth Networks. A comparable project by US West (www.uswest.com) offers DSL-based Internet access in Arizona. To head off fragmentation of the DSL market, the Universal ADSL (Asymmetric Digital Subscriber Line) Working Group (www.uawg.org) recently proposed a single framework designed to compete with cable modems. This emerging standard will have always-on 1–1.5Mbps connections with monthly access as low as $40. These systems are very promising, since they may allow webcasters to deliver high-speed data from locations with unimproved phone lines. More information is available at the ADSL Forum (www.adsl.com).

Leased-Line Connections

The bulk of medium-distance, point-to-point connections on the Internet utilize rented phone lines with circuits that are always open. These *leased-line* connections provide much greater reliability than modem and ISDN lines. A fixed circuit must be installed by the phone company, like ISDN connections, making these lines impractical for on-location webcasts unless venue operators decide to install their own connections. The cost of leased lines generally runs $200 to $1,000/month for the phone connection and $400 to $800 for the Internet connection. These prices make installation practical for hotels and business complexes but too expensive for performance clubs and other webcast venues.

The most common leased line in current use is the *T1* connection, roughly the equivalent of 24 56K modem connections. Higher-speed connections, such as *DS3* and *OC3,* are generally restricted to the downtown region of large metropolitan areas. In some cases, several T1 lines may be aggregated via a procedure called *inverse multiplexing* to create the equivalent of a single higher-speed connection.

LAN Connections

Some fortunate webcast groups will host their productions in an ISP's *local area network (LAN),* giving them direct access to a high-speed network. Virtually all LANs today use 10Mbps or 100Mbps Ethernet, and 10/100 cards are becoming standard on most computers. Running the upload over a LAN provides an essentially seamless connection between production and media server. Unfortunately, Ethernet connections are severely limited in distance, and running a LAN much beyond the front door of the ISP is usually impractical. The cost for hosting within an ISP's LAN is similar to general web hosting fees—typically between $100 and $2,000 per media server installed on the network. For a list of webcast ISPs, see Table 4.3 later in this chapter.

Cable Modem Connections

For end users with the right cable company, fast Internet access is a reality today. Cable modems used by services such as MediaOne Express (www.media one.com) in Los Angeles and @home/Cox (www.cox.com) feature download speeds up to 10Mbps. Upload speeds are more variable, with some services relying on dial-up modems for this purpose, rendering them useless for webcasting. Other cable companies include Time Warner's Roadrunner (www.rr.com), which provides 3Mbps upload speeds. Since cable modems share a common connection with the ISP, these high speeds are theoretical and often drop as more users log on. Typical performance is somewhat superior to dual-channel ISDN. Cable operators can become Internet providers by using the services of companies like Community Networks, Inc. (www.cni.com), PerkInet (www.perki.net), and Cable Access America (www.caa.net), which provide turnkey Internet integration.

Like DSL, cable modems are always on and have a price point near $40/month. Though service is still spotty, cable modems may offer useful webcast upload services. Long term, the potential for competition between the broadcast-oriented cable company and the independent webcaster may curtail their use for this purpose.

Wireless Connections

The availability of an Internet connection from virtually anywhere is a tempting promise of wireless Internet connections. Currently, although this ideal is far from realized, several vendors including Motorola (www.mot.com/MIMS/ WDG/modemsDir/pm100cDir/) have recently introduced wireless modems. Low-speed wireless connections of up to 28.8Kbps are available from Metricom's Ricochet ISP service (www.metricom.com). The bandwidth is too low for video, but it is adequate for wordcasts and possibly voice-only webcasts. Ricochet service is available in several U.S. metropolitan areas, and its web site, shown in Figure 4.4, publishes maps of the current service areas. A similar service was recently announced by GoAmerica (www.goamerica.com).

Figure 4.4 Map of Ricochet Wireless Service in Santa Clara County (www.metricom.com).

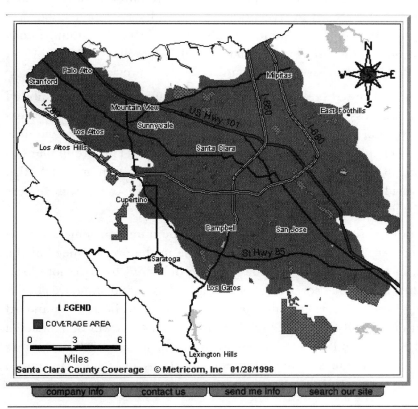

For higher bandwidth, *line-of-sight* systems that beam radio signals to the ISP are likely to become more common in the future. Unlike lower-frequency wireless modems, the signals cannot bend around obstacles (such as buildings), and consist of directional sender and receiver antennas connecting the production studio and the media server hosted at the ISP's location. Examples of these systems include Warp Drive Networks LLC (www.warpdrive.net), an easy-to-install wireless service providing ISDN-level connections to the event site. Most sites are used for business installations. Access is through UHF and microwave links, which confines the service to Warp's operating area in Silicon Valley and Seattle. Faster connections are supported by Multipoint Networks WaveNet IP wireless routers (www.multipoint.com/ProductindexT.html), which provide Ethernet-speed Internet traffic over distances of a few miles. Inficom's Infilink modem (www.inficom.com/product.html) may be of particular interest to webcasters. This advanced system supports T1-speed Internet access at distances of up to 10 miles. Unlike many other products, a standard antenna rather than a directional dish may be used for reception. Similar T1-speed connections are available through Internetix (www.innetix.com) and Winstar Communications (www.winstar.com). More information about wireless suppliers is available on the Wireless Provider Page (www.well.com/user/lawtech/provider.html).

In the past, incompatible hardware and data routing protocols inhibited the growth of wireless Internet links. Recent developments by the Wireless Application Protocol Forum (www.wapforum.com) may standardize wireless technology and enable rapid expansion in the near future. This group plans to create an open standard protocol called Wireless Markup Language (WML), which will provide a common communication language between web servers and wireless telephone networks.

It is tempting for webcasters to assume that the numerous emerging initiatives for high-speed access presage a quick rise in the overall speed of the Internet and in the types of media that may be delivered from remote locations. In reality, it will take several years of consolidation and standards building before high-speed Internet dial-tone or wireless access becomes standard in most locations. Until then, live high-bandwidth webcasts will be restricted to studios adjacent to an ISP or to large institutions such as convention centers that have already put in leased-line Internet connections for business purposes.

The rise of DSL may make it possible to webcast video from several locations, but the real-world performance of this technology over typical POTS systems is yet to be determined. Since current implementation is limited, webcasters recording live events will need to develop strategies that accommodate slow data uploads for some time to come (see webcast formats in Chapter 3, "Webcast Equipment and Authoring Environments").

Integrating Web Data with Traditional Broadcast

Web-television hybrids have recently become more common, and some predictions by Forrester Research (www.forrester.com) estimate that more than 1 million units will be installed by the year 2000. While varying in features, these *set-top boxes* (specialized computers providing Internet or other types of digital communication via cable or phone lines) all combine the capability to access Internet data with a standard broadcast television signal. Some versions restrict data to a one-way flow of web pages delivered in the *vertical blanking interval (VBI)*, the short amount of time between individual frames of the television signal during which data transmission may be sent. Others include full web access sharing a split screen with the television signal, which may also include VBI data linking the television show to particular web sites. Broadcasters use encoding hardware developed by companies such as eeg Enterprises (www.eegent.com). The following describes some of the connectivity technologies available to webcasters interested in using these systems:

> **WebTV networks.** In addition to a television tuner, a 1.1 gigabyte hard drive, a video effects engine, and a 56K modem, WebTV (www.webtv.net) contains a video/data integration system called VideoModem. The VideoModem system decodes standard television broadcasts and operates as a 10Mbps cable modem. Web information is placed in the video signal during the VBI. The end user may shrink or grow the video signal relative to the web page content. This technology gives over-the-air broadcasters the power to bypass cable/phone paths; they can continue to broadcast through conventional television signals.
>
> There is simultaneous support for standard dial-up Internet access. Microsoft and 12 television broadcasters/cable programmers are

working to provide data to WebTV in the VBI. Microsoft's VBI system is built around a custom Windows NT 4.0 server and software based on IP multicast technology. End users will need either broadcast-enabled PCs running Windows 98 or Microsoft WebTV boxes with a software upgrade that Microsoft plans to release late in 1998. More developer information is available on the WebTV site (www.webtv .net/primetime/TVLink.html).

Intel Intercast. Intel Intercast (www.intel.com/intercast/) is designed to promote PCs into television/web terminals. By adding a hardware board, a computer may be equipped to decode and process data encoded in standard television signals. In addition to Internet-style delivery, the system initiates file transfers and real-time data reports coupled with televisions. Intel has developed a set of tools that broadcasters can use to encode Intercast content. More information is available at the Intercast Industry Group (www.intercast.org). It is likely that this technology will receive significant use, especially since Intel and Microsoft recently announced plans to make Intercast and WebTV compatible with each other.

Worldgate. Worldgate (www.wgate.com) uses the VBI to send signals both upstream and downstream, eliminating the connection to a dial-up ISP. By concentrating computing resources in the cable head, this system allows access to Internet resources without computers or set-top boxes.

Currently, Internet audio/video is not comparable to standard broadcast, therefore the developers of data-enhanced television and webcasters have different goals. Most broadcast groups will focus on running interactive services such as chat or polling systems operated via standard web programming. For this reason, they are likely to have little interest in streaming Internet media that might compete with their broadcast. Ultimately, the WebTV hybrid technology will be of interest to traditional broadcasters rather than independent webcasters. The centralized nature of television broadcast makes it unlikely that webcasters will have much contact with these services.

Features of Webcast Media Servers

Compared to the production computers considered in Chapter 3, "Webcast Equipment and Authoring Environments," webcast servers require greater speed; in addition, they must efficiently support data requests from many users at once. Even if the media server is an outsourced item in the webcaster's budget, it is still important to understand the features and limitations of systems currently on the market. First, hardware that is relatively similar in price and appearance may have widely different limitations. Second, if problems are encountered during the webcast, they will be more easily analyzed and diagnosed if the webcast engineer understands the particular hardware configuration used. The following provides a brief summary of computer hardware components relevant to webcast delivery, and Table 4.1 shows possible configurations for low-, medium-, and high-performance webcast servers. At the low end, systems similar to the production equipment serve effectively. Resources such as PC Webopaedia (www.pcwebopedia.com) are useful in finding definitions for arcane hardware references from ISPs or retailers.

Table 4.1 Sample Configurations for Webcast Media Servers

Media Server Type	Bare Bones	Intermediate	NT
Mediacast Streams	15	50	75
Storage (hours)	4	10	20
Hardware	Pentium	Sparc 20*	Pentium II
Clock Speed	133MHz	80MHz	300MHz
Operating System	Red Hat Linux	Solaris (UNIX)	Windows NT
Disk Storage	4Gb	9Gb	9Gb
RAM	64Mb	128-256Mb	256Mb
Connectivity	10BaseT	10BaseT	10/100BaseT
Estimated Cost	$4,000	$8,000	$10,000

*remanufactured

(Continues)

Table 4.1 Sample Configurations for Webcast Media Servers *(Continued)*

Media Server Type	High-End UNIX	Enterprise Webcast
Mediacast Streams	150	500
Storage (hours)	50	300
Hardware	Origin 200 (SGI)	Origin 2000 (SGI)
Clock Speed	180MHz	180MHz
Operating System	SGI UNIX	SGI UNIX
Disk Storage	50Gb	250Gb
RAM	256Mb	786Mb
Connectivity	100BaseT/ATM	100BaseT/ATM
Estimated Cost	$25,000	$100,000+

Processors

Virtually all midrange computers today use either Intel-based Pentium/ Pentium II-level processors for Windows or *RISC (Reduced Instruction Set Computing)* for UNIX. It is not practical to use older processor architectures with speeds of 486 or slower as webcast media servers. The features of RISC systems deployed by vendors including Sun Microsystems (www.sun.com) and Silicon Graphics (www.sgi.com) make them generally faster than Intel architectures running at the same clock speed. RISC systems show better scaling when run on multi-processor systems. For these reasons, a RISC-based system may have a lower clock speed than an Intel system and still deliver greater performance. On the other hand, RISC systems are generally more expensive than Intel. For midrange webcasts serving a small number of viewers, a fast Intel Pentium II, such as 300MHz, may show comparable performance to a slower but more expensive server based on RISC technology. It should be noted that very fast Intel processors may be limited in practice by the 33MHz speed of the *PCI bus* (the system that connects the computer's components). Webcast servers may be built by computer manufacturers including Compaq (www.compaq.com) and Hewlett-Packard (www.hp.com). Popular consumer enhancements for Intel systems such as MMX/Pentium processors have little effect on webcast performance.

Hard Disks

Most hard disks today operate using either the *ATA/EIDE* (also known as *Integrated Drive Electronics, IDE,* the default internal hard drive contained in most Intel-based computers) with an average data throughput of about 2–9Mbps, or one of the various *Small Computer Systems Interface (SCSI)* (www.scsita.org) standards with throughputs in the range of 5–80Mbps. Table 4.2 lists the various SCSI standards. A detailed technical comparison of the systems is available at AdvanSys (www.advansys.com/wpide.htm). In single-user mode, EIDE and SCSI are roughly similar; however, tests by PC labs (www.zdnet.com/pcmag/pclabs/report/r960702a.htm) indicate that SCSI disks have an advantage when heavy disk access is coupled with webcast-style streaming. Webcasters will always want to choose fast and/or wide SCSI standards with 20Mbps or greater throughput. SCSI systems have the additional advantage of supporting several internal or external high-speed drives at once, which is important for supporting system backups. The current generation of high-capacity SCSI drives includes standouts such as the Seagate Cheetah and Barracuda (www.seagate.com) series with capacities in the range of 4.5–30Gb or greater. SCSI drives cost approximately $100/Gb.

For even higher performance, necessary for real-time video delivery, *redundant array of independent disks (RAID)* arrays should be considered. Produced by companies such as American Megatrends (www.ami.com), Artecon (www .artecon.com), and Buslogic (www.Mylex.com), these systems stack a series of

Table 4.2 Features of Various SCSI Standards

SCSI	Bus Width	Devices On Chain*	Mbps*
SCSI-1	8	8	5
Fast SCSI	8	8	10
Fast/Wide SCSI	16	16	20
Fast/Wide Ultra	16	8/16	40
Ultra (narrow)	8	8/16	40
Wide Ultra-2	16	16	80

*maximum

hard drives that pass data in parallel as a single drive. This gives RAID throughput speeds that are multiples of the disk number. Depending on the array design, RAID drives may also offer automated data backup. Such systems will be increasingly in demand as webcasting invades traditional broadcasting and supports multiple megabit webcast streams.

Backups

To some extent, disk capacity has surpassed standard tape storage devices. While high-capacity drives and tape arrays such as Procom's Jetstream (www.procom.com) have the capacity to support several webcast servers, backup times may last several hours and impose a speed penalty on the systems served. To increase performance and save money, many webcasters prefer to archive their information to a second hard disk. The use of hot-swap plugs that allow drives to be added and removed from SCSI chains such as SCSI Pro (www.scsipro.com/01fs_main.htm) facilitate this process. Other backup options include Iomega's 1Gb and 2Gb Jaz drives (www.iomega.com) and the SyQuest (www.syquest.com) 4.7 removable drive using UltraWide SCSI. Other systems such as MicroNet's DataDock 7000 (www.micronet.com) allow mixing a variety of drives ranging from hard drives to CD-R and DAT systems. If such a system is used, the engineer should confirm that the presence of slower devices, such as tapes, does not hinder transfer from the hard disks.

Memory

Media servers supporting hundreds of webcast streams require great amounts of memory, and adding memory is generally the best way to increase server speed and reliability. Webcast servers should run with an absolute minimum of 64Mb of RAM; 256Mb or more will improve performance. The webcast engineer should consult a memory guide for the processor to select the right type of memory.

Recently, some hardware companies have begun to deliver integrated systems optimized as webcast servers. The Silicon Graphics Origin200/MediaBase system (www.sgi.com) shown in Figure 4.5 is a good example of this new breed of high-performance media server. This system integrates extremely fast UNIX-based hardware with standard webcast encoding, authoring, and

Figure 4.5 Silicon Graphics Origin200/MediaBase webcast server.

delivery software. As such, it forms a one-stop solution in the $20,000 price range combining the webcast production studio and media server. High-end versions of the 200 series provide for up to four processors, 4Gb of shared memory, and more than 20Tb (terabytes) of storage; the enterprise-level 2000 series supports a remarkable 128 processors and 58Tb of storage. A unique feature of the system is the bundled MediaBase database designed specifically for indexing media archives. The system supports H.263 videoconferencing, MPEG-1, MPEG-2, and RealNetworks. Webcasters wishing to use RISC technology on a lower budget might check remanufacturers such as Rave Computer (www.rave.com), which sells reconditioned Sun servers at a fraction of their original cost. For webcasters using Intel architecture, the fastest systems are recommended; multiprocessor systems should be avoided because their speed improvement is too small to justify the increased cost.

Operating Systems

In addition to hardware, media servers are also characterized by the software used by the operating systems. Because the original Internet ran almost exclusively over UNIX-based systems, these form the bulk of the servers used by webcasters; however, recent improvements in Windows NT have made it a viable alternative for at least some forms of webcasting. Both these systems are characterized by their support of a protected-mode multitasking environment. Among other things, this means that bugs in individual programs will not cause the entire system to crash. This gives the systems the required reliability necessary for webcasts. Let's take a look at the advantages and disadvantages of these operating systems and compare them to other minor and forthcoming systems.

> **UNIX.** The UNIX operating system has developed in close association with the Internet, and currently still is the best choice for a webcast platform. High-end versions of UNIX using RISC technology are available from vendors such as Silicon Graphics (www.sgi.com) and Sun Microsystems (www.sun.com). Recently, RealNetworks and Sun announced an agreement that will closely integrate RealMedia technology into Solaris, Sun's version of UNIX. Other versions of UNIX capable of running on Intel processors (486 and Pentium) have become popular in recent years, particularly BSDi (www.bsdi.com) and Red Hat Linux (www.redhat.com). These relatively low-cost platforms, ranging from $40 to $400, provide most of the power of UNIX using relatively inexpensive hardware.

> **Windows NT.** Microsoft's network solution shares with UNIX a protected-mode multitasking operating environment similarly resistant to system crashes. In developing NT, Microsoft successfully combined this feature with access to the enormous range of software available for the Windows platform. For those already familiar with Windows,

installation and maintenance of an NT webcast server presents a smaller learning curve than mastering UNIX. The tight integration of most NT Internet software with the operating systems also allows administrators to use standard tools to monitor the performance of a webcast. These advantages somewhat offset the reduced scaling of NT relative to UNIX. There is also limited support for clustered server networks with dynamic load balancing, though Microsoft's Wolfpack system (www.microsoft.com/ntserverenterprise/guide/wolfpack.asp) should provide this functionality in the future.

Other platforms. Currently, Macintosh and Windows 95 are not viable webcast platforms. Despite the intrinsic speed of the PowerPC RISC hardware used in Macintosh systems, the operating system is inefficient when handling multiple audio and video streams, and it is not protected against system crashes. The upcoming Rhapsody operating system announced by Apple may help to correct this problem by providing modern features such as preemptive multicasting and protected mode operation. A similar crash problem exists with Windows 95. The new BeOS (beos.newdream.net) operating system is a protected-mode multitasking system that could be used to build robust webcast media servers, but it is a recent development, so the software necessary to create a server is just beginning to appear.

Despite the current battle among operating systems, it is possible to select UNIX or NT servers depending on the strategy developed by the production team. Webcasters with limited budgets should generally consider Linux systems, which provide credible performance on consumer-level Pentium servers. UNIX is also the best option for high-end webcast production that demands the best available performance of hardware and software. In these cases, Sun or SGI servers are the best choice. If webcasters have a Windows orientation, or want to take advantage of many low-cost software programs for Windows, an NT platform is an alternate possibility. If NT is chosen, however, webcasters should plan on buying hardware that is approximately twice as fast as UNIX systems. Many webcasters employ a mix of platforms, UNIX for heavy-duty streaming and NT for hosting the associated web site.

Server Management Tools

During the webcast, webcasters will generally need to monitor their servers for a variety of parameters that affect performance and reduce its impact on the network as a whole (see Chapter 6, "Webcast Promotion, Commerce, and Analysis," for details). For example, if the webcast occurs over an intranet, it is important that streaming media services do not disrupt mission-critical operations such as database updates. On the Internet, effective server management may be used to partially compensate for traffic and end-user problems. The major classes of server administrative tools likely to be encountered by the webcast production team are as follows:

Webcast encoder utilities. All major streaming media vendors supply administrative packages that allow live uploads of streaming media. Most of these packages also provide monitoring systems that enable the administrator or engineer to allocate media streams and control bandwidth.

Server bandwidth management. Servers from RealNetworks and VDO automatically confirm the end-user's bandwidth and send compatible data streams. The VDOMaster (www.vdo.net) software bundled with VDOLive 3.0 is a good example of a server management tool. It creates a control center that allows the provider to track streaming activity and performance; predetermine bandwidth for particular recipients; and control available bandwidth by time of day. The VDOLive video streaming technology can adapt to the measured bandwidth of a network connection from dial-up modems up to 512Kbps. Microsoft has announced similar bandwidth management tools for NetShow 3.0. Other companies, such as Packeteer (www.packeteer.com), Xedia (www.xedia.com), and Ipsilon (www.ipsilon.com), provide software tools and integrated solutions specifically targeted at webcasts run through intranets. They are also used by webcast ISPs providing guaranteed bandwidth. For intranet webcasts, products such as Vstream's (www.vstream.com) DEMAND software enable the regulation of bandwidth by users, groups of users, and segments of the company's network. VitalSigns Software (www.vitalsigns.com) has two tools—VitalHelp and VitalAnalysis—for analyzing problems detected by its Net.Medic program at end-users' computers. It is essentially for intranets where monitoring software can be installed onto each user's computer. In the future, the *Real Time Streaming Protocol (RTSP)* developed by RealNetworks and Netscape may become an important standard in this area. Running on top of the standard RTP discussed in Chapter 2, "Developing a Webcast Strategy," RTSP supports several bandwidth-reduction strategies, such as setting higher priority for certain types of Internet traffic relative to other types. This standard is currently supported by RealNetworks and Silicon Graphics.

HTTP server management. Since most webcasts are associated with a web site, it is also necessary for the production team to monitor the HTTP server. A wide variety of tools are available for this purpose, including Freshwater Software's SiteScope (www.freshtech.com), which allows administrators to monitor URL availability on several web servers. They can also receive reports for CGI script execution, mail server access, disk usage, and delivery efficiency of web data. SiteScope also provides automated fixes for some problems and creates manual alerts for others. For sites anticipating very high traffic, products such as RadView Software (www.radview.com) offer packages that simulate heavy loads and flag bandwidth bottlenecks.

Access statistics. In order to determine the features of the webcast audience, it is necessary for the webcast engineer to monitor usage during webcasts. Standard media servers normally write access logs for web traffic, which may be supplemented by reporting software such as Webtrends (www.webtrends.com) and Marketwave HitList (www.marketwave.com). Interestingly, no webcast-specific access analysis tools have been announced, though RealMedia and other servers write access logs separately from the web server.

Despite the availability of software tools for monitoring webcasts, it is important that the webcast producer assigns an engineer to routinely check the system. Webcasters will need to expect the unexpected and assume that hardware or software problems may arise to impact the quality of uploads or server delivery at any time. Ideally, the engineer will have a portable computer to log in to the production and media servers and an open standard ISP account for monitoring the webcast as it appears to end users. The engineer should communicate with a representative from the ISP level, maintaining email and phone contacts in case problems occur.

Webcast ISPs

The rising interest in webcasting has helped to create a new group of Internet service providers (ISPs) specializing in the medium. Depending on the ISP, this may mean anything from reliable bandwidth to access to broadcast-style production studios. Services provided may run from server hosting and high-speed lines to a complete outsourced solution for webcasts. Webcasters can check for these services on the ISP's home page, as shown for InterVU in Figure 4.6. A list of some of the companies currently offering specialized webcast delivery support is shown in Table 4.3.

Figure 4.6 Home page of InterVU, a major webcast ISP (www.intervu.com).

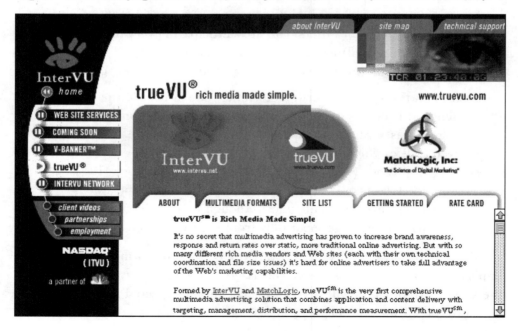

Table 4.3 Representative Webcast ISPs

Company	URL
DigitalNation	www.digitalnation.com
Concentric Network	www.concentric.net
Uunet Technologies	www.uu.net
MCI	www.mci.com
America Online	www.aol.com
InterVU	www.intervu.com
GTS	www.graham.com
AudioNet	www.audionet.com
Exodus	www.exodus.com
Digex	www.digex.com

The features determining an ISP's ability to support webcasts are somewhat different from standard ISPs:

Data replication and server networks. Since unicast web servers are limited to supporting very small audiences, webcast ISPs create multiple copies of the webcast data on widely separated server networks. This method is used when the webcast is prerecorded. For live streaming data, the multicast strategy introduced in Chapter 2, "Developimg a Webcast Strategy," is necessary. Some webcast ISPs support one but not the other form of replication, so the production team should check to see that their provider fills their needs.

Traffic redirection. ISPs supporting this service dynamically point webcast traffic to the media server on the network hub closest to the end-user's location. This reduces the number of hops taken by the data and may avoid congested national backbones and public *network access points (NAPs)*. Use of this method requires data replication across a server network.

Support for intermediate-speed connections. Virtually all ISPs support modem and leased-line connections, but only a subset have experience with ISDN and DSL systems. Webcast ISPs are generally more experienced with high-speed connectivity and can solve problems implementing Internet access in remote locations.

Multihoming. Internet traffic is exchanged between various ISPs, forming the Internet at NAPs. These public exchange points are typically overloaded, and packet loss through a NAP may run as high as 30 percent. While suitable for text and graphics delivered on web pages, this level of loss is unacceptable for streaming media. To avoid this, national ISPs have increasingly turned to creating private access gateways between each other independent of the NAPs. This *multi-homing* greatly increases the reliability of the webcast, since the media server and end user are more likely to share the same network backbone. However, multihoming is expensive and therefore is generally not supported by very small ISPs. The increased cost of multihoming may also require concentrating all servers at one point to eliminate paying connect chargers for multiple ISPs at several geographically dispersed points.

Load balancing. Simply put, load balancing refers to software-based strategies that detect net traffic increases and distribute the traffic evenly across the available bandwidth and media server network. Cisco's DistributedDirector (www.cisco.com) router software and the hardware-level systems provided by HydraWEB Technologies (www.hydraweb.com) allow an ISP to distribute traffic among multiple dispersed servers. These systems are still relatively rare, and their presence at an ISP is evidence of a commitment to provide webcasting and other high-bandwidth support.

Guaranteed bandwidth. ISPs that combine all aspects of webcast delivery are able to provide clients with constant bandwidth despite traffic ebb and flow in their networks. These options allow webcasters to design for a specific audience size with the assurance that they will have the capacity to support them regardless of other ISP clients. As might be expected, these options are expensive relative to standard server hosting, and it seems unlikely that current technology guarantees bandwidth across a network of multiple media servers. Webcasters electing for guaranteed bandwidth should make sure that the ISP provides a feature list explaining the service.

Security. Most ISPs enforce only minimal security, which is a potentially serious problem for their clients. While a hack into a webcast might seem like additional entertainment to some of the audience, it has the potential to damage the reputation of the production team or organization they represent. When signing up with an ISP, webcasters should ask when the last security audit was conducted and whether a summary report is available. Features to look for include the use of firewalls, support for a variety of encryption services, and physical security for the locations harboring the ISP's server network.

In addition to direct discussion with prospective ISPs, the production team may also take advantage of commercial services that rank webcast ISPs, such as net.Genesis' net.Sweep (www.netgen.com) and Inverse Network Technology (www.inverse.net). These services draw sophisticated performance profiles after placing random dial-up calls to the ISP from a variety of locations and then tabulating the statistics. Webcasters working on a smaller scale analyze access from individual users with low-cost software such as VitalSigns Software's Net.Medic (www.vitalsign.com). This software has the advantage of detecting problems on the end-user's computer as well as within the network.

Features Affecting Webcasts

In the preceding sections, the discussion centered on components of the webcast delivery system over which the production team has direct control. Getting the desired set of components is a matter of informed purchase. There are also components outside of the team's control that involve the general Internet and the audience's hardware and software; for these, the production team cannot buy their way into a particular solution, but must adapt the features of their production to the prevailing circumstances. Groups webcasting over intranets may have somewhat more control but will still have to adjust to available bandwidth and end-user configurations. In the following discussion, these factors are considered, along with adaptive strategies that may be used by the webcasters.

Features of the Internet

The Internet is truly a network of networks. Once the webcast stream leaves the media server and the ISP network, it must proceed through a variety of networks owned by competing groups. The webcast producers may not be able to control the groups that collectively operate the Internet, but they can plan around the bandwidth realities of their ISP and geographical location. In developing their webcast, producers should check the current state of the following global features of the Internet:

Bandwidth. Despite the rapid growth of the Internet, the available bandwidth has also increased at a rate that has rebuffed the doomsayers who predict a worldwide crash. Nevertheless, bandwidth will remain a key issue for many years to come. Since the majority of Internet users are concentrated in the United States, bandwidth rises and falls with day/night cycles for the East and West Coasts. Local bandwidth problems may be glimpsed at sites such as the Internet Weather Report (www.internetweather.com).

Latency. The time between a data request and actual receipt of information is referred to as *latency*. Webcasts typically consist of uninterrupted streams of data, so latency itself may not have a negative effect on a live event; but this feature becomes relevant when the connection is erratic. In this case, if the latency time exceeds the buffered information in the media player, webcast dropouts of audio or video signals will result.

Error rate. The reliability at which data is sent and received is referred to as the *error rate*. This feature measures the percentage of individual packets reaching their destinations. Since all Internet data is carried by these packets, knowing the error rate is essential to ensuring that the webcast data is being delivered efficiently.

To determine the effect on the webcast, the production team may check real-time analyses of the Internet as the webcast date approaches. Most national

ISPs also announce network outages and slowdowns on their web sites. During 1997, ISPs became more reliable, especially America Online, which started the year with a series of service outages. Thanks to this improvement, webcasters may rely on the majority of their audience having at least 28.8-modem-level access for extended periods of time. However, remember that a typical connection to an ISP still includes random disconnects and login failures. Some national ISPs may fail to match smaller, service-oriented organizations such as Earthlink (www.earthlink.com) and Mindspring Networks (www.mindspring.com).

Features of Consumer Hardware and Software

Other features important to webcast delivery concern the state of hardware and software on the end-user's computer. While the webcasters have little direct control over this aspect of the project, knowledge of the current state of consumer equipment is very useful.

Windows computers comprise virtually all of the consumer hardware equipment being sold today. New systems normally come with Windows 98 pre-installed, though a significant fraction of older systems still have Windows 3.x software installed. Since streaming media is generally not compatible with Windows 3.x, the potential market is automatically restricted. A comparable situation exists with hardware. For example, media players generally do not run on 486 and slower systems, so the available webcast audience actually comprises less than one-third of the total Internet audience. Macintosh users make up only a small percentage of the total market, though recent improvements in Apple's fortunes led to an increase in new users for the platform. Although 6800-based Macs cannot support media players, virtually all PowerPC-equipped Macs should be able to handle audio and video by default.

While these are significant problems, the most vital issue facing webcasters is consumer player software itself. Despite the promise of Java-based players, current webcasts require users to download and install software on their computers. Since only a fraction of users will download software, webcasters appeal to a very limited audience. These restrictions do not apply to older webcast systems such as the server push method used to send still images from webcams to a web site. One interesting use of this technology is provided by GTS Inc. (www.graham.com), which has developed custom webcasts using CGI-based video animation delivered by server push. Since this is supported by any recent web browser, webcasts hosted by this provider are ensured the widest possible audience. For those with Java installed on their systems, a custom real-time player provides audio.

The best way to determine current statistics for end users is to check sites that aggregate a variety of reports related to Internet use, such as CyberAtlas (www.cyberatlas.com). It is also useful to consult yearly studies that list demographics along with hardware statistics, such as GVU's WWW Internet User Survey (www-survey.cc.gatech.edu/). For webcasts aimed at a large audience, such information will be handy for answering the inevitable "Why doesn't it work?" questions received from the public.

Next . . .

This concludes the discussion of the various hardware, software, standards, and services that webcast production teams need to understand. The following chapters deal with preproduction and production processes, which will convert these abstract concepts into an actual production plan of a live webcast.

PLANNING, LICENSING, AND MANAGEMENT

5

Webcast producers manage a juggling act that involves both advanced network audio/video and real-world aspects of content creation. These two areas come together in the production process, during which the producer organizes hardware, software, personnel, and other resources by creating a timetable for managing various aspects of the webcast. In this chapter, general production issues common to all webcasts are considered, including developing production schedules, writing scripts and storyboards, working with performers, licensing content, and managing the webcast as it occurs. Later chapters will focus on the production details of wordcasts, audiocasts, animacasts, and videocasts.

Planning the Webcast

Coordinating a webcast production is more difficult than standard web development. The real-world requirements for organizing people and equipment impose an additional layer of complexity and time constrictions that require greater effort. Production coordination ideally involves creating databases, checklists, schedules, and an overall production timetable to keep track of equipment, connectivity, personnel, and budget. All schedules and databases should be kept on an intranet or an accessible computer so that all participants in the webcast may access them.

Equipment checklist. Maintained by the technical engineer, this contains an inventory of each physical object, hardware, and software required for webcasting. Examples include computers, cameras, microphones, cables, mixers, modems, routers, headphones, encoders, authoring systems, server software, and small tools.

Connectivity database. Maintained by the technical engineer, this lists contact information for the webcast ISP and phone lines/network protocols needed during the webcast.

Personnel database. Maintained by the producer, this contains email addresses and phone numbers for all members of the webcast production team, performers, temporary help, and the venue operator if the webcast is on location.

Financial schedule. Maintained by the producer, this includes salaries for employees, taxes, payments to consultants, venue operators, utilities, leases, and direct purchases. A small-scale schedule may be created in a spreadsheet program such as Microsoft Excel (www.microsoft.com/excel). For large productions, the complexity of the financial schedule may require using software such as Intuit's Quicken or QuickBooks (www.intuit.com) to create a formal financial statement, or special-purpose software developed specifically to manage production budgets, such as Screenplay Systems' Movie Magic (www.screenplay.com).

Once these databases, schedules, and checklists have been developed for the production, the producer should generate an overall timetable listing production milestones and individual tasks within the production. This calendar ensures that tasks associated with listed items are carried out in the correct order. The production timetable should be duplicated and made available to each member of the development team. A sample production timetable is shown in Figure 5.1.

Choosing a Webcast Performance Format

Early in the production process, the webcast team must decide on a webcast performance format; this is an extension of the basic bandwidth-imposed webcast formats discussed in Chapter 2, "Developing a Webcast Strategy." Following is a list of possible webcast performance formats:

Figure 5.1 Example of a production timetable.

"The Apartment": Week of 10/10/98

	MON	TUES	WED
8:00	—	NYC call	Move equipment.
9:00	Visit club; check phone lines.	Test live encoder.	Set up /w film crew.
10:00	Visit club; check phone lines.	Promote on Yahoo events page.	Scene 2: "An apart
11:00	Confirm ISP 310-293-4498.	—	Scene 2: "An apart
12:00	—	Cast meeting/lunch.	Cast meeting/lunch.
1:00	HOME PAGE UPDATE!	Scene 1: "Finding the apartment"	Set up /w film crew.
2:00	Meeting with sound engineer.	Scene 1: "Finding the apartment"	Scene 2: "An apart
3:00	Add 2.0 software to server.	Scene 1: "Finding the apartment"	Scene 2: "An apart
4:00	Add 2.0 software to server.	Test results of encoding.	Scene 2: "An apart
5:00	NYC call; test remote connection.	Pack on-location hardware.	Scene 2: "An apart

- Text stream
- Ambient webcast
- Voice-quality audio
- AM radio-quality audio
- Small-screen slide shows
- "Talking head" videos
- Quarter-screen animation
- Slide shows with sound or music
- FM radio-quality audio
- Broadcast-quality audio
- High-quality small-screen video
- Near-CD-quality audio
- Full-motion, full-screen video

These formats depend on the number of participating actors and the number and location of input devices. The following common webcast performance formats are compared in Table 5.1, which may be used to help the webcast team analyze the hardware/content requirements and choose the correct format for the production. Often, this may require rethinking the method used to present the content. For example, music-oriented webcasts may involve a solo musician singing to an audience (monologue narration) or a fantasy story constructed around the music (sketch). Webcasters on a budget will find it easier to produce the former. News and sports may be effectively presented in monologue and interview formats, avoiding bandwidth-hogging action scenes. The production team will need to consider technical abilities when choosing a performance format. In general, it will be much easier to set up cameras, microphones, and a stage for a narration-style webcast than one using sketches or

Table 5.1 Comparison of Webcast Performance Formats Relative to Bandwidth and Production Complexity

	Ambient	Monologue	Hands-on	Interview	Skit/ Sketch	Multimedia/ Data
Performers	None-to-many	1	1	2	2-to-many	None-to-many
Cameras	1	1	1–2	2	2-to-many	1-to-many
Microphones	1	1	1	2	2-to-many	1-to-many
Narration	No	Yes	Yes	No	Yes	1-to-many
Dialogue	No	No	No	Yes	Yes	No
Interaction	No	No	No	Yes	Yes	No
Camera Mounts	Fixed	Fixed	Move	Move	Move	Fixed
Microphone Locations	Fixed	Fixed	Worn	Fixed	Multiple	Fixed

integrating multimedia, The team may want to reconsider the basic strategy developed in Chapter 2 to choose a performance format more effectively. More specific factors, such as the available number of cameras, microphones, and performers, should also be taken into account.

Ambient

The ambient performance format is unique to the Internet. It employs a fixed camera or microphone that is pointed at a specified area, passively recording what transpires there. Content of ambient webcasts are generally quite simple because there is no defined script, and little may change from moment to moment. "Slow scan" technologies, discussed in Chapter 3, "Webcast Equipment and Authoring Environments," are typically used to send ambient performances to the Internet. Performers do not narrate or otherwise speak to the audience, but drift in and out of the webcast independent of audience observation.

Some successful videocast sites using this methodology include the infamous Jennicam (www.jennicam.org) site that contains a camera pointed into Jenni's bedroom. Audiocasts of this form are rare because they require a burst of high-bandwidth streaming when visitors request the audio. A slow-streaming visual slide show does not require this level of bandwidth. Ambient webcasts work best when embedded in a structured concept (e.g., a location-specific weather report) that is of interest in its own right. This also means that ambient webcasts work best for conveying information sampled on an occasional basis. For this reason, webcasters providing access to traffic reports, skiing conditions, and peeks at famous locations can use the ambient format to their advantage. In contrast, webcasters trying to repurpose traditional narrative stories or provide original Internet entertainment should avoid the ambient format. Few visitors will be interested in sitting through the functional equivalent of a long slide show.

Content depending on motion rather than appearance (e.g., sportscasts) will not work well in ambient performance formats, whereas a gallery tour might. Novelty entertainment, such as the Notorious Spam Cam site (www.fright.com/cgi-bin/spamcam), is also well-served by ambient webcasts. Due to the modest hardware and software requirements of ambient webcasting, it makes a good first choice for developers not yet committed to the

Choosing a Webcast Performance Format

These questions will help you narrow your choices when searching for a webcast performance format.

- Is the primary purpose of the webcast entertainment or information?

- How many cameras, lights, and microphones are available?

- Will the available bandwidth allow for a real-time webcast?

- Does the team have a camera/microphone operator trained in recording live performances?

- Is content accessed intermittently by the audience, or does the audience stay through to the end of the event?

- How big is the performance space? Is there room for standing/walking, or will performers need to remain in one place?

- Will the performers need professional acting ability? Will one or more performers be well known to the audience?

- Does the webcast involve showing, fixing, taking apart, or otherwise manipulating an object?

- Will the webcast include animation or other computer-generated multimedia?

- Will a question-and-answer session be part of the webcast?

- If the webcast is live, will the audience be able to interact with performers?

medium. As Internet connectivity improves, ambient audiocasts are likely to become more practical. It is not difficult to imagine individuals and companies tuning into a "nature sounds" webcast to enhance relaxation and improve productivity.

Monologue Narration

The monologue narration format includes an individual performer who reads from a prepared text. Cameras and microphones are typically in fixed positions pointed at the performer, who does not move from the location. The performer speaks directly to the audience, typically with little or no body movement except possibly shuffling papers and other desk props. The background behind the narrator in a videocast may be neutral or it may be replaced with other images via bluescreen or similar techniques. Depending on the content, it may be useful to alternate between close-ups showing the performer's reaction to the narration and shots showing the head and upper body.

Broadcast has made this format quite familiar to the web audience, and many webcast productions deliberately adopt monologue narration to increase their similarity to radio and television. Newscasts and sportscasts are common examples of monologue narration, which works equally well with audio and video webcasts. Many good examples of this format may be found in audiocasts from Sports Byline USA (www.sportsbyline.com) and videocasts on major media sites such as NBC (www.nbc.com). Simplicity is a major factor in choosing this performance format. Compared to more active performances, monologues have simple production requirements. Effective presentations may be possible with a fixed-position, and fixed-focus camcorder, microphone, and light. Novice performers who find it difficult to act onstage may be comfortable reading directly into the camera. The limited movement reduces bandwidth, allowing for sharper images and clearer sound over consumer equipment.

Monologues have far fewer applications in arts and entertainment. Since the tiny screen of a webcast seldom conveys the ambience of the event, monologues of spoken word, theater, or poetry are likely to be boring to the audience. Similar problems exist with music videos that do little more than show the face of a vocalist singing. Monologue narration is best suited to direct, to-the-point reporting—a style that is increasingly popular with major sites such as CNN (www.cnn.com) and MSNBC (www.msnbc.com).

Hands-On

The widely used hands-on format comprises scenes of an individual who is speaking about an object, alternated with images of the object itself. This format is common in online education and infomercials where products or services are being demonstrated. The performer speaks directly to the audience. A variation of this format is seen in news reports when the action alternates between an ongoing event and the commentator. Typically, the camera jumps abruptly between the object and the speaker. In audio-only productions, a change in background music may symbolize the transition between narrator and subject.

If cuts between scenes do not employ elaborate transitions, it is possible to make hands-on webcasts that run in low bandwidth. The increased movement and clear jumps between points of view make hands-on more like standard broadcast. Demands on performers remain minimal, since full-body acting (e.g., walking) is not required. In many cases, the decision to use this performance format may lie in the size and detail of the object of interest. For example, a hands-on webcast showing how to insert a toner cartridge into a laser printer might be effective since the components are fairly large. In contrast, a video detailing brushstrokes used in creating an oil painting are less likely to work, since the changes on screen are more subtle. Like ambient and monologue formats, hands-on webcasts are generally not appropriate for storytelling or entertainment. In contrast, an audio-only webcast featuring car engine tune-ups might exploit the relatively high quality of Internet sound to illustrate the subtle changes in engine noise.

Currently, the hands-on format is not common; but this is likely to change. Given the widespread availability of training videos and infomercials using hands-on techniques, it is a safe bet that many webcasts will follow this pattern in the future. Examples of hands-on videocasts are available at C|Net's The New Edge (www.cnet.com/Content/TV/Newedge/Webcast) feature.

Interview

In the interview format, two or more individuals have a question and response dialogue. In audiocasts, the speakers are distinguished by the tone of their voices; in videocasts, two cameras are typically used, making camera operation more complex. The performers speak to each other instead of the audience. A more complex version of this format is the "round robin" discussion found in political commentary television shows.

There are two largely webcast-specific reasons for excluding the audience from interviews. In most cases, the audience will need dedicated microphones and/or cameras, which increases the complexity of the production. More important, in current webcasts, wide-angle shots of an audience are likely to appear as indistinct blurs. Panning over the audience will introduce movement over the entire screen, which in turn increases bandwidth requirements. In general, webcasters should confine audience participation to the audio portion of the webcast.

Interview performance formats are more complex than ambient, monologue or hands-on webcasts, but they are still within the capability range of very small production teams. Fixed cameras and microphones are practical, since the interview usually occurs in a confined space with the performers seated. Novice performers may feel more comfortable with the give-and-take of an interview, as opposed to memorizing lines for a script. This makes the interview format ideal for live webcasts. Some webcasters have produced interview-style webcasts in which the performers receive and respond to user email during the program, a rare example of an interactive, participatory format using the two-way features of the Internet. Talk show type entertainment using this format is practical, and it is only a matter of time before this form of content is regularly delivered via webcasts. A good example of this format is provided by Hazardous Media (www.hazardous.com/europa) with its popular series of live webcasts featuring science fiction writer Arthur C. Clarke.

Sketch

For fictional events, reenactment, and comedy, the sketch, or skit, format supports interaction between several individuals who often move freely throughout the performance space. Audiocasts may present compelling sketches simply by combining several voices and sound effects, as done in classic radio programming. By contrast, videocasts require sophisticated camera work; multiple cameras are necessary to show individual performers, and any physical movement may require timed pans and zooms by the operators. The appearance of the performers is also more important, since their entire bodies are visible, not just the "talking heads" found in other performance formats. Examples of this format include music videos, concerts, plays, and rebroadcasts of films and television shows.

By virtue of their complexity, sketch-style webcasts present the greatest potential—and the greatest challenge—for the webcast production group. The team will need to include professionals skilled in lighting, sound, and direction of groups of performers wandering freely throughout the stage. Sketch formats also require effective acting and body language, which in turn often necessitates using professional performers. Despite the complexity, the chance to create broadcast-style shows is a strong reason for exploring this format. Effective implementation just might result in the first broadcast-style "hit" on the Internet. Production teams familiar with the demands of film and television will find their skills most valuable for this format, though they may have to unlearn some of them in order to cope with the primitive nature of current webcast technology.

To date, the most common sketch-style webcasts are repurposed film trailers such as those provided by VideoDome (www.videodome.com). Original sketch content is available at webcast ISP InterneTV (www.internetv.com); and music videos following a similar format may be seen at sites such as Streamland (www.streamland.com).

Multimedia

The multimedia format is unique to computer systems; it involves an interactive combination of computer-generated interfaces, images, sounds, and animation. The webcast content usually contains short segments of audio or video that present a single concept or image and contribute to a larger interactive whole. Performers usually play a subordinate role in this format, and content organization is done within the overall multimedia environment rather than within the webcast stream.

Production of multimedia webcasts requires a substantially different makeup for the production team. Computer-oriented individuals skilled in animation, graphics, and sound editing are very important, and knowledge of cutting-edge web technology is a virtual necessity. However, in many cases, these skills may be combined in one or two individuals, thereby making the production team smaller than in other formats. A good example of this is shown on the Real Education site (www.realeducation.com), which showcases multimedia webcasts often designed by a single instructor. Multimedia-format webcasts may have less utility in entertainment. Computer games do use multimedia, but they derive their impact from interactivity, a feature that is reduced or missing from most webcasts.

As the newest entry in a new field, multimedia webcasts are relatively rare, but good examples may be found on Macromedia's Shockrave site (www.shockrave .com). Flash-based animation is attracting the attention of traditional animators, many of whom had been avoiding multimedia. Examples of trends for this kind of webcast may be seen at Spumco (www.spumco.com) and Smashing Ideas (www.smashingideas.com).

Developing Scripts and Storyboards

Developing a plan that coordinates events during the webcast will be new to many webcasters. Fortunately, writing for an event draws on the long history of storytelling in performance and broadcast which precedes this new medium. Most events will require a combination of *scripts* and *storyboards*, as shown in Figure 5.2.

Scripts are text-only descriptions of scenes, transitions, performer cues, narration, dialogue, stage props, camera directions, and lighting/sound cues. Essential for audio-only webcasts, scripts are also used when the spoken word is a significant part of a video webcast. As might be expected, custom software supporting script and screenplay writing is produced by companies such as Screenplay Systems (www.screenplay.com) and Hollywood Cinema Software (www.scriptwriting.com). Resources, products, and links relevant to script and screenplay writing may be found at the Internet Screenwriters Network, shown in Figure 5.3, and Screenwriters Tips in RealAudio (www.teleport.com/ ~cdeemer/tip-home.html).

Storyboards comprise a series of line drawings depicting scenes within the webcast, usually with commentary and/or script elements indicated below each drawing. Storyboards are usually hand-drawn, though some companies, including Ezone (www.ezone.com/beast/index.htm), produce electronic storyboard

Figure 5.2 Combining scripts and storyboards.

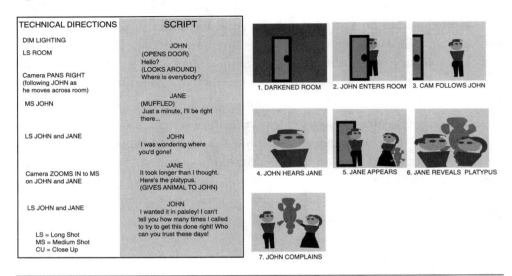

TECHNICAL DIRECTIONS	SCRIPT
DIM LIGHTING	
LS ROOM	JOHN (OPENS DOOR) Hello? (LOOKS AROUND) Where is everybody?
Camera PANS RIGHT (following JOHN as he moves across room)	
MS JOHN	JANE (MUFFLED) Just a minute, I'll be right there...
LS JOHN and JANE	JOHN I was wondering where you'd gone!
Camera ZOOMS IN to MS on JOHN and JANE	JANE It took longer than I thought. Here's the platypus. (GIVES ANIMAL TO JOHN)
LS JOHN and JANE	JOHN I wanted it in paisley! I can't tell you how many times I called to try to get this done right! Who can you trust these days!
LS = Long Shot MS = Medium Shot CU = Close Up	

1. DARKENED ROOM   2. JOHN ENTERS ROOM   3. CAM FOLLOWS JOHN

4. JOHN HEARS JANE   5. JANE APPEARS   6. JANE REVEALS PLATYPUS

7. JOHN COMPLAINS

software adapted for computerized production environments. Storyboarding allows the production team to analyze visual aspects of the webcast, including entrances and exits, scene composition, and continuity of events. They are also useful for describing the blocking and positioning requirements of a scene to performers and equipment operators.

Developing scripts and storyboards requires creativity, even when the subject is nondramatic, such as a corporate presentation or online lecture. Since webcast teams are usually quite small relative to standard broadcast groups, scripting and storyboarding will typically be assigned to someone who is already involved in the production in another capacity. These tasks should not be an afterthought. Care should be taken to choose individuals with excellent writing or visual art skills and who have an interest in the artistic challenge of telling a story. Here are some guidelines that may be used to create effective scripts and storyboards:

Determine the overall purpose. Define the goals of the webcast before writing a script. This will help avoid wasted writing effort and keep the script lean and focused. People with an analytical bend may

Figure 5.3 The Internet Screenwriters Network (www.screenwriters.com/hn/writing/screennet.html).

elect to create a short, bulleted outline of each key concept that will be communicated by the webcast. Others may decide to visualize the webcast and run through a series of imaginary events in their mind. This latter approach to scripting and storyboarding is particularly effective if the webcast mixes audio and video with animation and multimedia.

Outline components. Write out the individual components of the webcast after the goal is established. To prevent one part of the script from becoming too detailed relative to others, use a top-down approach; begin with a brief outline of the webcast based on major physical changes, and work down to individual lines within scenes.

Simplify. Watching a webcast is currently challenging enough for the audience without webcast producers including unnecessary complexity at the scripting level. Concepts should be introduced in short, easily understood phrases. Television audiences in particular have become used to short sound bites, and scripts need to appeal to this expectation. Complex information is best served outside the webcast on related web pages.

Use repetition. The typical webcast audience member will have tuned in sometime after the beginning of the program. For this reason, extended webcast scripts need to frequently reintroduce the content and performers in a manner similar to commercial radio or television. Alternately, this information may be displayed on the web page containing the link to the webcast. Each concept presented during the webcast should be reiterated using the *same* words, rather than phrases with similar meanings, because rewording may confuse a webcast audience member who is already missing words due to interruptions in the data stream. Simplicity in writing should also extend to features such as character and place names.

Edit. Most writers create first-pass scripts that are much too long. While it may seem that a lengthy script is necessary to cover everything, it is far better to leave a few points unaddressed if it reduces the size of the script. An audience is interested in highlights rather than a blow-by-blow account—and this is doubly true for an Internet audience. Hyperlinks promote rapid jumping from topic to topic, and the typical Internet audience member is likely to click to a new web site at the first sign of boredom. With the advent of MTV, television has adopted an increasingly fragmentary approach that even includes partial sentences. This style is even more acceptable over the web, where the audience is used to clicking quickly in and out of sites and gathering bits and pieces of information. Email protocol has also favored the use of incomplete sentences. There's nothing wrong with being a stickler for grammar; but it may come across as unnatural in the webcast medium.

Cue cards and teleprompters. The written script must be formatted for easy readability by the performers. Contrary to common belief, most television reporters are not reading from the news items in their hands; they are reading text that is positioned next to the camera that is filming the event. This text may be provided on static pages with large lettering or on electronic systems called *teleprompters* that scroll text on-screen. For live events, it is especially important to provide this much-appreciated safety net, even if the performers have memorized their lines.

If the script is designed for a nonlive event and will require editing (e.g., a movie-style linear narrative), it is necessary to indicate when each scene will be recorded. This *shooting script* specifies a different scene order from the script itself. The reason for this is that several unrelated scenes may be shot as a group to take advantage of short-term equipment rentals, locations, or even weather conditions. An individual within the webcast group should be made responsible for preserving continuity in the finished product. For example, the continuity editor might make sure that performers wear the same clothes in scenes shot on different days, or that outdoor lighting is similar.

Some production groups may decide to outsource the process of script generation and storyboarding. Many consulting companies offer these services on the web, including Atlanta Video (www.telefilm-south.com/home/atvideoinc .html), CR Advertising (207.208.113.113/bud.html), and Crandal's Comps and Storyboards (home.earthlink.net/~jimmy57).

Managing the Webcast

After the various components of a webcast—the hardware, software, personnel, strategy, and performance format—are arranged, attention must be paid to the day-to-day management of the production. This requires skills beyond technical expertise, which may present a major challenge for some groups. In general, the qualities needed to manage a webcast are similar to other ongoing events requiring effective coordination of personnel and resources. This section considers various aspects of webcast management. These topics are more mundane than installing the latest high-tech system, but the success of the webcast is no less dependent on successful execution.

Managing Equipment

Previous chapters have considered hardware and software in the abstract, dwelling on their various advantages and disadvantages. As production begins, webcasters will need to make concrete decisions and acquire the equipment.

Depending on the experience of the production team, it may also be necessary to plan a training schedule and rehearsals using the equipment.

Purchasing versus Renting

During budgeting, the producers will need to determine whether to rent or buy equipment outright. Small-scale webcasts (e.g., ambient) may use inexpensive consumer equipment totaling a few hundred dollars, but groups planning broadcast-style productions frequently require tens of thousands of dollars of hardware. Due to the expense involved, most production teams will probably elect to use a mixture of rentals and purchases in their budgets. The following lists the relative merits of rental versus purchase for each major class of webcast hardware:

Authoring computers. Most webcasters will want to purchase *authoring computers*, since they will be used during and after each webcast. Though it is possible to lease computer equipment, the long-term cost of doing so is often much higher than a direct purchase. Typically, renting computers for webcast capture and authoring will run several hundred dollars per day—hardly a bargain when these same systems may cost less than $2,000 if purchased outright.

Webcast server computer. Smaller webcasting groups may elect to pay a webcast ISP a monthly fee for server space, along with the necessary bandwidth to handle the webcast. Groups intending to reach a very large audience usually rent time on an IP multicast or distributed server network. In contrast, corporate and educational webcasters may decide to purchase the server, which is usually installed on a local LAN, and offers direct access.

Cameras, microphones, mixers, and lighting equipment. Unlike computing equipment, this production-specific equipment should be rented. Since the monetary return of webcasts is at present unknown, it may be difficult to justify the cost of an expensive camcorder or sound system, and most groups will not need high-end equipment other than for the event itself. Furthermore, the rapid advance of technology may render some items (such as digital video camcorders) obsolete before they are paid for. Going a step further, some groups may hire companies that provide a one-stop solution, including the equipment and the specialists needed to run it. A good introductory resource for issues surrounding live show production is available at Playbill's Theater Central (www1.playbill.com/cgi-bin/plb/central?cmd=start) and Entertainment Technology Online (www.etecnyc.net).

Because webcasters work in a digital world, they should carefully analyze their production strategies to see whether a low-cost digital system may be substituted for expensive analog hardware. For example, a software program such as Adobe Premiere (www.adobe.com) may be substituted for extremely expensive nonlinear editing systems using videotape. High-end computer sound cards provide built-in mixing board functions, and represent an alternative to purchasing freestanding systems.

Webcasters should also purchase the many smaller—but absolutely essential—items of equipment they will need during the webcast, including duct tape for securing cables and equipment, cables and connectors, power extension cords, phone cords for reaching distant phone jacks, light meters, equipment covers, extra batteries for equipment, surge suppressors, cords for microphone attachment, tripod stands, and even gloves for handling hot stage lights. Other equipment includes instrument stands, marking tape, a soldering gun, extra power cable plugs, phone jacks, and fire extingushers. A toolkit containing wrenches and screwdrivers is always helpful.

Testing and Transport

Whether the webcast is shot on location or transmitted directly from the office, all equipment must be in place and running properly when the show begins. After confirming inventory via the equipment checklist, the webcast team should set up the equipment and stage a complete dry run orchestrated with their webcast ISP. If the webcast occurs away from the office, the team should assemble and test everything as a unit before leaving. This will allow the team to discover missing components and problems with hardware/software compatibility before it's too late to fix them. If possible, the webcast engineers should travel to the venue in advance and make sure that the required Internet connection is actually available. More than one webcaster has appeared at a

CAMCORDER TROUBLESHOOTING

Common reasons that a camcorder may not work include:

- Lens cap is on.
- Batteries are dead or improperly recharged.
- Incorrect f/stop values; high values will result in a dark image.
- Audio output plugged into video—or vice versa.
- Camera is in character generator mode.
- Broken or loose connections to the computer or video mixer.
- Fade button is pressed.
- Output selector is not on.
- Camera is not turned on, or AC adapter is not turned on and/or plugged in.

club or auditorium only to discover that the supposedly free phone lines are being used to validate credit cards, or that the ISDN line was ordered but was never actually installed. Even if available, the plug for the Internet connection may be some distance from the event, requiring running many feet of shielded cable.

The on-location power requirement is also an issue for webcasters. If the location is outside, keep enough camcorder batteries on hand to run the equipment throughout the event. Nickel-cadmium (NiCad) batteries may be difficult to find on short notice. Indoors, the engineer should make sure that the venue can supply the power needed. Most computers use several hundred watts of power in operation, amounting to several amps. Adding more than three computers to a single socket is likely to trip standard 15-amp fuses. Power surges and brownouts during the event may drastically affect computer equipment. In the worst case, a momentary flickering of the lights may interrupt the webcast while the computers are rebooted and reconfigured. To avoid this, all computer equipment should be plugged into an *uninterruptible power supply (UPS)* system designed specifically to protect against surges and momentary power loss.

The producer should also check the rules and regulations governing the use of the performance space. Many large auditoriums, venues, and convention halls have agreements with local unions that restrict use of outside personnel. The webcast producer should contact the venue operator well in advance and determine whether they need to hire local or union-only help. Staging certain types of productions may also require permits from the local government, and regulations may restrict noise levels or use of certain equipment in public places. Since the groups providing these permits are generally not online, webcasters should be prepared to use other means such as phone calls and snail mail to get the information they need. It may also be beneficial to check out web sites devoted to independent filmmaking such as CinemaWeb (www .cinemaweb.com) and Webcinema (www.webcinema.org), since these groups often face similar issues.

Webcast production teams new to handling broadcast-style equipment may benefit from public access television. Due to a law enacted in the 1970s, cable companies must allocate a channel on which anyone may produce a show independently, and must provide the equipment and studio. Developing a public access show provides an opportunity to write production schedules; test scripts and storyboards; learn to use cameras, microphones, and lights; and to gain experience working with limited budgets. To take advantage of this service, the webcast team should contact the local cable company and attend the production classes offered. After developing a public access show, it is usually a relatively small jump to creating webcasts. And because the show ultimately becomes the property of the creators, it might be possible to directly repurpose it for webcasting.

Managing Performers

Obviously, animation-only webcasters only have to manage performers of their own creation. But when the production team requires the services of real-world talent, webcasting enters the world of show biz, with all that implicates. Before becoming too star-struck, the producers should develop a strategy for working with performers during webcast production.

For small groups, individuals within the webcast production team often double as performers. As for other real-world aspects of webcasting, finding performers should not be an afterthought. Webcasters are already constricted by limited bandwidth and infant technology; they can do without a tongue-tied performer impacting production. Acting takes training and experience, even for the simplest roles. Fortunately, potential actors are not in short supply. Webcasters with a limited budget might find friends or acquaintances with acting experience. Despite objections on the performers' part, the producers should consider doing a screen test of the candidates to ensure that they can play the part. A basic screen test might consist of the performer reading the script while facing cameras or microphones. Webcasters who require more professional talent might try taking out small ads in local weekly events newspapers and industry trade publications in their area. For many performers, the appeal of appearing in a new medium such as the Internet may outweigh low or nonexistent payment for their efforts.

Performers may also be found on the Internet itself, which is increasingly becoming a viable way to scout professional talent. Many talent agencies have gone online, and sites such as Castnet (www.castnet.com) maintain actor databases open exclusively to casting directors and talent agents. (Note that using professional actors from these services will involve payments according to standard industry rates.) For groups looking for new and unrepresented actors, sites such as Actor's Worldlink (members.aol.com/aworldlink/index.htm) and World Wide Stars (see Figure 5.4) may provide an alternative. In all cases, the webcasters should make sure their performers understand exactly how their work will be used online.

During a live webcast or during performance times in a recorded webcast, the production team will pass through several distinct stages. What follows is one possible breakdown for the webcast event once the team is at the webcast location. The producer may want to add these stages to the overall production schedule:

Assembly. In the assembly stage, all equipment is plugged in and checked out. The Internet connection should be established, and test data should be sent, possibly through a secondary web page not linked to the main broadcast. Depending on the nature of the webcast and the time available, performers may also go through a rehearsal.

Opening. In most cases, the opening stage of the webcast will be indicated by a verbal announcement or titles flashed across the

Figure 5.4 World Wide Stars (www.worldstars.com).

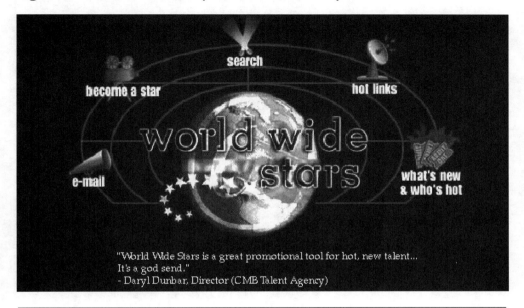

screen. On the web, the page linked to webcast data is frequently swapped with a default page, as shown in Figure 5.5. This allows rapid shifts between an open and closed state for the webcast area.

Monitoring. During the actual webcast, the engineers need to constantly monitor the capture, authoring, and upload computers to verify that data is actually being encoded and delivered to the webcast ISP. A separate monitor should be maintained using a standard Internet account to determine the webcast quality being received by end users. Local monitors tied into the webcast stream are not sufficient, since these only illustrate how the webcast looks from the origination point, not what it looks like to the Internet audience. The engineer may want to try connecting through a set of national ISPs to compare quality. If the webcast is being recorded, the engineer should frequently check disk capacity to make sure it doesn't fill up and affect the encoding programs.

Customer support. There are likely to be people interested in viewing or listening to the webcast who, for one reason or another, are not

Figure 5.5 Swapping on and off pages during a webcast.

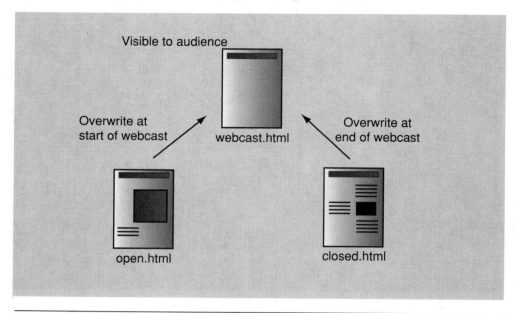

Visible to audience

Overwrite at
start of webcast

webcast.html

Overwrite at
end of webcast

open.html

closed.html

able to connect or configure their players for acceptable performance. They are likely to turn to email or the phone for customer service. Unlike regular email, these messages need to be answered immediately. One individual from the production team should be designated (separate from the engineer monitoring the webcast itself) to answer hardware and software questions related to webcast reception.

Event chaperones. If the webcast includes participatory elements (e.g., a chat room), it may be necessary to install *virtual chaperones*. A chaperone is given administrator-level access to the webcast, and often has the power to lock out unwelcome or offensive visitors. In some cases, chaperones "lurk" in the background, while in others they act as moderators and manage discussions with the guests. These individuals may prevent problems from arising for some of the guests, and may supply technical support as well. Most chat rooms assign administrator rights to specific individuals, allowing them to provide special services or kick out hackers, spammers, and potty-mouths who worm their way into a discussion group.

Closing. Normally, a webcast is closed by an announcement or set of visual titles similar to those used at the opening. At this point, the web site is updated and an altered page is substituted for the one linking to webcast data. At the same time, new hyperlinks may be made to the completed webcast data for an archive. This should be done as quickly as possible, since audience members will frequently continue to stream in well after the announced time for the webcast. To avoid embarrassment, announcements on the site also need to be updated to reflect that the webcast is over.

After the event is over, it is usually necessary to take down, or strike, the set and store materials related to the webcast. The producers should consult the scripts and checklists to make sure that critical hardware or software is not accidentally left behind. They should also police their work area and return it to its original state. Groups leaving behind a mess are unlikely to be invited back. If the group has rented a temporary Internet connection, it is important to ensure that the connection is closed. More than one webcaster has received a surprise bill for a connection left running after the show was over.

Licensing, Copyrights, and Fair Use

Many webcasts will use material from another source, often film and television content repurposed for the Internet. Webcasters who have become accustomed to the open, freewheeling environment of the Internet will find that licensing and copyrights will have an increasing impact on their work.

In simple terms, copyrighted material cannot be used in a webcast without permission from the *copyright* holder. In order to use copyrighted work, it may be necessary to pay royalties to the copyright holder. Copyright applies to a wide variety of situations:

- Making copies/duplications in any form.
- Creating a new work based on an existing work.
- Distributing copies of the work by rental, lease, sales, or lending.

- Public performance at all levels, including performance in front of an audience, and delivery through media including broadcast, CD-ROM, and the web.

- Modification of the work (e.g., parody lyrics set to a popular tune).

These rights apply equally to text, images, audio, video, and multimedia, and content pulled from the web is no exception. According to copyright law, protection starts once the pen is on paper, image is on film, sound is on tape, or programs are on disk drives. Penalties set by U.S. law permit the copyright holder to recover between $500 and $100,000, depending upon the circumstances, and criminal infringement can result in five years in prison with a $250,000 fine. Clearly, any organization providing public performance must pay close attention to copyright! Information is available from the U.S. Copyright Office (lcweb.loc.gov/copyright), the Copyright Website (www.benedict.com), and the World Intellectual Property Organization (www.wipo.org). Additional sites useful for researching copyright and obtaining clearance are shown in Table 5.2.

Rights accorded by copyright frequently overlap. Consider a production group that wants to use an exciting rendition of a famous jazz standard by a local artist. Legal use of the work requires clearance from the artist who rerecorded the song, plus a second clearance from the copyright holder of the song itself. Licensing the work may require paying an additional fee to unions representing studio musicians and background singers. The broad overlapping applicability of copyright, combined with the absence of any clear guidelines for Internet-based broadcast, has made may webcasters justifiably cautious. For example, webcasts of sports often cut out the commercials, thereby avoiding potential royalty payments to the actors.

In regard to the inclusion of material in journalism and education, the notion of *fair use* has become part of the legal copyright lexicon. Fair use allows limited use of certain works without contacting the copyright owners. Typical examples include short quotes made by book reviewers, short clips from a long movie, and political speeches reported by a newspaper without consulting the participants. Fair use also applies in limited cases to teachers creating course content that includes copyrighted material. To observe fair use, most developers provide an excerpt of a copyrighted work, rather than the work in its

Table 5.2 Sites Useful for Researching Copyright and Obtaining Clearance

Description	Function	URL
The Copyright Clearance Center	General clearance	www.copyright.com
Broadcast News Licensing Service	News	www.copyright.com/ BNLS/product.html
WWW Multimedia Law	Web-specific	www.batnet.com/ oikoumene/
Public Domain Materials	Public domain	www.benedict.com/ public.html
Fair Use: Educational Guidelines	Fair Use	www.indiana.edu/ ~ccumc/mmfairuse.html
Copyright Clearance Center	Copyright	www.copyright.com/stuff/ mira_online.htm
Digital Future Coalition	Digital copyright	www.ari.net/dfc/

entirety. Fair use is usually set on a case-by-case basis; for this reason, most commercial webcasters will want to take a conservative approach and contact the copyright holder in virtually all cases. Nonprofit and educational institutions may be less strict, but they should remember that they are bound by the same copyright law as commercial organizations. Current copyright law does not assign an automatic excerpt size that will be judged as fair use. This means that fair use may not apply to a sampled song—even if the material used was a single note from the work. For this reason, webcasters must be extremely cautious when incorporating material in their webcast under fair use guidelines. For more information about copyright and fair use law, check Stanford University's discussion of these topics (fairuse.stanford.edu).

A group of laws designed to compensate musicians when their work is played by others is known as *performance rights*. Examples of play include cover bands, radio airplay, and even in venues such as restaurants and movie theaters. Until recently, the issue of Internet performance rights has been moot since audio was usually provided by the artists themselves specifically to promote their work. With the rise of Internet radio stations and other webcasting forms, Internet performance will increasingly come to resemble the broadcast industry. In these environments, broadcasters keep a record of airplay to submit to performance rights organizations. These organizations use this information to collect royalties, which are forwarded to the artist. Current collection practices are based on aggregate statistics, but digital webcasts and performances raise the likely prospect of exact, database-driven accounting for performances. A free resource specifically pertaining to use of music on the web is available at Kohn Music (www.kohnmusic.com).

Clearance

To use material in a webcast, the producers must get a waiver from the responsible party or pay royalties. Educational and nonprofit organizations seeking clearance should send an institutional request on official letterhead explaining why the waiver is being requested. A sample request is shown in Figure 5.6. The letter should include a description of the intended use of the material, along with the relevant portion of the copyrighted work. If the webcast team decides to obtain clearance for a popular work, they may have to contact several organizations that specifically provide this service to ensure that the various overlapping rights are accounted for.

Musicians seeking to use published musical work may contact the Harry Fox Agency, Inc. (HFA), a branch of the National Music Publishers Association (www.nmpa.org), which provides an informational, clearinghouse, and monitoring services for licensing musical copyrights. Contacting this organization is necessary when a copyrighted work of music will be performed during a webcast. Additional music clearance services are listed in Table 5.3.

Table 5.3 Music Clearance Services

Company Name	URL
The Harry Fox Agency	www.nmpa.org
The Parker Music Group	www.musicclearance.com
EMG Musical Services	www.clearance.com
Signature Sound	www.signature-sound.com

Figure 5.6 Sample copyright clearance request for nonprofit use.

LETTERHEAD

Copyright holder or publisher
Permissions Dept.
Address

To Whom It May Concern:

We are requesting permission to use the following material for an educational/nonprofit presentation we plan to make via "real-time" video on the World Wide Web:

    Title of work:
    Author(s):
    Copyrighted material used:
    Method of distribution:
    Request list: (listing pages, chapters, images, frame number and/or audio timings)
        Indicate the method of webcast to be used and whether the webcast media
        will be in a form that can be saved to hard disk by the end user.

Project information:
    Contact person:
    Position:
    Project number:
    Duration:

We request a waiver, as these materials will be used solely for nonprofit educational purposes.

Sincerely,

_____
(Webcast Producer)

COPYRIGHT OWNER REPLY:

Permission granted _____ Permission denied_____

Indicate charge (if any)_____

Indicate special conditions /restrictions:

To use recorded music in a webcast, the producers will have to find the performance rights organization that represents the artists whose work they are planning to use. In the United States, the two largest organizations are the American Society of Composers, Authors, and Publishers (ASCAP) (www.ascap.com) and Broadcast Music, Inc. (BMI), shown in Figure 5.7. BMI began distributing royalties for Internet performances early in 1998. Comparable organizations exist in most countries. All of these nonprofit organizations have systems in place for working with Internet broadcasters. Producers should contact these organizations and draw up a licensing agreement. In the case where the musicians are willing to provide a release for their work directly, producers will need to create a separate contract that waives performance rights. As an alternative to paying royalties, webcasters may elect to use royalty-free music libraries distributed by companies such as SuperSound (www.supersound.com). Unlike individual license arrangements, the buyer receives a one-time, 99-year music license for performance. A large number of companies provide licensed stock film footage, including BBC Library Sales (www.bbcfootage.com), Footage.net (www.footage.net), and Global Village Stock Footage (www.videosource.com).

Obtaining clearance extends to performers. For example, a webcast team working on location might select performers from casual passers-by. In this case, a simple release form such as the example in Figure 5.8 is sufficient. Clearance may seem excessively formal to webcasters working with friends or relatives, but it is better to be safe than sorry! Obtaining clearance for commercial events (such as sports or television shows) usually requires more elaborate contracts, and frequently will include paying compensation to the studio, performers, or an organization representing them. Given the relative novelty of the Internet, many commercial groups may be reluctant to participate at all.

By definition, an ambient webcast, or "spy" camera, records and transmits everything in its path. While this might not be a problem for a site like the Maui Camera (www.mauigateway.com/~rw/video/index.html), whose camera is pointed at the Pacific Ocean, a webcam recording the events on a movie set may have special clearance problems. Since pay scales in the entertainment industry are frequently related to appearance in a medium, the potential exists for crew and maintenance workers caught by a spycam to ask for performance

Figure 5.7 BMI (www.bmi.com).

royalties. Webcasters wishing to provide such a service should research the situation thoroughly and be prepared to develop releases or pay royalties.

In the long run, the production team will need to consider whether the extra work and potential hazards of copyright material are worth the trouble. While it may be tempting to include a famous song or film clip in the webcast, it should be remembered that alternatives exist. Because they are working in a new medium, webcasters might opt to focus on new and relatively unknown media in the production. Ideally, all content will be created within the production group itself, reducing copyright issues from external problems to internal agreements.

Protecting Webcast Content

A live performance or recorded work streamed over the web may be copyrighted like any other work. Under current law, copyright is assigned when the work is created; but keeping that right requires monitoring for and challenging unauthorized use. Webcasters interested in protecting their own work should use the following methods to establish their rights to the production:

Figure 5.8 Basic release form for "casual" performers.

COMPANY LOGO

COMPANY
ADDRESS

Actor Release

I hereby give COMPANY the absolute right and permission to publish, copyright, or use photographic or video scenes in which I may be included in whole or in part, in conjunction with my own or fictitious name, in reproductions delivered over the Internet or through advertising or any other lawful purpose.

I waive any right to inspect or approve the final product or any advertising copy that may be used in conjunction with the creation of the finished product.

I release COMPANY from any liability including but not limited to distortion or alteration that may occur in the capturing or use of said images, or in processing to finished product.

DATE: _____

ACTOR NAME: _____
ADDRESS: _____
                       _____

PHONE: _____

EMAIL: _____

On-screen copyrights. All pages of web sites associated with the webcast should contain a copyright notice, usually in the address field at the bottom of the page. For this purpose, page designers should use the specific "&copy" HTML command instead of a copyright symbol from their word processor. This ensures that the symbol will appear correctly in different browsers and with all keyboard character sets. Since streaming audio and video may be duplicated independent of web information, it may be appropriate to list copyright at the beginning or end of these works.

Digital watermarking. To help enforce their copyright, the webcast production team may decide to encode a "hidden" message in their streaming data. Digital *watermarks* work by encoding a specific registration number or phrase directly into the media. The message/phrase may be a copyright notice, or it could encode the purchaser's information at the time of download. This allows immediate determination of whether a copy of a product is authorized. The altered data bytes are randomly scattered throughout the image, sound, or video file, and are essentially undetectable. Companies providing digital watermark services include Digimarc (www.digimarc .com) for images, and Blue Spike (www.bluespike.com) for images, audio, and video. Other companies such as NEC (www.nec.com) have announced comprehensive watermarking technologies for their electronics and multimedia products. It is important to remember that watermarks are not a cure-all—programs that can remove them are already posted in public software archives.

Copyright spiders. To detect unauthorized copyright use on the Internet, several companies are currently developing automated systems that scan files for watermarks or other signs of illicit use. Digimarc, shown in Figure 5.9, offers a Marcspider service that automatically "crawls" the Web looking for unauthorized images on Web sites. A similar service for music has been announced by Solana Technology Group and is currently used by the Liquid Audio (www.liquidaudio.com) online music distribution system. BMI

Figure 5.9 Digimarc (www.digimarc.com).

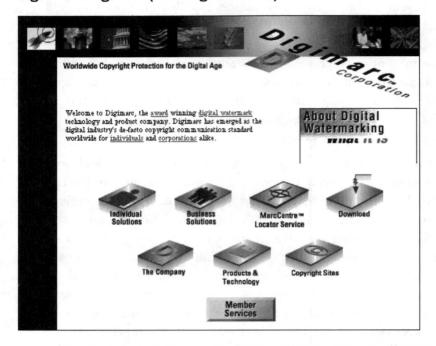

recently announced its MusicBot service, a *spider* program specifically designed to crawl the web in search of illegal music use.

Built-in software protection. Many player programs such as the RealNetworks RealPlayer (www.real.com) offer the capability to disable the "save" option. This means that the performance, once delivered, disappears in a manner comparable to traditonal radio and television. Using this option is a good way to prevent unauthorized use of webcast information.

Protecting the intellectual property represented by a webcast is ultimately an issue of time, money, and resources. An unlimited budget would allow the webcasters to monitor the fate of each broadcast stream sent out over the Internet, but in reality this is not practical. The producer will need to define guidelines for protecting the webcast in a way that keeps time and expenses low while quickly detecting large-scale misuse of the data. For most webcasters, copyright notices and watermarks represent effective strategies, whereas running copyright policing programs may be overkill.

Next . . .

Chapter 6, "Webcast Promotion, Commerce, and Analysis," focuses on the nonproduction elements of a webcast, including publicizing the webcast, storing webcast data for on-demand archives, and evaluating the effectiveness of the webcast in promoting the desired content, products, or services.

WEBCAST PROMOTION, COMMERCE, AND ANALYSIS

6

Even when a webcast is successfully developed and delivered to the Internet audience, additional steps are necessary to ensure that the overall project is a success. These include promoting the webcast, determining the practicality of a commerce model, and evaluating the overall impact of the webcast. While peripheral to the actual production effort, these steps are essential if the webcast is to be more than a novelty act or technology experiment.

Features of Webcast Promotion

Compared to regular web site publicity efforts, promotion for streaming media places additional challenges in front of the production team. These challenges are primarily due the fact that webcasts have a substantially different format from standard web design. This necessitates a change in strategy when promoting a live webcast or an on-demand archive. Some unique features of webcast media influencing the publicity effort include:

Unique content. Webcasts feature an event-oriented stream of information that is distinctly different from the page-centered presentation of the web. Content is less likely to include general reference material and is more likely to include information that must be viewed in a particular order to make sense. Storytelling, documentary, and music video—all which are difficult or impossible to implement through HTML—are possible in webcasts. For this reason, publicity techniques developed for web content may need to be modified. For example, the netpublicist describing webcast news might choose to emphasize the ability to see and hear content over the specifics of the content itself. Promotion strategies might emphasize the potential for passive viewing of concentrated information instead of active surfing for isolated bits of information.

Player download and installation. Since most webcasts require software that extends the function of the standard web browser, publicity must encourage installing this software as a prerequisite for viewing the webcast. Many users find these steps difficult, and publicity must frequently educate as well as promote.

Time dependence. Many webcasts provide content that must be seen or heard at a particular time. This stands in stark contrast to the web, where most content is relevant whenever it is viewed. The netpublicist must do more than simply drive traffic to the site; visitors must also know when and where to tune into the webcast. Time dependence also offers a chance to promote the unique, one-time aspect of the content. If a webcast is only available for a limited time, audience members may feel greater urgency to visit the site—as opposed to standard web content that they may assume is always available.

Monitoring issues. The nature of webcast data streams differs significantly from web downloads, and new monitoring software is necessary to determine real-time access to the site and to develop statistics on site visitors. In the context of webcasts, simple "hit" counting is nearly useless, because the administrators also need to know when the audience tuned in and how long they stayed. Unlike web pages (which have the same final appearance whether delivered over fast or slow connections), the quality of a webcast depends critically on available bandwidth. For this reason, determining user connection speeds is valuable to the webcaster.

Payment models. Webcast content often requires higher production values than standard web development, and pressure to make it a paying proposition is likely to increase. Collecting pay-per-view for a webcast stream requires fundamentally different tools from those used in online product catalogs, since users are buying access to connection time instead of to a discrete product. Webcasters interested in commerce will need programs that can meter user connections and charge accordingly. Several of these systems are discussed later in this chapter.

Integrating promotion efforts is the job of the marketing/promotion member of the webcast team. If promotion efforts are focused on Internet-based publicity, the web developer/administrator may be responsible for much of the actual promotional work. Larger groups will probably have to outsource publicity and advertising efforts to dedicated online promotion networks. Methods for accomplishing effective *netpublicity* are listed in the following section and in Table 6.1.

Netpublicity Methods

Fortunately for the netpublicist, there are many ways to effectively promote Internet content, including:

- Mailing lists
- Messaging software
- Online event calendars

Table 6.1 Netpublicity Methods

Type of Service	Reach	Response	Cost
Paging service	Medium	Very high	Very low
Offline advertising	Low	High	Very low
Posting software	High	High	Low
Posting service	Very high	Medium	Very high
Banner advertising	Medium	Low	Medium
Associate programs	Low	Very low	Low
Reciprocal links	Medium	Medium	Very high
Mailing lists	Low	High	Medium

- Reciprocal links
- Link-based associate programs
- Link submission services and software
- Banner ad networks
- Push channels
- Offline publicity

As a group, these methods apply targeted publicity to a relatively small set of individuals, as opposed to mass marketing that is aimed at a "lowest common denominator" demographic. Before beginning a netpublicity campaign, it is important to create a description of likely audience members and determine where they may be found online and offline. Along with targeting comes a requirement for two-way interaction. Internet publicity is almost never exclusively one-way, and it usually requires interaction between the audience and site operators. Even banner ads (the web equivalent of billboards in airports and bus terminals) typically invite the viewer to select them and explore additional linked web pages. The methods for promotion, considered in terms of the unique features of webcast content, are discussed in the following subsections.

Mailing Lists

Promoting through mailing lists is the oldest and most reliable method for developing fan communities on the Internet. Despite the negative reputation of junk or spam email, highly targeted lists whose members voluntarily asked to join can form the core of a dedicated webcast audience. Mailing lists work particularly well for long-term projects. For example, if a webcaster is running a weekly show for an entire year, a mailing list would remind show fans each time the show was airing over the Internet. Mailing lists are also a good way to encourage the audience to discuss webcast material among themselves and provide feedback and commentary to the content developers.

Mailing lists may operate in three modes. In the *one-to-one* mode, a single sender and recipient interact. An example of this occurs when a list member asks the list administrator technical questions. A more common mode uses the *one-to-many* strategy, in which the administrator sends a message that is received by the entire list. This broadcast-style format is good for publicity and announcements. Another form of communication unique to Internet lists is the *many-to-many* format. In this mode, any member of the list may send messages that are forwarded to everyone else on the list. Having elements of a "cocktail party" style, it is good for audience discussions, helping to build fan interest and online communities.

Small one-to-many lists (approximately 100 members) may be managed by copying email addresses into the blind carbon copy (bcc:) field of a standard mail program. Use of the carbon copy (cc:) field should be avoided, since recipients are presented with a list of all list member email addresses along with the message. For larger groups, and to support many-to-many communication, specialized programs are necessary. Most mailing list software requires UNIX-based servers to operate. Examples include L-soft International's (www.lsoft.com) software based on the venerable LISTSERV program, Majordomo from Great Circle Associates (www.greatcircle.com), and the Shelby Group's (www.shelby.com) Lyris list server. Macintosh users may take advantage of Starnine's Liststar (www.starnine.com) mailing list processor, and Windows users may develop mailing lists using the built-in features of Microsoft's SiteServer 3.0 (www.microsoft.com/siteserver). Filemaker Pro 4.0 (www.filemaker.com) provides Mac and Windows users with built-in support for integrating mailing lists with database records. Platform-independent list software based on Java is available from Sockem Software's LLC (www.sockem.com). Webcasters may also outsource their mailing lists to companies such as The PostMaster General (www.postmastergeneral.com) and Stargame Mailing List Services (www.stargame.dyn.ml.org).

The most common way to attract members to a mailing list is to place an online registration form on the web site associated with the webcast. Invitations to join may also be supplied in the signature line of email sent out by the site operators. It is not a good idea to subscribe individuals to mailing lists without their knowledge, even if they have indicated interest in the past. To confirm continued interest, and to check whether the email address still works, the webcaster may send out a one-time mailing asking the group whether they want to join the list. In general, avoid at all costs so-called bulk email with thousands to millions of anonymously collected addresses. The strong negative reaction associated with junk email will damage any webcast effort.

Messaging Software

Messaging software systems combine functions associated with email, phone pagers, and Internet chat, and may be viewed as an expansion of the mailing list concept. These systems are usually implemented as freestanding software clients that must be downloaded by the end user. Registered users compile lists of individuals they want to contact. When logging in, the messaging software automatically detects the Internet connection, announces the users' presence to other members, and alerts them when other members sign on or off. Once connected, users may control the software to initiate chat, implement URL transfers, and send one-to-one or one-to-many messages. Like traditional mailing lists, these systems are extremely effective at bringing together small groups for live webcasts. Examples of messaging software use include an instructor paging online students at the start of class, or a company calling attendees to a virtual conference staged over their intranet.

Many messaging services such as Yahoo! Pager (pager.yahoo.com) and AOL Instant Messenger (www.newaol.com/adc00.html) require users to register with a centralized service. Webcasters wishing to develop messaging as part of their netpublicity strategy will need to buy a specialized server to handle the requests. In contrast to mailing lists, the webcasters should expect to spend several thousand dollars for the enhanced features found in messaging servers. A popular messaging system is available from Mirabilis' ICQ (www.mirabilis.com). This system includes a high-performance messaging server, client software, and administration tools in a well-integrated package running on UNIX and Windows NT systems. Another highly developed product is Ichat's (www.ichat.com) Internet Edition Paging System (IPS). The IPS package includes the Ichat Paging Server, a firewall proxy server, the ComHub server (which centralizes user registration), and the ROOMS server (which converts pages/messages sent to multiuser chat forums). An administrator module provides control over use of the service, user access privileges, and user events.

Online Event Calendars

Since many webcasts are time-dependent, it is reasonable to promote them in web-based event calendars similar to television programming guides. Currently, there are only a few guides that reach a significant audience, and only a few of them are specifically designed for webcast media. An example of such an event calendar is found at OnNow, an event site that regularly posts webcast events using the interface shown in Figure 6.1. Fortunately, getting a listing on event sites is usually free and may be accomplished via a standard web browser. After logging on to the event site, the netpublicist simply fills out a web-based form listing the event and submits it to the site operators. Other sites do not use forms, but accept submissions via regular email. Table 6.2 lists sites enabling postings of upcoming webcast events.

Table 6.2 Webcast Event Listing Sites

Site Name	Category	URL
Yahoo! Events	General	events.yahoo.com
Netguide Events	General	www.netguide.com/Happenings/Add/Entry
OnNow	General	www.onnow.com/SubmitEvent.shtml
Webcam Central	Ambient webcasts	www.cameracentral.com/add .htmlWebcams/ambient
Earthcam	Ambient webcasts	www.earthcam.com/ADD.HTM
Timecast	RealAudio/ Video	www.timecast.com/help/addevent.html
Real Planet	RealAudio/ Video, international	www.realplanet.com
NetShow Events	Microsoft NetShow	nssubmit@microsoft.com
VDOGuide	VDO	www.vdoguide.com
Web Times Network	Webcast audio/video	www.webtimes.com/info/submit.asp
Mediachannel	Webcast audio/video	webmaster@mediachannel.com

Figure 6.1 OnNow (www.onnow.com).

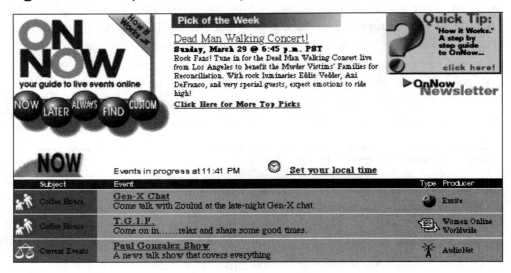

Sites running large numbers of webcasts may consider creating their own event calendars. It is relatively simple to do this using CGI programming; and calendar software is available for free or at low cost from sites such as the CGI Resources Index (www.cgiresources.com). Some event guide sites will automatically include information listed on local event calendars, provided that it follows certain organizational guidelines.

Reciprocal Links

Another way for webcasters to direct highly qualified traffic (as opposed to random surfers) to their webcast is through link exchange. By swapping links to each other, the sites involved (even when competitors) share traffic and receive visitors more likely to be interested in their content. Reciprocal links also have the advantage of directing visitors to a specific page, which can include webcast-specific information such as player download links. Many groups that use reciprocal links to generate publicity develop a specific page on their sites to manage these relationships.

Developing a reciprocal link program is inexpensive and takes little more than an Internet connection and an email account. This makes link exchange a practical promotional option for webcasters working on a limited budget. On the other hand, securing reciprocal links is generally very time-consuming. As a rule of thumb, the netpublicist should expect to spend at least 30 minutes per reciprocal link; the web developer will have to spend additional time confirming that the reciprocal link was placed on the other site.

Link-Based Associate Programs

Many companies on the Internet have formed formal relationships that compensate web sites that provide links to them. Payment may be in cash or discounts on products or services. These programs perform extremely well relative to other forms of Internet advertising, and they have been used very successfully by many commerce sites. In a recent example of this netpublicity technique, Talk City (www.talkcity.com) instituted a program that invited its chat room users to put HTML code on their web pages. The code led users back to relevant areas of the main site. Within a short time, approximately 20,000 web sites had registered and placed back-links to Talk City.

Managing an associate program will take considerable time, and may require a full-time employee for a large site. For groups interested in outsourcing this service, companies such as Submit-It's ClickTrade (www.clicktrade .com) is a central clearinghouse that matches advertisers with linking sites. The service currently has more than 7,000 members.

Link Submission Services and Software

In addition to reciprocal and associate links, most webcasters will want to register their sites with major search engines and directories, including Yahoo! (www.yahoo.com), AltaVista (digital.altavista.com), InfoSeek (www.infoseek.com), Lycos (www.lycos.com), HotBot (www.hotbot.com), and Excite (www.excite.com). Reciprocal links are not required to maintain these postings. After the webcast URL is posted, a *spider* program (software that "crawls" the web, automatically indexing content from web sites) might index specific text and keywords encoded in the site's *metatag* (data written into the invisible header of a web page that provides information accessible to spider programs). In some cases, search engine staff members assess the suitability of the link by visiting the site personally.

Performed manually, postings of this sort are very tedious and require the skills of a full-time netpublicist. Fortunately, many organizations offer outsourcing for web postings. Basic posting services usually guarantee to add web URLs to the major search engines and a few hundred smaller directories. More sophisticated posting programs evaluate the site's content, seek out potential reciprocal link contacts, and adjust metatag information to improve search rankings. Posting services are offered by thousands of independent web developers and a few commercial groups such NetCreations' Postmaster service (www.netcreations.com/postmaster) and Submit-It! (www.submit-it.com). As an alternative to hiring a commercial service, the netpublicist may purchase software that automates the process of link submission. Examples of these programs include MSW's SubmitWolf engine (www.msw.simplenet.com/swolf), Power Solutions www.SitePromoter (www.SitePromoter.com), and Viper Spider (viperinc.com). These companies advertise their software primarily by the number of automated submissions it makes—a dubious proposition considering the obscurity of many of the sites accepting links. However, for groups that regularly need to post new web addresses to major search engines, these software packages are an inexpensive alternative to hiring a submission service.

Banner Ad Networks

Webcasters with an advertising budget may elect to purchase ads on other sites using graphical banners. This method is a useful way of contacting the public; it encourages *click-throughs* of approximately 1 percent of those viewing the page to a site specified by the webcaster. Like reciprocal links, this gives the webcaster a way to lead visitors to specific informational pages. For webcasters working on a budget, Internet Link Exchange (ILE at www.linkexchange.com) forms a viable banner option. ILE extends the concept of reciprocal linking by providing a free service that allows member web sites to share each other's banners. More than 200,000 web sites participate in the service.

Groups that want to post to high-traffic web sites may hire commercial banner ad networks. A representative list of these companies is shown in Table 6.3. These groups typically provide a full-featured service including market analysis, evaluation of banner placement, and even banner ad design. Webcasters may be particularly interested in MatchLogic (www.matchlogic .com), which recently formed an alliance with webcast ISP InterVU (www.intervu.com) for the delivery of streaming video and multimedia adver-

Table 6.3 Commercial Banner Ad Networks

Network	URL
24/7 Media (Commonwealth)	commonwealth.riddler.com
Central Ad Software	www.CentralAd.com
Doubleclick Software	www.doubleclick.com
Netgravity	www.netgravity.com
Adknowledge	www.adknowledge.com
Narrowline/NMX	www.narrowline.com/nmx
MatchLogic	www.matchlogic.com

tising. The service, hosted at the TrueVU (www.truevu.com) web site, uses MatchLogic's proprietary ad-targeting technology to serve, monitor, and measure advertising traffic. It also uses InterVU's high-speed Multimedia Advertising Network to deliver multimedia banner ads that incorporate streaming audio, video, and multimedia. TrueVU delivers all major formats of streaming media, including InterVU's V-Banner, GEO Emblaze, Microsoft NetShow, Narrative Enliven, and RealNetworks' RealMedia across a wide range of sites. The server software tracks clicks and mouseover activity; and because it uses Java applets, no plug-ins are required. Groups interested in exploring Internet media buying should also check Microscope (www.microscope.com), which features regular case studies of web banner buying, sometimes with short webcasts by the company representatives.

Push Channels

In 1997, push *was* webcasting. The expansion of the web and difficulties in finding information via browser had spawned a whole series of technologies designed to filter and automatically deliver a stream of information to the end-user's desktop. While sharing broad similarities with the streaming media discussed in this book, push has become less important in planning webcasts. Nevertheless, some push programs incorporate utilities borrowed from mailing lists and messaging software, and they may be useful for contacting a webcast audience. Push programs that are potentially useful for webcast promotion include:

Marimba Castanet (www.marimba.com). The new version of this all-Java application builds on multimedia push delivery by adding secure communication and administrator-level control of channel use and content. While highly suitable for corporate intranets, the complexity of designing Castanet content make it overkill for webcast promotion.

Wayfarer Communications (www.wayfarer.com). This push system has been adapted for drag-and-drop Internet publishing to a folder, and it is specifically designed for business organizations that need to provide notifications of relevant information. Wayfarer might be useful for sending out class schedules or meeting dates over a university or corporate intranet.

Backweb (www.backweb.com). This advanced system consists of a client and a specialized push server. Information pushed to subscribers may be displayed via change of screen background, screensavers, or Flash technology (not to be confused with Macromedia's Flash program), which puts a small animated symbol as an alert on top of other programs. Clicking on this icon launches a web browser leading to the new information.

Several factors have led to a decline in the popularity of the push concept, but the most telling reason is the nature of push itself: It attempts to convert the on-demand interactive content of the web into a one-way delivery system. Most users report being irritated by automatic content delivery and prefer web-based interaction. In order to avoid the fate of push, webcasters will need to address this concern and ensure that their webcasts provide a two-way interactive experience for their audience.

Media Contacts

As online media matures, it becomes increasingly useful to invite Internet-based media contacts, such as reviewers, to a webcast. The goal of such publicity efforts is to secure favorable comments that may be used in future promotions, as well as to create additional exposure on other media web sites. To explore this option, the netpublicist should check major media sites and author bylines for email addresses. The netpublicist should then write a letter to reviewers inviting them to the upcoming webcast and offering to provide technical support if necessary. Getting reviews is a risky process, however; a bad review could cause problems, but any exposure may serve to legitimize the webcaster's content in the eyes of the public. As the novelty factor wears off, audiences are increasingly likely to rely on reviewers to choose between different webcast events.

Offline Publicity

Due to their similarity to conventional broadcast, webcasts may benefit more than most Internet content from offline promotion. Large media companies should consider adding webcast information to ongoing promotional efforts in radio, television, and print. Due to the small and scattered nature of the typical webcast audience, extensive offline promotions are frequently not economical for smaller groups. These webcast groups should explore getting reviews in the offline press. Many small- and medium-circulation weekly newspapers now have cybercolumns whose authors might be interested in covering a webcast. In many cases, it is possible to submit story ideas by submitting a query via the publication's web site.

Timing

Many of the publicity methods described in this section take several weeks to take effect, so webcast promotions should begin well in advance of the actual event. Reciprocal web link requests and search engine postings should start three to four weeks before the webcast, and event calendar listings should be completed one to two weeks before the webcast. And because community-building is a major feature of many netpublicity strategies, netpublicists should continue working after the initial promotion and direct their efforts at consolidating the initial burst of interest. As an example of this strategy, a banner ad series might be followed by invitations to site visitors to join a mailing list. The netpublicist should also keep records of the various kinds of promotion that were applied during a particular project. This will help the team avoid later duplication of effort (e.g., reposting a link to a site) and make it easier to evaluate the long-term impact of the publicity effort.

Commerce Models

Despite the primitive nature of current webcasts, there are already groups developing pay-for-view services. For example, a college instructor might produce a series of online courses featuring streaming media content, and require payment from students and/or other colleges for its use. On the commercial side, a well-known comedian might release previously unseen stand-up comedy appearances via webcast. Emerging technologies that may be used to turn a webcast into a commercial venture are discussed in the following subsections.

Banner Ad Software

High-traffic webcast sites might consider selling banners on pages leading to the webcast. To determine the banner potential of the site, webcasters should divide the total number of hits they receive in a given time by 1,000 and multiply by the advertiser's CPM (cost per thousand), which translates to dollars paid per 1,000 page views. According to a July 1997 study by Focalink (www.focalink .com), average CPM rates paid by advertisers hovered at $30.27 (audio sites charged $63.93), and web serials (HTML-based storytelling) charged $250. The higher rates for audio and narrative sites suggest that future webcasts will be able to command higher advertising CPMs than average web sites. Even with higher rates, banner ads cannot provide sufficient revenue to operate a webcast site. In the case of a high-level audio webcast with 10,000 users logged in viewing two ads, the revenue could be calculated as follows:

10,000 viewers × $60 CPM / 1,000 page views per CPM = $600

Since webcast ISPs such as InterVU (www.intervu.com) quote costs of several thousand dollars for webcasts of this size, it is evident that developers will require large audiences (on the order of 200,000) or command very high CPMs (> $500) to support themselves via advertising alone.

In choosing a banner network, webcasters should determine how comprehensive the service is. Many banner ad networks provide support options that include inventory management, traffic, research, metering, ad serving, reporting, billing, and collection services. To join these networks, the webcasters often need to install custom reporting programs on their web servers that connect over the Internet to dedicated ad servers providing the banners. Large sites might consider installing their own banner ad software from vendors such as Intelligent Interactions (www.adfinity.com), NetGravity (www.netgravity.com), Clickover (www.clickover.com), and IMGIS Starpoint (www.imgis.com). Though these integrated systems give the developers greater control, they usually cost tens of thousands of dollars per installation, and the webcasters will still receive banners from a third-party network.

Embedding Advertising in the Webcast Stream

A compelling alternative to standard banners puts multimedia-style advertising directly into webcast content. This has become practical with the introduction of RealNetworks' RealServer G2. The commercial version of this system (but not the basic free version) contains built-in ad management routines that include insertion of multimedia ads at the beginning, middle, and end of an on-demand clip, or at the beginning of a live webcast.

Ads are generated using RealMedia tools and are automatically served from a specified directory on the media server. They may sequentially rotate through a specific list or be assigned unique presentation frequencies. During operation, ad viewing data is automatically recorded to log files. RealServer G2 includes a streaming media *Application Programming Interface (API)* for integration with third-party ad servers and database applications from all major banner ad software companies, including NetGravity, Clickover, Intelligent Interaction, and IMGIS Starpoint. A comparable solution has been announced by Microsoft for its NetShow 3.0 system, which integrates ads into streaming media using Microsoft Site Server (www.microsoft.com/siteserver) functions.

Implicit Payment

For sites that want to receive per-view fees (as opposed to advertising payments), it may be simplest to collect funds independently of the Internet. In this implicit payment strategy, access to the webcast is unrestricted, but diplomas, awards, and certificates gained by viewing the webcast are contingent upon payment elsewhere. For example, the media files of an online class might be accessible to anyone on the Internet, but receiving credit would require a separate registration and payment at a local campus office. This strategy allows groups using basic webcast tools to receive money for their efforts.

In a related strategy, a site may report use of copyrighted content for later payment to the correct individual or group. In a recent example, the American Society of Composers, Authors, and Publishers (ASCAP at www.ascap.com) formed an alliance with Liquid Audio (www.liquidaudio.com), which will

TIP — INTERFACES FOR COMMERCE-ORIENTED SITES

Commerce-oriented webcasts need to satisfy visitor concerns about security and use of information provided during the online transaction. Here are some ways site designers can make their site more "commerce friendly":

- Make buttons and graphics linking to payment areas obvious but not obtrusive; avoid a "hard sell" appearance.

- Provide links to information describing the complete payment process, how paid content will be received, and any product guarantees.

- Provide a link to consumer privacy information.

- Make online payment forms multistep, with the service or product being ordered shown on the first screen and the contact/payment information shown on the second screen.

- Provide confirmation via email that the payment was processed within 24 hours.

- Create a contact page that allows customers to check their current account status; if a direct link to account information is impractical, send the consumer an email reply from the orders department.

encourage web sites using their webcast technology to obtain ASCAP licensing. Liquid Audio will automatically report webcast delivery of music to ASCAP and facilitate the collection and payment of royalties.

Access to a "Hidden" Directory

When viewing webcast content is an end in itself, an implicit payment strategy cannot be used. As an alternative, some webcasters hide their files in an obscure directory on the media server. Users who receive authorization are then supplied with the path to the directory. This system fails for general use, however, since it is very easy to share the directory path information with non-paying viewers.

User-Based Authentication

Slightly greater security for webcast commerce may be provided using the standard authentication system built into most web servers. To implement this strategy, the web page and/or media file is placed in a folder that cannot be accessed unless a specific name/password is provided. Paying customers are given a password they can use to access the information. This method, while preventing random or accidental access by casual web surfers, has the same problem as hidden directories: passwords are easily shared.

As the popularity of webcast media grows, companies producing media servers are building in their own authentication schemes. More sophisticated than generic name/password schemes, these strategies allow username/password control of access to the media stream itself, instead of to the file storage directory. Server-based authentication may also include other features such as passwords that only work a single time (eliminating password sharing) and limiting access by date or time.

Player-Based Authentication

Systems using player-based authentication perform much of the commerce work in the background, outside the user's control. After an initial setup, they store names/passwords and payment information (e.g., credit card numbers) within the media player software on the end-user's computer.

On subsequent access, authentication occurs without user intervention via a unique player ID. This method limits the user to a single computer and may be easier for new computer users to understand. Security is high in some respects (only a single computer may be used for logins) but low in others (anyone using that computer has instant access to the content).

Digital Watermarking

Because users often have the capability to save downloaded webcast data, the possibility of producing unauthorized copies poses a problem. To prevent this, commerce systems have begun to support digital watermarking strategies, similar to those discussed in Chapter 5, "Planning, Licensing, and Management," that record user name/password, player IDs, and copyright information related to the work.

In most cases, watermarking does not prevent unauthorized copies from being made, but it does make it possible to rapidly identify any copy as legitimate or pirated. This makes Internet commerce more practical, particularly for all-electronic content, including webcasts. Since sites may identify unauthorized copies and demand their removal from the Internet, legitimate copies become more valuable to their audience. Installation and use of watermarks requires no special effort by the end user, making it easier to implement than many other solutions. While much has been made of the widespread piracy on the Internet, watermarking coupled with online searches actually creates a more secure copyright protection system than exists in any other medium.

Webcast Software Supporting Commercial Transactions

Currently, only a few systems provide the tools necessary to support online commerce. The current leader in this area is the RealNetworks CommerceServer G2 (www.real.com). The software has built-in username/password support for accessing streaming media that is implemented independently of web-based authentication. Passwords are restricted to a single media stream and cannot be reused or shared. Authentication takes place directly in the media server independent of the web.

Support for online credit transactions is also provided via integration with CyberSource (www.cybersource.com), CyberCash (www.cybercash.com), VeriFone (www.verifone.com), and Open Market (www.openmarket.com) commerce products. Use of these systems through a web server supporting secure transactions coupled with the CommerceServer G2 allows for real-time validation of credit cards. A sample user interface for pay-per-view webcasts using CommerceServer G2 is shown in Figure 6.2. Access may be restricted to a specified number of minutes or allow unlimited access up to a particular closing date for the webcast.

The Liquid Audio (www.liquidaudio.com) system relies solely on player-based authentication. After users download the software, they register and supply demographic and credit card information, which is stored in the player

Figure 6.2 Sample interface for entering credit card information during a pay-per-download webcast.

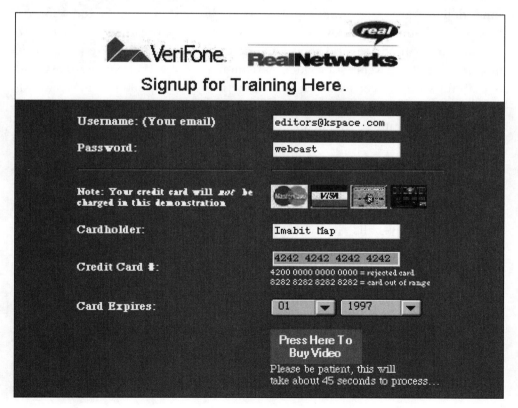

itself in the proprietary Digital Passport format. Access to protected content is mediated entirely through the player, and the user's interaction is limited to selecting audio clips to download for purchase. Webcast content that is purchased and downloaded contains a digital watermark that may identify its origin even if it is copied to an analog device such as a tape player. Credit information is processed via a link to third-party transaction services and deposited directly in the vendor's bank account. The server also keeps track of performances for reporting to performance rights agencies. Commerce support is also featured in Microsoft NetShow via tight integration with Microsoft Site Server. Commerce features include pay-per-view and pay-per-minute billing services.

Running a full-featured pay-per-download webcast service is currently an expensive proposition. The RealNetworks CommerceServer costs several thousand dollars, and the complete Liquid Audio system retails for $25,000. Integrating commerce hardware and software capable of supporting real-time transactions will add several thousand additional dollars. At these prices, it is important that the webcast production team makes sure that pay-per-download is a useful strategy. For example, audiences using older 6800-based Macintosh systems (common at many universities) will not be able to support authorization, and users connecting to the media server are likely to crash their computers.

Assessing the Impact of a Webcast

After the webcast, those handling marketing/netpublicity will need to determine the success of their efforts. Some webcasters will be concerned only with the number of eyeballs that viewed the program, while others will want to determine how the webcast affected purchasing and creation of fan communities. In determining this, the following factors should be considered:

Who logged on? This is the most basic measure of the number of individuals who actually downloaded the webcast stream. Hit quantity alone tells little about the audience, but extremely high or low hit counts are a measure of success or failure. To properly interpret hit quantities for events such as live webcasts, it will be necessary to compare statistics to the daily rise and fall of normal traffic to the site.

Where did they come from? Analysis of the addresses of the visitors will reveal the ISP providing the Internet connection—as well as the country of origin, commercial, educational, or nonprofit status. In addition, checking the *referrer log* of the web server will indicate the last web site visited prior to joining the webcast. If the visitor was directed to the site from a search engine, it will be possible to capture the query term they typed, which will give additional clues to their motivation.

Who stayed on? Typical Internet surfers stay on individual pages for only a few seconds before moving on. For this reason, determining the average time a webcast was viewed is more important than absolute numbers. Analysis programs such as WebTrends (www.webtrends.com) provide averaged estimates of time spent on the site; media server software, including RealSystem G2 and Microsoft NetShow, may provide precise timings of how long each visitor tuned into the webcast stream. Long visits are essential to appreciate narrative content, such as Flash-generated cartoons or repurposed film or television. In contrast, news stories on sites including CNN (www.cnn.com) are typically a few minutes in length; short visits may be compatible with interest and appreciation of the webcast.

What kind of equipment do they have? Access log data may provide information on the operating system, general hardware class, and installed webcast software on the end-user's computer. Analysis of error logs will show if there were compatibility problems, and transmission statistics will reveal the web connection speed.

What else did they do? By tracking visitors, it is possible to determine what impact viewing the webcast had on subsequent surfing. For example, tracking statistics might record the percentage of the webcast audience that bought a related product, or the number of people who added themselves to the site's mailing list.

A variety of methods may be used to determine the impact of a webcast. Currently, these solutions are found in several types of software, but consolidation into a single system seems likely in the near future. Major classes of software that may be used to access the success of a webcast include:

Exit polls. These are web-server-based programs that create a fill-out form for webcast viewers. On the form, it is possible to ask questions about the value of the webcast and provide automatic sign-up for mailing lists. Forms are easily implemented by web developers using CGI or JavaScript programming. Results are usually emailed to the appropriate recipient in the webcast team.

Web analysis software. These programs take the standard access logs generated by web servers and convert them to easily understood charts and tables. Currently, the leader in the field for low- and mid-size sites is WebTrends (www.webtrends.com). This comprehensive package for Windows systems provides general access statistics, user demographics, and a list of common paths users took through the web site. A Java-based, cross-platform alternative is provided by Aquas, Inc. (www.aquas.com) with its Bazaar Analyzer software. This tool combines access log analysis with automatic notification by email when certain pages on the site are accessed by a particular kind of user. The PathView option provides a graphical look at visitors' clicks as they move through the site. It also indicates entry and exit points, page view order, and time spent on each page. For larger corporate sites, the preferred choice is Net.analysis Pro by Net.Genesis (www.netgenesis.com). In addition to standard statistics, its ReportSite option allows daily and weekly analysis results to be distributed throughout an organization using an online calendar.

Banner ad access and tracking. Banner ad management software usually creates a separate log file detailing user interaction. This is primarily useful for relating advertising results to absolute page views during the webcast. Virtually all commercial banner software writes custom access logs; and banner networks provide detailed tracking reports to their clients. Simpler freeware and shareware banner software programs, available at sites such as the CGI Resources Index (www.cgiresources .com), also generates logs for direct analysis by the webcasters.

Streaming media access analysis. All standard media servers write their own access logs independently of the web server. These logs provide additional information beyond selecting the webcast for play. For example, via a record of which media file was sent, the RealServer access log provides information about the users' hardware and operating system and connection speed. To evaluate this information, it is necessary to use the supplied software, which analyzes user viewing habits and traffic over time.

Real-time analysis. This form of tracking shows the number of streaming media files being accessed in a rapidly updated display. The web administrator/engineer may use this to determine whether demand for content is exceeding server capacity. Marketers may be able to correlate logins and/or logoffs during the webcast with the particular content being displayed at that time. RealServer and VDO administrators may monitor how many connections, users, and files are being accessed in real time. A similar service is provided in Microsoft NetShow via its integration with Microsoft SiteServer.

Email feedback. Webcasters should regularly monitor their main email boxes (e.g., webmaster@webcastsite.com) for messages related to their webcasts. On large sites, the developers should create a set of department-level email addresses to forward messages received through the main box. Many complaints will require interaction with the customer to discover the actual problem, so time has to be allocated for two-way communication.

Checking online. Standard search engines may be used to determine whether a webcast has resulted in increased mention of a word, phrase, or web site URL. Since most search engines currently take several months to complete an indexing pass through the Internet, access to this information will be delayed. Submit-It! provides a commercial PositionAgent system (www.positionagent.com) that may be used to monitor search engine rankings. Webcasts aimed at strong fan communities may show their impact by postings to Usenet and other discussion groups. An easy way to check Usenet is to become a member of the DejaNews (www.dejanews.com) site and search its archives by topic and keyword.

After the preliminary analysis of the webcast, the next step is to convert the raw numbers into a judgment of its failure or success. This evaluation will be somewhat subjective since webcasts may succeed or fail at many levels. For example, a music webcast that attracts a tiny audience might still be considered a success if the visitors become members of the artist's fan club. Conversely, a webcast attracting tens of thousands of viewers might be a failure if server capacity was exceeded and part of the audience was unable to connect. For many groups, the primary benefit of running a webcast will be derived from the experience the production team receives.

Privacy Considerations

Webcasters who collect mailing lists, promote to a large audience, and monitor visitor behavior are faced with informing the public as to how this information is used. Web information is both more and less informative than traditional

---

Broadcast.com's Criteria for a Successful Webcast

Broadcast.com (www.broadcast.com) lists the following criteria for a successful webcast, determined by checking access logs, real-time monitoring of webcast streams, and email feedback from the audience:

- The broadcast goes live at the right time with proper audio/video feed.

- Viewers can easily find the broadcast from the home page and other links.

- Viewers are able to successfully view and listen to the event without interruption.

- The client receives positive feedback from the broadcast.

- The client desires to archive the broadcast for future viewing.

---

information about consumers. On one hand, access logs allow the equivalent of tracking every turn taken by shopping carts in a supermarket. On the other, users are typically anonymous unless they specifically provide basic information linked to tracking data. In early 1998, no U.S. federal laws set limits for sharing access data or selling it to third-party marketers. Privacy violations are an increasing concern of consumers, and many users routinely sabotage the link between anonymous tracking and demographics by providing false information. According to the "7th User Survey" of the Graphic, Visualization, & Usability Center of the Georgia Institute of Technology (www-survey.cc.gatech .edu), almost 40 percent of respondents indicated that they falsify data in web site registration; and 60 percent indicated that they don't trust web sites that collect personal information to use it responsibly. Reflecting this concern, the European Community (EC) is developing rules that will prohibit web sites from collecting user data from European countries without direct communication with the user each time.

Typical positive comments include statements by the client that their audience has been expanded. In recent statements by Robertson, Stevens & Company (www.audionet.com/events/rsco/121097/) and The Gartner Group (www.audionet.com/inter/gartner/), increased access to company presentations were a major positive factor in adding webcasting to the service.

According to Broadcast.com, failures usually occur due to the following:

- Advanced planning didn't take place between the client and AudioNet.

- Technical problems prevented even a small number of viewers from enjoying the event.

- Negative feedback was received from the client and or their targeted audience.

With the increasing shift toward protecting end-user privacy, webcasters will need to display a privacy policy on their own sites. Using the following guidelines, it should clearly state how user information is handled:

Privacy statement. This should be a short paragraph summarizing the site's privacy policy. For example, it might indicate that user demographic information would not be sold to other sites.

How information is gathered. This section of the statement should indicate how information is gathered, either through passive (access log analysis), active (registration), or implicit (contact information for individuals who order products from the site) methods. Tracking methods, including IP addresses, cookies, browser types, and originating Internet domains, should also be documented.

How information is used. This section reveals how end-user information is used by site operators. For example, a webcaster might indicate that statistics of repeated logins by a user are pooled anonymously and used to rank long-term interest in content.

How information is shared. This section should name any groups with which consumer information is shared, and how they in turn plan to use the information.

Opt-out and information deletion. Virtually all sites should have a policy in place allowing the end user to prevent data from being collected. Most sites also provide a way for consumers to delete any existing information stored by the company.

Certification. This indicates whether the site is a member of a privacy organization, and specifies that it has been cleared and meets their standards for disclosure.

Security. Information about how information is collected and stored should be listed in this section. For example, sites might indicate that all commerce-oriented communication is conducted using a secure server, and that personal information is not stored on public web servers.

Contact information. An email address, phone, or postal mail contact should be supplied for those with further questions.

Organizations providing a privacy assurance include TRUSTe, an independent, nonprofit privacy initiative dedicated to building users' trust and confidence on the Internet. The organization, whose symbol is shown in Figure 6.3, helps web operators create a privacy statement, and upon approval, encourages them to display the TRUSTe logo on their sites. TRUSTe is sponsored by major companies including IBM, CyberCash, MatchLogic, Netcom, InterNEX, Excite, Wired, and AT&T. Other groups providing useful guidelines include the Electronic Frontier Foundation (www.eff.org), The Direct Marketing Association (DMA; www.the-dma.org), and the Interactive Services Association (www.isa.net). Up-front declarations of privacy policies and information sharing have been highly successful in increasing user confidence at HotMail (www.hotmail.com) and CyberGold (www.cybergold.com). Looking to the future, Netscape and other companies are developing an Open Profiling Standard (OPS; developer.netscape .com/ops/ops.html), which will allow users to store personal information locally in their web browsers and specify what portion of it is available online. The Platform for Privacy Preferences Project (P3P) is a privacy mechanism being developed by the World Wide Web Consortium (www.w3c.org).

Figure 6.3 TRUSTe (www.truste.org).

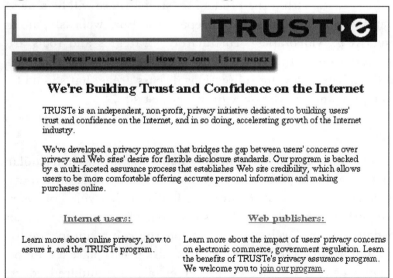

When complete, it will allow Internet users to set default preferences for disclosure of personal information.

Archives and Searching

Once a webcast is complete, it is necessary to determine how material will be archived. In many respects, the decision of how to archive and index content for searching is an implicit rating of the impact of the webcast. Provided the content generated interest in its first showing, the webcast team may increase its long-term impact and value by developing archives and allowing the Internet audience to request past events on demand. The archive also provides a "second chance" for poorly received content, and opens additional opportunities for user tracking. Long-term patterns of access to "legacy" content will help the webcasters plan their next production.

Archives strategies on the Internet generally follow one of three strategies. In some cases, the webcasters will remove the material from the site and replace it with new content. This is most appropriate for time-sensitive material that rapidly and permanently loses its value. More frequently, they will organize it into on-demand media archives available to those who couldn't attend the original webcast. Within the production studio there will be a need to archive audio and video samples used to prepare the final webcasts, along with physical assets (e.g., videotapes). Fortunately, strategies and tools are available to webcasters to help them effectively plan for storing webcast content online and offline. The following subsections discuss areas that should be considered in developing an archive policy for a webcast site.

Planning Archive Space

Though media destined for webcasts have much smaller footprints than similar material used in CD-ROM and broadcast environments, they will still require extensive storage space. As shown in Figure 6.4, ISDN-quality video or near-broadcast audio require at least 10 megabytes per hour of storage. For media archives receiving daily inputs of webcast information, this can result in a multi-gigabyte archive in a matter of weeks. Current hard disk drives place a limit on the maximum amount of material per media server of a few hundred hours. Beyond this, multiple servers will be necessary to deliver content to the web.

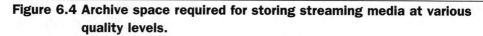

Figure 6.4 Archive space required for storing streaming media at various quality levels.

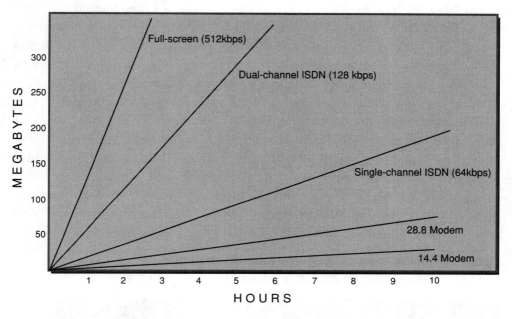

Due to the constraints imposed by media file sizes, the webcast production team will need to make strategic decisions about the level of archive material to provide on the web. Some sites may restrict their offerings to webcasts from the past week or month, which is recommended for sites with a very large amount of content such as news reports. Others may choose to highlight "best of" webcasts; this method is most appropriate for entertainment-related sites. A third strategy periodically rotates a subset of total archives, which could be used for content that does not go out of date or has value in being rewebcast (similar to television syndication). This strategy has the advantage of supplying regular updates to archive pages, encouraging frequent returns by the audience.

Media Search Engines

Conventional search engines may index text (e.g., title of a video clip) but they cannot index audio and video data. With the growth of video on the Internet and elsewhere, several new products have set the extremely ambitious goal of automatically indexing audio and video by its content. While most of the products are currently geared toward video, audio support is included in all of them. At the low end, Imagine Product's Executive Producer is distributed free with video editors from Avid (www.avid.com). This entry-level product detects scene changes in video and creates a series of thumbnail images for searching or storyboard creation. The product is currently restricted to searching text provided along with the video, but newer versions will index video data itself. A more advanced product is Magnifi's (www.magnifi.com) SmartMedia, a specialized web spider that checks audio, video, multimedia, and web assets; it then extracts attributes, indexing them across an entire intranet. While indexing the content, the software also creates thumbnail images and audio/video bites, presenting them along with the text index. The software is currently being used by NASA (as shown in Figure 6.5) and CNN Interactive (cnnplus.cnn.com). A similar product developed by Virage (www.virage.com)

Figure 6.5 NASA's use of Magnifi's SmartMedia software (marsindex.jpl.nasa.gov/msearch/).

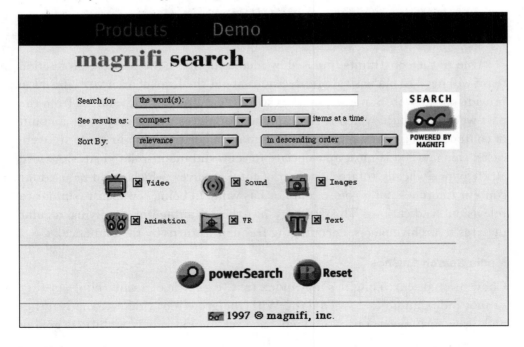

automatically determines where scenes in video begin and end based on color, composition, and texture. After identifying scenes, it generates a set of thumbnails and indexes any closed captioning so that the video archive may be searched by keyword. Both products also provide asset management and allow users to control whether they access earlier or later versions of the same work. Drawing on a library metaphor, users may check content in and out for personal use. Media archives are capable of handling webcast-format media and may enable searches through streaming content archives directly from the web. Additional companies offering software for media archiving and searching are listed in Table 6.4.

Currently, media archiving is relatively primitive, but this is likely to change in the near future. The ever-increasing amount of nontext media on the web, along with a desire for finding relevant information in streaming media archives, ensures that development will continue in this area. Long-term, effective indexing of media archives will be essential to reduce the total amount of streaming media downloaded, thereby reducing bandwidth. Indexing will also need to become personalized. For example, a developer may need to search for particular graphic styles and encoding, while a producer may need to examine clips for potential copyright violations. It may be that webcasting will not take off until the interactive, "hunter-gather" model for web browsing is successfully applied to streaming media.

Table 6.4 Companies Offering Media Archiving and Searching Software

Company Name	URL
Virage Video Cataloger	www.virage.com
Magnifi Enterprise Server	www.magnifi.com
ISLIP MediaKey Digital Library System	www.islip.com
Excalibur Visual Retrievalware	www.excalib.com
Cinebase Visual Asset Management System	www.cinebase.com
Imagine Products Executive Producer	www.imagineproducts.com

Next . . .

This concludes the discussion of the various aspects of webcast production. In Part Three, "Forms of Webcast and Live Event Production," these principles will be applied to webcasts incorporating specific media: text (wordcasts), data (datacasts), sound (audiocasts), animation (animacasts), and video (videocasts).

PART THREE

FORMS OF WEBCAST AND LIVE EVENT PRODUCTION

DATACASTS AND WORDCASTS

7

Datacasts and wordcasts form a unique, nontraditional area of webcasting specifically enabled by the Internet. Although still relatively unknown, this area is growing rapidly, and it may become one of the dominant categories of webcasting in the near future as noncomputer devices such as pagers and notepads are connected to the Internet.

A datacast consists of a stream of numerical or symbolic information broadcast to the Internet. Depending on the implementation, datacasts may contain audio, video, or animation in addition to the symbolic data. Examples of datacasts include:

- Weather patterns
- Traffic reports
- Thermometers
- Light sensors
- Seismometers
- Stock reports
- Real-time sports scores

A good example of datacasting is provided by the U.S. Geological Survey (USGS) Real-Time Water Data Site. As shown in Figure 7.1, the home page displays a graphic map of the United States that is updated in real time with hydrological data from throughout the United States.

Figure 7.1 U.S. Geological Survey (USGS) Real-Time Water Data Site (water.usgs.gov/public/realtime.html).

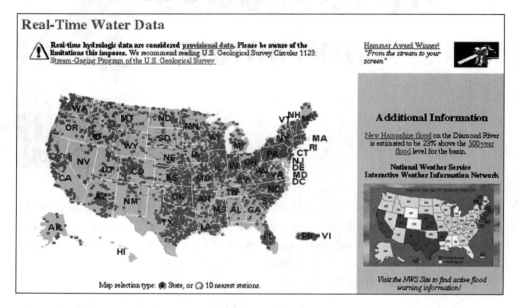

While relatively difficult to implement, and frequently requiring "home-brew" programming for success, datacasts are becoming increasingly popular on the Internet. A good list of sites providing these features is found at Anthony's List of Internet Accessible Machines (www.mitchell.net/ant/machines.htm#status) or Thingys on the Net (www.oink.com/thingys/).

In a wordcast, a continuous stream of text is transcribed from a live mono-logue or dialogue and uploaded to a media server for delivery over the Internet. For example, a sportscaster might type a running game commentary on a lap-top computer and have the text relayed to Internet audience members in real time. Compared to the more familiar Internet chat, wordcasts are one-way (though audience members may be able to forward questions to participants). Examples of wordcasts include:

- Classroom lectures
- Minutes from business meetings
- Sports commentary

- Audiobook transcripts
- News reports

A live wordcast is similar to close-captioned broadcast services. Sports sites such as ESPN (www.espnet.sportszone.com) provide streaming wordcasts featuring the latest scores. News sites such as ABC (www.abc.com) allow other web sites to display streaming wordcast tickers containing news from their sites. The Wordcasters site, as shown in Figure 7.2, focuses on longer forms of streaming text content, including live speeches, seminars, and educational lectures.

Wordcasts may be found on many sites, frequently in the form of small windows of scrolling text on such sites as Netscape (home.netscape.com) and MSNBC (www.msnbc.com). Certain push services such as PointCast (www.pointcast.com) are functionally equivalent to wordcasts. Currently, longer wordcast transcripts are confined exclusively to the Wordcasters site; no lists or compilations exist.

This chapter discusses the unique features that define wordcasts and datacasts, along with important applications in use on today's Internet. Case studies

Figure 7.2 Wordcasters (www.wordcasters.com).

of sites running these webcasts will demonstrate the relative importance of word-casts and datacasts in the webcast paradigm. This chapter also addresses the question of who may benefit most from running a wordcast or datacast; specific production principles needed to make wordcasts and datacasts accessible to the public; and additional concerns such as cost estimation and archiving strategies.

Unique Features

It is important to distinguish among the methods used to present a wordcast or datacast and the information itself. Unlike other kinds of webcasts, word-casts and datacasts stream symbolic (words or numbers) information. This information has no sensory equivalent, so it is processed and presented using audio, video, or animation. Although the site visitor will see words and num-bers, the actual streaming mechanism is most likely some form of animation. Due to this, wordcasts and datacasts share the following unique features, which do not appear in other webcast media:

Conversion process. Interpreting information in datacasts often requires more than simply recording environmental information. Instead of data compression used for streaming audio and video, datacasts require calculations such as normalization, scaling, or amplification.

Transcription. Like most other webcasts, datacasts have an analog/digital conversion step; but they often require an engineer with expertise in handling unusual equipment such as thermometers or radiation detectors. Wordcasts must be transcribed from a live monologue or dialogue, possibly with condensation and grammatical corrections done "on the fly" prior to delivery.

Storage size. Since wordcasts and datacasts represent, rather than reproduce, content, they may be stored in very compact formats. Whereas a few paragraphs of audio might occupy 200K or more when compressed, the same sentences would amount to less than 1K if sent as text. This minimizes bandwidth requirements relative to other webcasts.

Low bandwidth. Wordcasts and datacasts may operate effectively even with very slow Internet connections. This allows users with older equipment or bad Internet connections to access these webcasts. Servers providing datacast or wordcast information typically support much larger audiences than normally possible for streaming audio and video.

Programming. Datacasts often require specialized media players that need to be modified for each data type. Since each data has a unique format, a special programming algorithm will be necessary to display it intelligibly. This requires more high-level programming expertise within the webcast production team. New versions of streaming animation programs such as Flash Generator (www. macromedia.com/software/flash/) may simplify datacast player programming in the future.

Datacasts and wordcasts are extremely flexible formats. Many sites have used datacasts and wordcasts to present content found in other media such as stock tickers and sports scores. Furthermore, the unique characteristics of wordcasts and datacasts encourage experimentation with novel types of data found nowhere else but on the Internet.

Applications

Wordcasts and datacasts offer access to a wide array of information frequently unavailable in other forms of webcasting. This wide content range is due to the ubiquity of symbolic and numerical data in daily life. The audience for wordcasts and datacasts is also very general. Unlike entertainment-oriented audio and video webcasting, wordcasts and datacasts appeal to web users who view Internet access strictly as a tool. The following list includes some key areas in which wordcast and datacasts are used, along with characteristics of the audience accessing this information.

Education. Wordcasts and datacasts have a strong place in education. The flow of a wordcast closely emulates a real-world class lecture. Datacasts complement the wordcast by providing direct access to supporting data. For example, students studying traffic patterns via a datacast may examine real-time changes for their city, instead of reading a printed summary with dated information.

Case Study: USGS Real-Time Water Data Site

URL: water.usgs.gov/public/realtime.html
Contact: Kim Fry (kfry@usgs.gov)

The USGS site is an example of a datacast site integrating information from a very large number (4,000) of collection points. The purpose of the site is to provide a graphical display of water levels and water flow through the various lakes, streams, and rivers in the United States. Currently, the site delivers more than 200,000 real-time hydrographs every month. As shown in Figure 7.3, water levels are initially measured at hydrologic stations. The sensor's information is then transmitted at four-hour intervals to two geostationary operations environmental satellites (GEOS) operated by the National Oceanic and Atmospheric Administration. These data are then retransmitted by means of a domestic satellite; the resulting signal is received by the USGS district offices and other users.

Figure 7.3 Design of the USGS Datacast system.

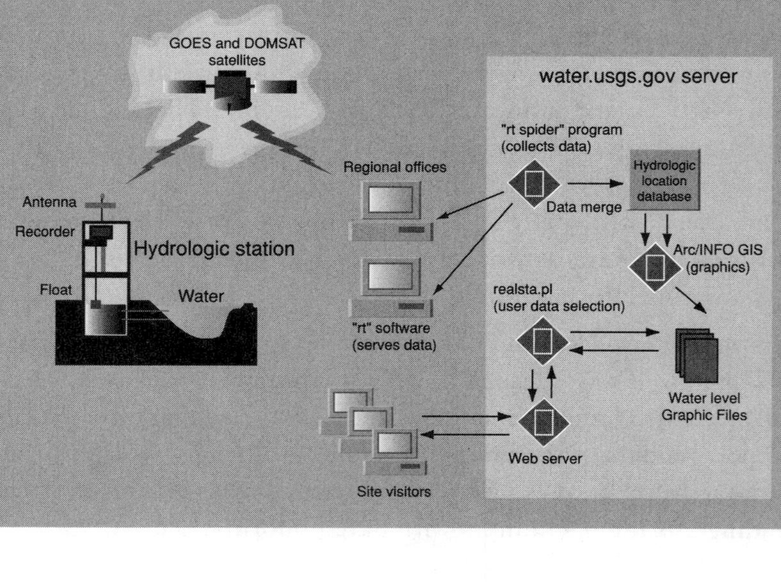

Each of the 60 or so district offices serves its own real-time data using "rt" software developed by USGS. The current version of rt posts new data every few minutes. To move this information to the web, the water.usgs.gov web server runs an internally developed software robot that checks each of the district rt sites to compile a daily list of active stations. This list is merged with a local database of station locations. The resulting dataset is used to create a graphical image map using ESRI's (www.esri.com/) Arc/INFO GIS (Geographic Information System) software.

The image and text-only versions of the data are delivered to the web by a Perl script called "realsta.pl." This program allows users to examine water levels at a particular station by pointing to the map or typing keywords for states, hydrologic units (watershed), or station numbers. The graphic image map is connected to a custom program that runs much faster than the standard image map program found in many web servers. The overall system requires considerable back-end programming by USGS.

The developers estimate that the rt program took two programmers approximately two weeks to implement, while the graphic conversion routines took about four weeks of effort by a single programmer experienced in working with GIS. To handle daily maintenance, the USGS team rotates personnel through a duty officer, whose responsibility is to monitor the real-time data and identify reporting stations that have gone offline. Support for the system at the district offices typically takes about one-fourth the total administration time of the local webmasters. While the site has not received extensive publicity, it interacts with a large community of scientists and white-water enthuasists—and it provides a focused service to this niche audience.

Business. Wordcasts are excellent for delivering lectures and speeches to large audiences. As a rule of thumb, a wordcast may support audiences 10 to 50 times larger than audiocasts or videocasts. Wordcasts are a good choice for highly focused business situations such as seminars and corporate policy speeches. Datacasts can provide graphical representations of processes important to the business, such as the condition of an internal network or the statistics of incoming or outgoing calls.

Infotainment. Datacasts and wordcasts are often used to provide information-based entertainment such as sports scores or audience votes on the performance of a celebrity. Examples of sites mixing information and entertainment include ESPNET Sportszone (www.espnet.sportszone.com) and Livest@ts (www.livestats.com). Scientific data displayed in an interesting way may also qualify as infotainment, such as the real-time monitors of spacecraft health on the Lunar Prospector (lunar.arc.nasa.gov) site.

Finance. Datacasts featuring stock tickers are a popular form of content on the web. Typically, the information is provided as a scrolling wordcast ticker, although a few sites provide graphical datacast information as well. Datacasts of stock quotes and related information are available from around the world from sites such as Real-Time Swiss Quotes (www.swissquote.com), World Online Quotes and Trading System (www.woqats.com), InterQuote Stock Service (www.interquote.com), and Thompson Real-Time Quotes (www.thompsonrtq.com/index.sht).

Science. Datacasts provide a way to get information to the public that would otherwise be too tedious or difficult to understand. For example, the DataViz section of the Lunar Prospector site, shown in Figure 7.4, displays data originally designed for review by specialists. The engaging graphical presentation of the data encourages the general public to study this area for themselves.

The types of information that may be effectively displayed by wordcasts and datacasts is only limited by the developer's imagination. For example, a project on the National Zoo Satellite Tracking Collar Test Site (www.si.edu/elephant)

Identifying a Wordcast/Datacast Audience

Not all web surfers will benefit equally from attending a wordcast or datacast. The following provides some rules of thumb that may be used to determine whether your audience is suitable for this type of information.

Is the audience online? A datacast aimed at information technologies (IT) personnel managing a corporate Intranet is much more likely to succeed than one aimed at computer-phobic employees.

Is the audience technicially sophisticated? Appreciating abstract data such as spacecraft telemetry requires the audience to understand the source and meaning of the information.

Does the audience have suitable hardware and software? Many datacasts require that the end-user's system support Java or animation programs such as Macromedia Flash (www.macromedia.com/software/flash/).

Is the audience available at the required time? Educational wordcasts aimed at students may be inappropriate if the wordcast takes place outside of school hours.

Can the audience be contacted easily? Random surfers are unlikely to be interested in most datacasts and wordcasts. For this reason, it is important to develop a strategy to identify and reach potential audience members effectively.

Is the audience interested in interacting? For full appreciation of a datacast, the audience often needs to adjust on-screen controls—and wordcasts may allow chat-style conversation between the wordcasters and the audience.

allowed visitors to monitor the movements of animals wearing wildlife tracking collars. Programs tracking user movement through the web itself may be displayed in real time by web-based log analysis programs, which effectively qualifies them as datacasts. It is likely that the current samples of wordcast and datacast represent only a fraction of the full potential of the medium.

Aspects of Production

Datacasts and wordcasts present a unique challenge for production at the levels of media capture, encoding, and delivery. The unique content and the necessity for sophisticated visualization lead to production strategies significantly different from other webcast formats.

Figure 7.4 The Lunar Prospector DataViz Site (lunar.arc.nasa.gov/dataviz/ index.html).

Case Study: The Lunar Prospector Site

URL: www.lunar.arc.nasa.gov
Contact: Ken Bollinger (kbollinger@mail.arc.nasa.gov)

This outstanding site is the first to provide web access to live, real-time telemetry from a working space probe in a graphical datacast format. Launched in January 1998, the Lunar Prospector is designed to map the mineralogical resources of the moon using a variety of high-tech instruments. The site developers at NASA's Numerical Aerospace Simulation (NAS) Center's Data Analysis Group (science.nas.nasa.gov/Groups/VisTech/) have developed a datacasting presentation that allows users to tune in directly to spacecraft operations. The site also features ambient webcam video, on-demand audio/video, and live videocasts.

As shown in Figure 7.5, data is received from the spacecraft via NASA's Deep Space Network and is routed through the Jet Propulsion Laboratory (www.jpl.nasa.gov) in Pasadena, California, to the NASA/Ames Research Center in Mountain View, California. There, the data receives initial processing by Sun workstations and is written to an archival microVAX via a shared NFS volume. At the same time, a Perl script (www.perl.com) writes the last few minutes of the raw data to a separate file for use by a PC running National Instruments' LabView (www.labview.com) software. The LabView application writes an ASCII text file every 32 seconds in an NFS volume shared between the web server and the PC that is running LabView. The DataViz Java applets read the ASCII data in order to construct graphs for online display. An example of the highly sophisticated presentation used on the Lunar Prospector site is shown in Figure 7.6. In this example, the initial hyperlink to "Spacecraft Health" launched a Java applet displaying an image of the spacecraft, along with buttons for selecting individual components of its

Case Study: The Lunar Prospector Site *(Continued)*

Figure 7.5 Organization of the Lunar Prospector datacast (lunar.arc.nasa.gov/dataviz/index.html).

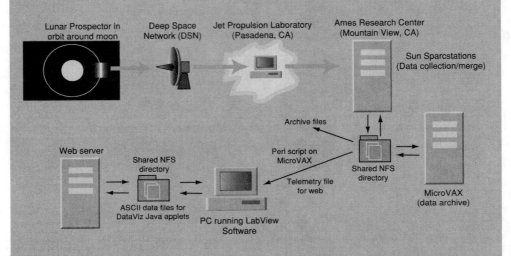

hardware. Selecting a component brings up two more Java windows: one showing a numerical display of the time of the last download from the spacecraft, and another showing a graphical display of the component data. This graphic is updated on a timeframe of several seconds and generally lags only two seconds behind NASA's Mission Control.

As a first-time effort, developing the complete datacast system took considerable time. Three individuals were required to develop the Java applets, for a total of 1,500 hours of work. The system transferring data to the web server in real time took a single programmer about 600 hours. In practice, this translates to a year's worth of development time. The total system requires administrative

Figure 7.6 Java applets displaying real-time data on the Lunar Prospector DataViz site.

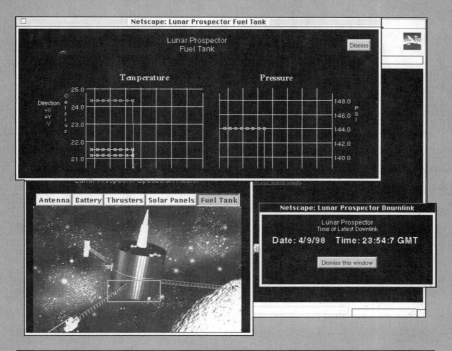

support from 12 to 13 individuals, two of whom are directly involved in the DataViz portion.

Due to the highly abstract nature of the data relayed from the Prospector probe, the designers have embedded the datacast links in a series of educational web pages describing the scope and purpose of the project. Information is provided as text, graphics, and Shockwave movies. The latter is used to illustrate points (such as phases of the moon) that are difficult to visualize via a text-only

Team Design

More than any other webcast form, datacasts require the expertise of hardware engineers and software programmers. For example, installation and proper use of environmental sensors require trained specialists who can connect sensing, telemetry, and data-logging devices to computers on a case-by-case basis. Sophisticated datacasts will require the support of an electrical engineer experienced in hooking analog equipment to computer serial ports. Some remote sensors are designed to transmit information over cellular telephone networks, so the production team may require an expert in converting this data to Internet-ready form. Since datacasts frequently pool information from a wide variety of sources, the webcast production team may have to split into two parts: a local editor group actively producing the webcast, and a larger external group of reporters supporting content collection. Datacast groups will also need a web designer with special skills. Since interpreting the data may require educating the audience, it is important that the designer creates an online tutorial complementing the datacast.

Wordcasts do not require special engineering support at the point of data entry. Instead, the webcast team will need to hire personnel who are capable of transcribing speech in real time. Support will be required for teams who want to copy/fact-check wordcast streams "on the fly" and for development of wordcast players.

Capture Systems

The methods used to capture information for datacasts vary widely. Usually, an environmental sensor supplies analog or digital information to a capture computer. In some cases, the sensor's connection may run directly to the web server, while other sites may aggregate data from many computers over modem or network connections. The diverse range of sensors used in datacasts includes devices measuring temperature, seismic activity, water level, water turbidity, chemical detection, lighting, wildlife telemetry, soil moisture, and radiation. Table 7.1 lists a representative group of companies providing the hardware for developing environmental sensors; and discussion of electrical engineering is available at The Electronic Engineer's Toolbox (www.eetoolbox.com/ebox.htm) and John's Electrical Engineering Page (www.ecn.uoknor.edu/~jspatric/ee-info.html).

Table 7.1 Companies Producing Environmental Sensors

Company	URL	Sensor Type
Environmental Sensors, Inc.	www.envsens.com	Soil moisture, GPS, wildlife telemetry, weather, water quality
Spiderplant	www.spiderplant.com/about.htm	Thermal
AIL Systems, Inc	www.ail.com	Air quality, radar, gamma-ray
Global Water	www.globalw.com	Water level, flow, quality
Chelsea Instruments, Ltd.	www.chelsea.co.uk	Oceanographic instruments
Campbell Scientific, Inc.	www.campbellsci.com	Weather and environmental
Herian Proffer	members.aol.com/herian/index.html	Ultrasonic object detection
Photo Research	www.photoresearch.com	Light and color
SensoMotoric Instruments	www.smi.de	Eye movements
Quantum Research Group	www.interquant.com	Water, proximity

Instead of using existing equipment, some datacasts have modified equipment not originally intended for data reporting to act as sensors. Examples of this approach are found in Anthony's List of Internet Vending Machines (www.mitchell.net/ant/machines.htm), and include Internode's Internet Toaster (www.internode.com.au/) and the MIT Random Hall Laundry Report shown in Figure 7.7. This Java-based datacast shows washer/dryer use in real time.

Information generated by data sensors typically reaches the datacast system via direct serial connections, modems, or through the Internet. Currently, most datacast systems simply read the contents of output files generated by a custom *datalogger* program that collects and stores data in a file. Recently, some companies, such as Phar Lap Software (www.pharlap.com), have developed integrated datacast systems for Internet use. Phar Lap's World's Smallest Web Server (smallest.pharlap.com) is a 486-based single-board computer measuring 3.8 by 3.6 inches that combines a dedicated web server with environmental sensors. The system allows users to access the sensor directly through the web rather than passing through an intermediate datalogger stage.

In contrast to other datacasts, wordcasts normally require little more than a standard computer keyboard for data collection. Some wordcasters simply capture text from a console or Telnet session and write the output to a data log, which is in turn served to the web. Standard Internet chat programs such as ichat (www.ichat.com) may be adapted for one-way wordcast, or the software may be outsourced to third-party vendors such as Wordcasters. The capture stage requires a skilled typist who can accurately transcribe dictation from an ongoing monologue or dialogue, often while listening over the telephone. To acquire these input skills, webcast producers might check companies such as All-Around Secretarial Services (www.jps.net/aass), which provides transcription over 24-hour phone dictation lines. As computer voice recognition software improves, this step is likely to be automated.

Encoding

Converting datacast information into a form usable on the web frequently requires considerable skill and technical training. Commercial programs are generally unavailable for this step, and it is usually necessary to create custom software specific to each datacast. In some cases, the webcast team's programmer

Figure 7.7 Java-based datacast on the MIT Random Hall Laundry Report (spleen.mit.edu/LAUNDRY/laundry_java.html).

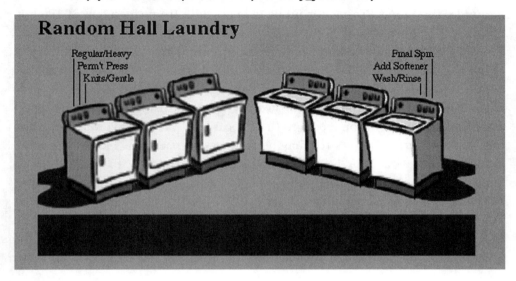

will also have to specify encoding parameters in an existing datalogger program. Use of the data may require additional processing or merging with database-derived information such as map coordinates. In the past, programmers have created custom programs in C++ or other languages to encode the data, or have used data analysis and display packages such as National Instruments' LabView (www.labview.com) as a starting point for their efforts. The recent introduction of Macromedia's Flash 3 Generator (www.macromedia.com/ software/ flash) provides the first web-centric solution for datacasting. Using Flash streaming animation, the Generator allows real-time, automated data-driven creation of graphics and animation.

Wordcasts typically do not require specialized encoding or compression. Since the wordcast stream consists of simple text, it may be received by browsers that do not display graphics at all. At normal speaking or typing rates, the required bandwidth is measured in tens of bytes per second, and the 1,200 bytes/second of the slowest 14.4 modem may carry dozens of streams.

Internet Connection

Datacasts often produce effective results over very slow connections. As an example, the Lunar Prospector probe delivers data from the moon at 100 bps or less. This contrasts with the 9600 bps of the slowest consumer modems. Wordcasts also have low-bandwidth requirements. This opens possibilities for delivering wordcasts and datacasts from unique locations where the available connection speeds may be very slow. For example, a wordcaster could type messages while driving through a newsworthy location, using a very slow (2400 baud) cellular modem connected to the webcast ISP. Live interviews from clubs and other entertainment sites may be sent to end users via 14.4 modems, in contrast to the ISDN or leased-line connections necessary to send audio or video. However, the datacast web site will need a high-speed connection. Efficient operation is important, since most users will be contacting the site for educational/background purposes related to the datacast. Depending on the type of web-based supporting material, web traffic may contribute more to total bandwidth than to the datacast itself.

Presentation

Unlike audio and video, datacasts do not have a predefined means of presentation to the user; therefore, the production team will have to develop a custom look and feel for the datacast. Two approaches are generally used. On one hand, sites such as the Gary-Chicago-Milwaukee Corridor traffic page (www.ai.eecs.uic.edu/GCM/GCM.html) do extensive back-end or "behind-the-scenes" processing through databases, CGI, and other programs, and post standard HTML text and graphics to the site.

The limitations in HTML-based display has caused other datacasters to develop custom applications for presentation, as seen with the real-time Java-based display of Internet transmissions at the Ars Electronica Center, shown in Figure 7.8. This site dynamically posts the connections made throughout the world originating from the center. In order to have the lines drawn in real time without redrawing the entire page, Java-based programming was implemented. Shockwave and Flash programming have also been used to present datacasts. Wordcasters may use existing chat programs in a one-way mode or develop player software in Java or JavaScript. A variety of ticker programs suitable for developing wordcasts may be found on sites such as Gamelan (www.gamelan.com) and 24-Hour JavaScripts (www.javascripts.com). Because custom programming is often necessary for this type of webcasting, the production team should consider contacting other sites for possible software licensing and/or purchase. Certain push technologies may also be employed in a datacast mode. See Chapter 6, "Webcast Promotion, Commerce, and Analysis," for more information on push technologies.

Though many datacasts employ graphical maps and charts, it is not necessary to confine output to visual formats. For example, the Netsound Project (netsound.is.titech.ac.jp/netsound/english/inside.html) converts Internet traffic statistics into *Musical Instrument Digital Interface (MIDI)* files. This information

Figure 7.8 Ars Electronica Center datacast showing real-time Internet connections (www.aec.at).

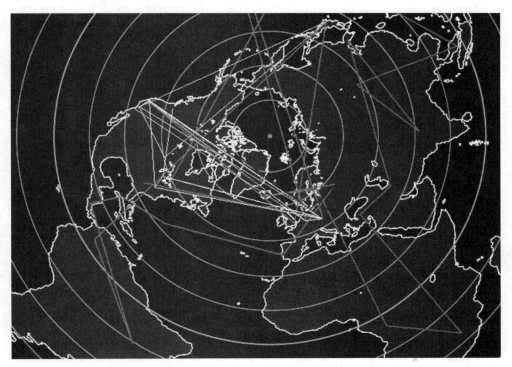

is streamed as MIDI data that may be played by a sound synthesizer or converted to RealAudio.

Due to the diverse array of possibilities for datacast and wordcast production, it is a good idea to have generalists on the development team. There are few hardware and software standards currently in use, so production teams will have to develop their own custom webcast solutions.

Publicity and Promotion

Datacasts typically do not involve personalities or celebrities. This means that promoters will have to emphasize the uniqueness and presentation of the data. The innovative features of many datacast sites often generate interest from groups giving awards for new technology. Netpublicists should be aware of the datacast's unique features and search for online and offline awards likely to acknowledge their site's accomplishment.

Since many datacasts are utilitarian, it may be effective to identify and contact a highly specific niche audience via email or offline promotion. For example, a traffic-monitoring datacast might be publicized by advertising in travel magazines; and banner ads might be effective on news-oriented web sites. Because wordcasts do not have an appealing graphic component, they may be harder to promote than datacasts. For this reason, netpublicists promoting a wordcast might choose to emphasize the live aspect, making it a one-time-only experience.

Archiving Strategies

The compact file size of datacasts allows enormous transcripts to be stored and archived with modest equipment. For example, a 1-gigabyte hard disk capable of storing only a few hours of webcast video might hold millions of wordcast transcripts. In many cases, the information will already be stored in an existing database, and therefore additional archiving plans may be unnecessary. Archiving should include links for any custom Java applets or media players needed to visualize the data. Wordcasts may be stored and accessed directly as web pages containing ordinary text. These archives may serve as a source for long-term promotion. For example, on the authors' Kspace site (kspace.com), there is a large archive of artist interviews. Visitors to the site

UNIQUE FEATURES OF DATACASTS AND WORDCASTS

In promoting a datacast or wordcast, the netpublicist should consider including the following in the press release:

Real-time. Unlike a static web page, this site has text or graphics that change during the audience member's visit.

Real-world. A wordcast provides a link outside the Internet to a real-world conversation. Datacasts that connect to environmental sensors in remote corners of the world provide telemetry from distant spacecraft.

Interactivity. The audience visiting the datacast may be able to customize the appearance of the datacast to suit their interest.

Low bandwidth. The audience doesn't need fast connections to receive wordcast or datacast streams.

Basic hardware. The audience may use older computer equipment with less memory and disk space. Wordcasts are available in libraries and universities that use text-only web browsers such as Lynx (lynx.browser.org).

Unique. Both the delivery format and the content of datacasts and wordcasts have no counterpart outside the Internet. Wordcasts and datacasts illustrate that the Internet has capabilities not found in other media.

frequently read the transcripts and attempt to contact the artist, apparently thinking the wordcast is still running! Sites storing wordcast archives on their media server should be prepared to identify messages related to the archive and respond appropriately.

Estimating Costs

Since storage and delivery of datacast information do not require high-end equipment or large amounts of bandwidth, these components will be moderate contributors to the webcast budget. On the other hand, webcast producers will need to budget for the services of programmers and hardware engineers. Costs will vary widely based on whether the production team develops solutions in-house or outsources the work. For example, the Buzbee Bat House, shown in Figure 7.9, was created for less than $150 above the cost of the input computer. This was possible because the single developer had sufficient experience with hardware and software to develop a custom solution. Outsourced, the same level of development could easily have cost several thousand dollars. Larger datacast projects aggregating data from multiple sensors or incorporating checks on data security will carry price tags of $50,000 or higher. Because of this wide cost variation, the webcast producers will also have to define the features of a wordcast or datacast project accurately enough to realistically estimate the budget. Publicity and promotion carried out over the Internet (see Chapter 6, "Webcast Promotion, Commerce, and Analysis") will have similar costs, independent of site complexity.

Figure 7.9 The Buzbee Bat House (www.nyx.net/~jbuzbee/bat_house.html).

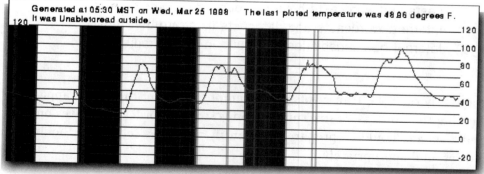

Generated at 05:30 MST on Wed, Mar 25 1998   The last plotted temperature was 48.96 degrees F.
It was Unable to read outside.

Case Study: The Buzbee Bat House

URL: www.nyx.net/~jbuzbee/bat_house.html

Contact: Jim Buzbee (jbuzbee@nyx.net)

This site is one of the oldest datacast locations on the Internet. It datacasts the temperature and light level of a dwelling designed to attract bats. Developed by bat fancier Jim Buzbee, the system consists of a set of hardware and custom programming implemented on a home computer. As shown in Figure 7.10, a Cryix P166 system running Linux acts as the capture and encoding system. The thermometer is a commercial product similar to a device produced by Spiderplant (www.spiderplant.com), and the light sensor was retrofitted from a joystick. Jim Buzbee describes the layout as follows:

"I took apart a joystick and replaced the Y axis indicator with a photo-sensitive resistor. . . . The thermometer is hooked to the serial port and the light sensor is hooked to the joystick port. A wire

Figure 7.10 Datacast design of the Buzbee Bat House.

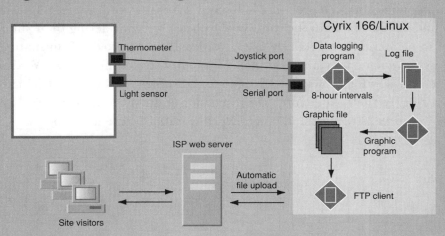

with a thermistor runs from the thermometer device out my window and into the bat house. A wire with the photo resistor runs from the hacked-up joystick to my window sill."

The software for reading the input was developed by Russ Nelson (www.crynwr.com/temp-plot.html), and runs automatically as a cron job at eight-hour intervals. Data is written to a log file where it is picked up by another process that creates the graphical plot. The completed graphic lists temperature in a coordinate plot, and light level as a text message at the top of the image. The completed presentation is automatically sent to an ISP via FTP.

Next . . .

Datacasts have not received the widespread attention that has been paid to audiocasts and videocasts, partly because there is no real analogy to datacasts in current broadcast media. It seems likely, however, that in the near future this will change. The proliferation of web servers into virtually every computer and electronic device during the next few years may make access to datacasts as commonplace as web browsing is today. Currently, wordcasts seem particularly underutilized within the context of webcasting, considering their simplicity of implementation. Properly used, wordcasts could provide information to end users, which partly makes up for low-quality streaming media. Wordcasts also offer a way for browser-challenged and disabled surfers to participate in webcasting. In the next chapter, the discussion shifts from these relatively new areas to the well-traveled and much-hyped world of Internet audio.

AUDIOCASTS

Audiocasts delivering music or spoken word are currently the most common forms of webcasting on the Internet. Tens of millions of users have configured their computers to receive streaming audio, and announcements by Microsoft (www.microsoft.com) and RealNetworks (www.real.com) ensure that virtually every Internet-ready system sold will have streaming audio capability during 1999. Sites providing access to on-demand audiocasts such as Broadcast.com, shown in Figure 8.1, are among the most popular destinations for web surfers, and sites such as RealNetworks' Timecast (www.timecast.com) have received high traffic simply by listing the ever-expanding numbers of audiocast events. Even groups already experienced with broadcast audio, such as the ham radio operators who tune into the Amateur Radio Listening Post webcast (speed.nimh.nih.gov/listener/listener.html), find that the Internet's unique features enhance their hobby. Audiocasts typically attract hundreds to thousands (rather than dozens) of viewers, and major entertainment, news, and sports organizations regularly supply streaming audio as part of their offerings. Sites such as LiveConcerts.com (www.liveconcerts.com) webcast music from popular clubs and are helping to define Internet entertainment.

To conduct successful audiocasts, developers must match their ever-increasing competition and satisfy a rising level of user expectations. This chapter examines the requirements for developing cutting-edge audiocasts, including content, audience, and production issues. It also provides case studies of audiocast sites that demonstrate real-world solutions for common problems. Developers may also con-

Figure 8.1 Broadcast.com (www.broadcast.com).

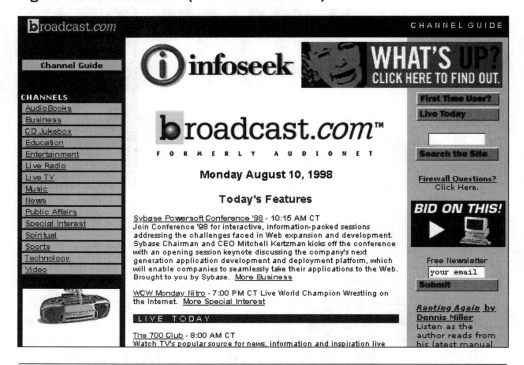

sult other audiocast sites on the Internet by checking RealNetwork's Timecast, Microsoft's NetShow Features (www.microsoft.com/netshow), and independent listings such as the Web Times Network (www.webtimes.com/main.html).

Unique Features

The favorable features of audiocast development are reflected in the tens of thousands of web sites incorporating the technology. The popularity of audiocasts is a result of the unique characteristics of digitized sound and the types of information traditionally delivered via sound. Taken as a group, the following features make it easy to design and implement audio-only webcasts:

Quality. Audiocasts deliver music directly comparable to AM radio at 28.8 modem speeds; and 14.4 modems support voice-only audio. This allows audiocasts to directly compete with traditional media such as traditional radio—as well as videocasts, datacasts, and wordcasts. In contrast to the extensive production budgets of videocasts, top-quality audiocasts may consist of little more than a single voice providing news, interviews, or drama, Content could also include sports events and concerts.

Production environment. Developing audiocast content is often simpler than producing webcasts that involve video and animation. Effective audio programming may require little more than a trained voice and a microphone, with no need to consider props, lighting, camera angles, costumes, and other visual production elements. Datacasts do not require lavish physical production, but they usually do need the often expensive services of programmers and/or data visualizers. Audiocast software and hardware requirements are substantially less than for video. Due to the popularity of audiocasts, many commercial "end-to-end" solutions exist for web production (see Chapters 3 through 6), and writing special-purpose programs is usually not required.

Hardware and software. Audiocasts demand less end-user hardware than videocasts. Since audio replay requires less memory and computing power than video, even users on older 486 and Quadra systems can receive basic audiocast content. This is an important feature for developers trying to reach a general consumer audience, as well as for companies providing content over intranets, which host significant numbers of legacy computers. On the production side, hardware and software needs are also reduced. Microphones are generally less expensive and complex to operate than cameras, and audio mixing and mastering for web delivery requires fewer powerful workstations.

Divided attention. Audiocasts may be played in the background while the user continues to focus on other tasks. This is in contrast to other webcasts that demand the user's undivided attention.

Similarity to existing broadcast. Audiocasts running over fast Internet connections are nearly identical to audio from other sources. Sound engineers who have created audio content for other media may directly apply their skills to web-based delivery.

Economic viability. The relatively high quality of Internet-based streaming audio allows companies such as Liquid Audio (www.liquidaudio.com) to charge fees for webcast music. Educational and business groups use RealServer (www.real.com) to deliver pay-per-listen instruction.

The relative simplicity of developing and implementing audiocasts makes them good candidates for developers just beginning to work in the webcast area. Rather than re-create a modern television broadcast studio, the webcast producers can emulate an old-style radio studio from the 1940s. Similarly, the expectations of end users are more realistic. Users who are disappointed by a tiny jerking video image are likely to be more impressed by an audiocast nearly identical in quality to the broadcasts they hear driving to work.

Applications

The relatively large audiocast audience is segmented into well-defined, specific groups. This enables webcasters to create audiocasts that target such groups while retaining the potential for a significant turnout. The following provides a breakdown of the main audience groups for webcasts, including possible content preferences specific to each group:

Education. Students frequently have access to computers with streaming audio, and instructors repurpose lectures and discussions for audiocasts by recording them to standard tape decks. Certain educational course materials (e.g., historical interviews and newscasts) require audio and thus are ideal for the webcast medium. Since students frequently access the web while on campus, a significant percentage of the audience for educational audiocasts will receive the information at intranet speeds, allowing high-quality sound to be delivered.

Music. Internet surfers interested in music form a major audience for audiocasts. As a group, this audience sees the Internet as a way to find and listen to music not found among the increasingly uniform radio playlists. Strong fan interest in certain artists or songs makes them attractive candidates for sites producing regular music audiocasts.

News. Audiocasts are becoming increasingly important for news delivery, particularly for short briefings aimed at technically sophisticated web users. By running a news-oriented audiocast in the background, these users may listen to the day's events while continuing to work at their computers. Audiocasting also has significant potential for individualized news reporting. For example, Earth Broadcasting's Earthmail (www.earthmail.com) provides to its members a daily five-minute streaming audio clip containing daily news; it is coupled with delivery of an email message containing follow-up web URLs. A somewhat similar service is provided by the RealNetworks Daily Briefing (cgi3.dailybriefing.com/welcome1_.html).

Business. Audiocasts running over corporate intranets have limited use at present. Though the intranet may provide bandwidth to stream the CD-quality pronouncements from management, in most cases these communications are delivered more effectively via text. Audiocasts may be more useful for external business communications as exemplified by AV Newswire (www.avnewswire.com), which hosts audio versions of corporate press releases, corporate overviews, product information, and audiocasts of interest to PR professionals.

International. The Internet gives audio content providers (radio stations in particular) a chance to reach new audiences. On the Internet, small, independently operated radio stations are not limited by regulations or station wattage, and therefore may provide their material anywhere in the world—allowing niche programming to thrive. Stations aimed at particular nationalities or ethnic groups audiocast content to listeners regardless of geographic dispersion. Sites including RealPlanet, shown in Figure 8.2, aggregate and organize international audiocast content for the Internet audience.

With the rise of electronic commerce, webcasters will be increasingly interested in which audience groups are willing to pay for content online. A recent study by Ernst & Young LLP indicated that e-commerce increased 30 percent during the last quarter of 1997, and a study by NUA Internet Surveys (www.nua.ie/surveys/index.cgi?blocknumber=1) indicated that nearly 20 percent of Internet users who had not made previous purchases made at least one

Figure 8.2 RealPlanet (www.realplanet.com).

during this period. This indicates increasing acceptance of e-commerce in general; but pay-per-view webcasts are still so uncommon that audience statistics are unavailable. Streaming audio has been used to promote music CDs with mixed success. Sites such as ValueVision (www.vvtv.com) are experimenting with live audiocasts of home shopping programs, in addition to listing a standard web-based catalog. Many of the purchasers indicated that they were interested in rare and hard-to-find items, and a study by Jupiter Communications (www.jup.com) indicated that 77 percent of purchasers went online with a specific purchase in mind. This statistic may indicate that pay-per-view webcasts are best promoted offline. As electronic commerce increases in popularity, it is likely that audio will play a more significant role in sales promotion.

Audiocast Formats

Webcasters planning to deliver streaming audio to their audience take a variety of approaches to formatting content. Popular formats are defined by the available bandwidth at the end-user level and by the Internet awareness of the listening public. Despite the diversity of available content, audiocasts may be divided into a few specific classes based on bandwidth and content type, discussed in Chapter 3, "Webcast Equipment and Authoring Environments," and elaborated here:

Ambient. These systems deliver background sound from unattended microphones in a variety of locations. As such, they are directly comparable to spy cameras hooked to the Internet (see Chapter 9, "Videocasts and Animacasts"). While few sites other than the Mars Microphone site (sprg.ssl.berkeley.edu/~gdelory/mm.html) plan to stream data from an unattended microphone, eavesdropping sites providing access to radio communications such as Policescanner.com (www.policescanner.com) are quite common. Ambient audiocasts may also be used for area surveillance, relaxation/mood music, and environmental sounds. However, unlike ambient video, as discussed in Chapter 9, ambient audio cannot be supported with extremely low bit-rate connections. The reason for this is psychological: while individual frames of a video sent on a scale of minutes can be interpreted by most users, isolated fragments of sound separated by long silences cannot be mentally assembled into a larger whole.

Voice-only. This format features speeches, conversations, or audiobook transcripts delivered without music. Since the human voice is confined to a modest range of frequencies, this allows for greater signal compression without loss of legibility. Voice-only audiocasts are highly effective as supplements to online education, especially when provided as short clips integrated with web-based information. Voice-only audio is also effective for news; audiocasts highlighting major news stories are routinely provided by online media sites including ABCNews.com (www.abcnews.com), MSNBC (www.msnbc.com), and CNN (www.cnn.com). Niche voice-only programming such as talk radio is available through sites such as Audiocast.net (www.audiocast.net).

Music-oriented. Many audiocasts draw content from the enormous number of records and live performances from singers, songwriters, record labels, bands, and industry professionals every year. Requiring higher bandwidth than voice-only audiocasts, music audiocasts are typically delivered over 28.8 or 56K connections. Major record companies such as Capitol Records (www.hollywoodandvine.com) regularly provide access to streaming music through their sites. Developers such as LiveConcerts.com (www.liveconcerts.com) and JamTV (www.jamtv.com) specialize in producing live audiocasts from music performance venues. Audio-based commentary on the industry is available through sites such as Addicted to Noise (www.addictedtonoise.com), and many of the independent music sites included in the Ultimate Band List (www.ubl.com) incorporate streaming audio on their pages.

Internet radio. Unlike audiocasts that intersperse sound clips among web-based information, virtual radio formats include titles, credits, and advertising in the webcasts. As such, virtual radio may be listened to independently of the web. Many Internet radio sites, including Broadcast.com (www.broadcast.com) and RadioTower (www.radiotower.com), repurpose standard radio broadcasts for the Internet. Other sites such as theDJ.com (www.thedj.com) and MetroRadio (www.metroradio.com) have adopted the virtual radio format without creating a "brick and mortar" radio station. The Amateur Radio Listening Post (speed.nimh.nih.gov/listener/listener.html), shown in Figure 8.3, provides access to a more interactive version of radio and gives its audience increased access to signals that are unavailable locally.

On many sites, relatively short audio clips are provided—even though there is no theoretical limit to the length of a streaming audiocast delivered in real time. Reasons for doing this include copyright/usage issues, the short attention span of many surfers, and the desire to provide nonstreaming versions of the audio with comparable content. As the ability to play streaming audio becomes more common and Internet users become comfortable with the webcast concept, it is likely that the length of audiocasts will increase. Shifts in content are harder to predict, though it is likely that music and radio-style formats will play an increasing role in the future as audiences turn to the Internet for entertainment as well as work.

Figure 8.3 The Amateur Radio Listening Post (speed.nimh.nih.gov/listener/ listener.html).

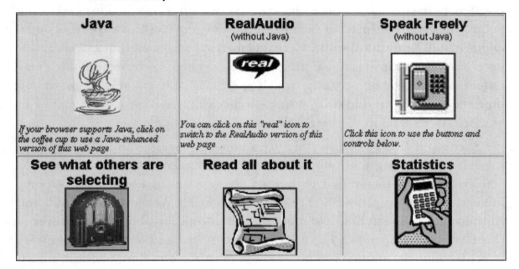

Aspects of Production

All audiocast production studios share common equipment sets, which include sound-enabled computers, editing software, audio encoding software, and a delivery system for putting completed content on the media server. If content comes from recorded media, no additional equipment will be required for production. In contrast, recording live audiocasts will require acquiring and learning to use additional equipment borrowed from the traditional broadcast industry. The production team will need to be familiar with microphones, mixers, PA systems, venue operators, performers, remote Internet connections, and even crowd control. The following discussion considers audiocast production in terms of team design, audio capture, mixing, encoding, and presentation.

Team Design

The key component of any audiocast production team is the sound engineer. This individual is responsible for transferring the audio from recorded or live formats into the final mix used for webcasting. For simple repurposing of recorded audio, an individual with computer-based sound editors may fill this position. Software skills must be balanced with a subjective feel for preserving audio quality at low Internet bit rates. As an example of this expertise, audio engineers at RealEducation (www.realeducation.com) sometimes deliberately lower the pitch of instructors during audio conversion. Lowering the pitch may reduce some encoding artifacts (which appear as sudden clicks, pops, or volume reduction in an otherwise normal audiocast stream), but it also gives an authoritative sound to the speaker's voice!

Successful live audiocasts require sound engineers who have extensive experience working with speakers, performers, and musical instruments. They will need to be familiar with microphones, power supplies, PA systems, mixers, and effects processors; refer to Chapter 3, "Webcast Equipment and Authoring Environments," for more more information about the features of this hardware. Depending on the complexity of the audiocast, the engineers may also have to understand how to mix multiple audio inputs onto multi-track recorders; they may also have to program comparable software-based systems such as Macromedia's DECK II (www.macromedia.com). The engineer must know how to place microphones within the performance space. Since the audio environment may change unpredictably during the event, the engineer will also need to monitor and adjust recording equipment in real time. Due to these responsibilities, live audiocast teams may elect to assign a second engineer to convert and upload audio data delivered by the sound engineer.

Fueled by cheap computers and other digital devices, the audio industry is currently undergoing a revolution during which many standard analog systems are being duplicated in digital form. Due to the recent introduction of these all-digital mixers and effects processors, their application has been spotty. If the production team will be using legacy audio equipment available at the webcast venue, an analog engineer is preferable. On the other hand, if a team plans to buy their own sound equipment, they may elect to go the all digital-route and hire or train a digital sound engineer. In general, expertise with analog and digital systems is not found in the same individual. For example, digital engineers are likely to be stymied by problems with phasing and feedback during a live webcast, while analog engineers may not be able to choose the best Internet audio compression and delivery strategies. It is important that the webcast production team define the skills they need from their engineers and make sure they match the requirements for operating their hardware and software. Developers looking for recording engineers might consider running classified ads in music trades such as *MIX Magazine* (www.mixmag.com), or in online listings such as MusicClassifieds (www.musicclassifieds.com), All AccessMusic Group (www.allaccess.com/members/jobs/), Musicians Connections (www.ccipc.com/MCS/), and Yahoo! Classifieds (classifieds.yahoo.com). Reference and training manuals for sound design are available through MIX Bookshelf (www.mixbookshelf.com) and Jerome-Headlands Press (kspace.com/jhp).

Audiocast teams will frequently need to assign personnel to interface with content providers and their representatives. In the case of recorded material, this may amount to little more than securing copyright clearance (see Chapter 6 for more information on copyright clearance). In other cases, the audiocasters will work with artists/bands, agents, managers, label representatives, music publishers, and performance rights organizations. Since many people in these areas are unfamiliar with the Internet, the webcast team may need to provide education as well as support.

Recorded Audio Capture

Recorded material includes the various media types discussed in Chapter 3, "Webcast Equipment and Authoring Environments," as well as live audio signals taken from radio or television receivers. In all cases, the webcasters do not have the luxury of adjusting the audio for maximum compatibility with their equipment, but must make due with the quality provided. On the other hand, using recorded audio eliminates the management of mixing, effects processing, and other live recording features. This feature has enabled sites such as Broadcast.com to aggregate hundreds of radio and television broadcast streams without building a large production studio. Small webcast groups may also be able to develop webcasts from recorded material without hiring a sound engineer. The following lists some of the areas that should be considered when converting recorded material, and provides guidelines for acceptable and unsatisfactory audio content:

Some people involved in the nontechnical side of a webcast (such as musicians, actors, narrators, and other performers) may be unfamiliar with—or even fearful of—the medium. This problem is often more acute for industry professionals, including managers, venue operators, and publicists. To assure these individuals, webcasters should refer to a set of basic statements like those below:

Webcasts are not television. The webcast will not appear on TV, nor will it be sent over broadcast channels unless separate arrangements are made.

Audiocast quality is comparable to radio. Even though much webcast audio falls short of CD-quality, many listeners hear conventional radio played through inferior equipment or in public places, and therefore experience comparable or lower quality.

The incidence of piracy is low. The Internet is much more accountable than other media. It is possible to embed digital watermarks (see Chapter 6, "Webcast Promotion, Commerce, and Analysis") in webcast audio, making unauthorized use easy to detect. Every visitor to a webcast may be asked to register—unlike a broadcast, which anyone in earshot can record anonymously.

No special equipment is necessary. Webcast recording technology is the same as conventional broadcast equipment, and it will not alter the performance environment or make it more difficult to perform.

Audiences are too small to support pay-per-view. Most webcasts have audiences in the hundreds or low thousands, and generate little or no revenue. It is usually unreasonable for performers to demand compensation, particularly at rates paid for national broadcast.

Sound quality. Musicians, interviewers, and news services often submit audio excerpts to developers on cassette tape. Webcasters compressing audio from this format may be surprised to discover that the quality is unacceptably low compared to samples from audio CDs or DATs. This is because streaming audio algorithms use high-frequency data during compression, even if the frequencies do not appear in the final clip. Sound captured from digital formats such as DATs and CDs varies in quality depending on whether it was transferred as a digital or analog signal. For example, most sound editors have separate menu options for copying digital data directly from a CD and for listening in when a CD is played through the computer's hardware. Webcasters recording near-CD-quality audio should always use the digital copy option. Audio captured from radio or phone feeds will generally be of much lower quality. Due to this problem, the webcasters may need to restrict the type of content they convert from these sources.

Storage. Converting recorded audio usually requires an initial step in which the audio signal is saved onto hard disk in a standard format such as Audio Interchange File Format (AIFF) used in most audio CD mastering. In some cases, the producers will want to save these initial high-quality samples for later resampling as webcast formats change. Since CD-quality audio typically takes up 10 megabytes of storage per minute, a team taking this approach must plan for high-capacity disc or tape storage, as well as develop an indexing strategy so that the clip may be easily relocated. In many cases, it will be easier to store the audio on the original CD or tape instead of copying to hard disk.

Variations based on audio source. Adjusting webcast audio compression for particular types of music takes considerable experimentation. For example, compression codecs that are good at picking up percussion (e.g., cymbals) may accidentally introduce artifacts into music using strings and horns. The reason is that high-frequency components of sound found in percussion are harder to encode than low-frequency ones. To catch potential quality problems, it is essential that the developer listen to the audio after converting it. The ease or difficulty of compressing particular kinds of music often runs counter to expectations. For example, music in industrial or metal formats may require higher bandwidth for acceptable sound quality than an acoustic or classical performance. This is because frequency components of the former are similar to white noise (audio containing random components of all frequencies), which is more difficult to encode than the few pure tones characteristic of most music. Audio signals sampled from broadcast feeds frequently have reduced high frequencies. For this reason, the developer may have to brighten the signal by emphasizing the remaining high-frequency component during encoding. Voice-only material such as speeches and audiobooks are usually much simpler to convert; the frequency range is smaller, and dramatic shifts in pitch and volume rarely occur.

Getting good results from recorded material is a highly subjective process. In most cases, it is not practical to set fixed guidelines for encoding unless content is highly uniform (e.g., a droning politician) or quality is not paramount. Since the recorded spoken word tends to be more tolerant of compression, some audiocasters set up batch jobs to automatically format large numbers of clips at a single time.

Live Audio Capture

The general public is so used to high-quality audio that few realize how difficult it is to get a good sound recording. Simply pointing a microphone at a live event on location is unlikely to produce acceptable results, and webcasters such as LiveConcerts.com (www.liveconcerts.com) are valued equally for their on-location and Internet expertise. The production team should consider the following rules of thumb when capturing live audio, but realize they are not substitutes for experience. Developers should plan to use a professional recording engineer for all but the simplest live audiocasts and should practice extensively before trying to produce a real-world event.

Signal isolation. Live performances are usually recorded using several microphones whose signals are combined though a mixing board (see Chapter 3, "Webcast Equipment and Authoring Environments").

Case Study: The Amateur Radio Listening Post

URL: speed.nimh.nih.gov/listener/listener.html
Contact: Andrew R. Mitz arm@helix.nih.gov

This site, shown in Figure 8.3, provides an example of a more specialized audiocast service requiring custom hardware and software solutions. Created by the NIH Amateur Radio Club, the site functions as a spy audiocast resource and allows users to tune in to UHF and VHF amateur radio stations in the Washington, DC, area by controlling an Icom R7000 radio receiver through the web. This qualifies it as a form of live audiocasting that does not require a studio or performance venue. As shown in Figure 8.4, the chief design element of the web site is a Java-based control interface

Figure 8.4 The Java-based control panel for Listening Post audiocasts.

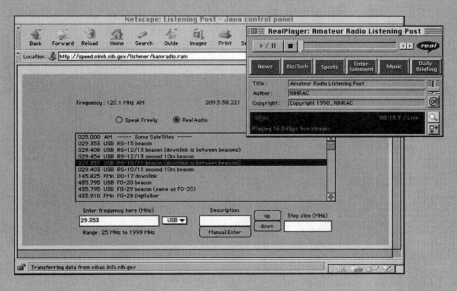

Case Study: The Amateur Radio Listening Post *(Continued)*

available from the home page. This control panel lists available ham radio frequencies used by hobbyists to communicate over the air and allows visitors to select either RealAudio (www.real.com) or Speak Freely (www.fourmilab.ch/speakfree/) versions of the audio-cast. Unlike RealAudio—but similar to ham radio—the Speak Freely media player allows two-way audio signaling. Originally, the Listening Post ran a Vosaic (www.vosaic.com) server using a Java-based player, but the developers replaced it in favor of the current setup. Casual visitors to the Listening Post may use a Java applet to view connections by other visitors to the site that are refreshed at 10-second intervals. The display does not use graphics, but this is unlikely to be a deterrent for the intended technical audience.

Integration of a tunable radio receiver with on-demand web access required a setup of some complexity. The overall layout of the final system is shown in Figure 8.5. The radio receiver is an Icom IC-R7000 (www.icomamerica.com), which is sensitive to frequencies between 25 and 2.0GHz; it supports AM, wideband FM, and narrow-band FM. The radio is connected to the serial port of a 233MHz Pentium PC running Red Hat Linux 4.0 via Icom's CI-V Level Converter. The web server is also hosted on this system. Audio streaming is via a shielded audio cable connected to a 200MHz Pentium running the RealAudio Encoder under Windows 95. The Pentium system encodes live audio from the receiver and sends the audio to a Sun SPARC 20 running Solaris 2.6 with a RealAudio Server. User interaction is mediated via HTML requests or Java applets that launch CGI scripts written in Perl. These custom scripts accept requests to access a particular frequency, return HTML

Possible arrangements for collecting and mixing input from live and recorded audiocasts are shown in Figure 8.6. In many cases, the performers will need headphones so they can hear the output and adjust their performance accordingly. Spoken dialogues usually do not pages to the user, log visitor requests, and command the Linux and Solaris systems at the shell (nongraphical command line) level. Depending on input, scripts may trigger the RealAudio server or launch programs for the Speak Freely player interface. By using low-cost Linux software (an inexpensive variant of UNIX) and creating home-brew programs for audio processing, the costs of implementation were kept very low. Andrew Mitz of the Listening Post estimates that upwards of 200 hours of programming were necessary to develop the various components of the site, including "a lot of research, testing, and learning."

Figure 8.5 Design of the Listening Post webcast system.

© *Reprinted with permission from February 1998 QST; Copyright ARRL.*

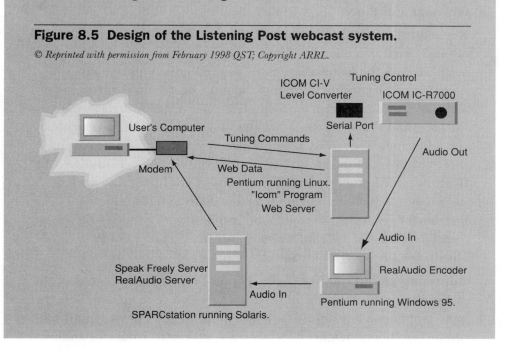

require headphones, but the engineer will still need to hear output from separate microphones. If the production team is building their own recording studio, they should create a separate, soundproof room specifically for the engineer to hear the mix.

Recording performers. If performers move, fixed microphones will be inadequate for sound pickup. In this case, the engineer will need to attach the microphones directly to the performers. Microphones, named for their methods of attachment, include the *lapel* (attached to clothing), *lavalier* (hung around neck), and *handheld*. The latter should be used for recording singers, since the sound quality of this microphone is usually better than the others. The engineer should also instruct less experienced performers to hold the microphone at least 12 inches from their mouths and not to fidget with the microphone and its cord, since these activities generate unwanted sound. If handheld, lavalier, and lapel microphones are impractical, the engineer may employ shotgun microphones (see Chapter 3) to record at a distance.

Recording musical instruments. The quality of the resulting sound of music used in audiocasts depends critically on where microphones are placed on the instrument. Some instruments require multiple microphone pickups for acceptable sound. For example, the sound of a guitar is a combination of wood resonance, air vibrations in the guitar body, and the overtones of strings and noises on the frets made by the performer. Therefore, recording an acoustic guitar may require three to four microphones. Many instruments, such as pianos, are difficult to record properly and require expert attention. An excellent instrument-based microphone selection chart and discussion of instrument recording may be found in *The Acoustic Musician's Guide to Sound Reinforcement and Live Recording* by Mike Sokol (Jerome Headlands Press, 1998; kspace.com/jhp).

Adjusting sound quality. Audio capture is strongly affected by the environment of the recording space, therefore the engineer will need to dynamically adjust the equipment to get a good signal. The production team may need to hire an engineer to scout out audiocast locations and determine microphone placement in advance. Wind, outside noises, instrument feedback, and vibrations from footfalls all may degrade output quality. To reduce these problems, it may be necessary to mount the microphone on vibration-absorbing

Figure 8.6 Sound-mixing strategies for live audiocasts.

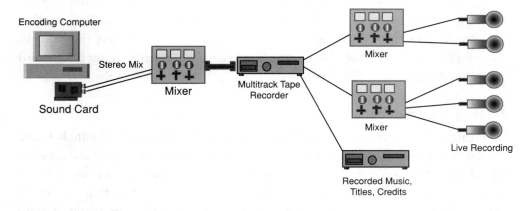

material such as foam rubber, and change the size of the windscreen placed over the microphone. Rooms used regularly for recording should have sound-deadening foam added to the walls, or have drapes and heavy carpeting installed. Noisy equipment should be turned off whenever possible during the recordings. In all cases, the sound quality should be tested during a sound check prior to the start of the webcast.

Phasing and feedback. Sound waves emanating from different locations of a performance space can interfere with each other. The resulting *phasing*, or inappropriate rise and fall in the volumes of the conflicting signals, reduces sound quality. To avoid this, the audiocast engineer will need to adjust the location of microphones relative to each other. *Feedback* occurs when an amplified sound drives its own amplification, typically because a microphone and loudspeaker (or monitor) are facing each other. Moving the microphones slightly usually eliminates this problem. If several microphones are pointed at one location (e.g., at an individual at a press conference), they generally should be put very close to each other to avoid phasing and feedback problems. Webcasters working without an audio engineer should minimize the number of microphones used, even if it reduces overall quality.

Live audio recording is not a casual process. Webcasters with expensive servers and high bandwidth may fail to produce quality output if they neglect this aspect of webcast production. New production teams might try recording voice-only audio first, since the demands on engineer expertise are fewer. After successfully producing the spoken word, the team will be in a position to record more challenging musical events.

Mixing Techniques

Creating a good mix from several live or recorded audio input channels is the area where professional experience is most necessary. With proper attention to detail, good mixing may partially compensate for poor acoustic environments or inadequate recording equipment. The following is a list of factors that commonly affect mix quality in audio-only webcasts. Mixing hardware is discussed in more detail in Chapter 3, "Webcast Equipment and Authoring Environments."

Volumes. Webcast audio compression codecs generally reduce the dynamic range of the incoming audio. Consequently, the engineer may deliberately reduce the *gain* (the ratio of signal to background noise) for particular mixing channels to provide implicit preprocessing of sound. Once recording has begun, the engineer should make sure that sound dynamics do not exceed the encoder's response; otherwise, a clipped sound will result. During equipment setup, mixing levels on all inputs should be set to zero and only raised after the microphones, power supplies, and effects processors are attached. If this is not done, microphones and computer audio-in ports may be damaged by the transient burst of power created by connecting live equipment.

Equalization. In addition to controlling the overall volume of each audio channel, the engineer must adjust the frequency range for each sound input. Most performance spaces emphasize some frequencies and dampen others, leading to distortion that may be compensated for by artificially adjusting their value in the graphic equalizer. For example, in live performance spaces, high frequencies often attenuate before reaching the microphones. The engineer may want to deliberately reduce the low frequencies in the mix.

Segues and cues. The audio equivalent of scene transition in film is the *segue*, consisting of a fade between one sound and another. Basic segues simply require the audio engineer to raise the volume of one sound in the mix while another is lowered. A common example of this is a fade from the opening theme of a program to the voices of the performers. More sophisticated segues may insert a *bridge* sound, such as music played between acts of a play. In the related *voice-over*, a much louder spoken word track appears over a quieter background track that does not disappear. Working with segues is relatively easy with recorded audio; but in live performance, one or more engineers will be needed to successfully manage the transitions. During the audiocast, particular mixing channels may be added or removed. In order to manage these events, the recording engineer will need to construct a *cue sheet* listing these entries and exits.

Cable and power management. The complexity of advanced audio equipment rapidly leads to a maze of *patch cords*, cables and connectors weaving through the performance space. The audio engineer needs to develop a strategy for keeping all the cables in order, as well as for keeping track of the ownership of particular cables; one way to do this is by tagging or wrapping masking tape at one end and writing on the tape with a felt marker. Duct tape is the engineer's best friend; plenty of it should be available to anchor cables and devices connected to cables. This will greatly decrease the possibility of someone tripping over the equipment. Cables should also be checked to make sure they have adequate shielding. The usual source of a low-frequency hum during a audiocast is lack of shielding in a cable, which allows it to pick up signals from computers, fluorescent lights, and other sources.

Sound check. Extensive preparation for audiocasts may be wasted if a particular component fails to work when ready. These problems may be avoided by conducting a sound check prior to the beginning of the performance. During the sound check, the engineer connects and powers up each audio component, testing them individually and in groups while coordinating with the performers.

Audiocast production clearly requires many specialized skills. Fortunately, extensive resources exist on the web for educating audio engineers within the webcast production team. Many of these were developed for independent musicians for home recording and combine simplicity with low equipment costs. Independently produced live audio guides are available at sites including The Live Sound Reference Page (www.il.net/~praetor/sound/sound.html), Chris Munro's Prostudio (prostudio.com/issues/chris/location.html), and The Cutting Edge of Music Technology (edweb.fnal.gov/linc/spring96/projects_linc2/allmusic/technology/cuttingedge.html). Home Recording (homerecording.com/) provides an extensive discussion of low-cost recording tips and runs a Mixmaster mailing list for ongoing discussion of these topics. Tutorials for preparing tape decks and microphones for recording are available at sites such as Analog Tape Recording (arts.ucsc.edu/ems/music/equipment/analog_recorders/Analog_Recorders.html) and Scott's PA System Tutorial (www.geocities.com/SunsetStrip/Stage/4241/index.html). Resources specific to digital audio and MIDI may be found at The Digital Sound Page (www.xs4all.nl/~rexbo/main.htm). A design for a small-scale recording studio suitable for a webcast production company or ISP is available at Recording Studio Design (www.mcs.net/~malcolm/). Books on this subject are available from Musicbooks (www.musicbooks.com) and Jerome Headlands Press (kspace.com/jhp).

Encoding

Unlike datacasts, audiocast encoding software is well developed. Several highly efficient standards for Internet audio encoding have been developed and proposed (see Chapter 2, "Developing a Webcast Strategy"). Encoding is primarily a matter of choosing the correct algorithm for the particular audio source. In most cases, the preset codecs have been designed for a specific format and may be selected directly. However, the developers will need to listen to the output to ensure that artifacts were not introduced. Coding for problematic audio will need to be set by trial and error. The webcast producers should also keep in mind that there are generally fewer real-time encoding options relative to those available for recorded audio. For example, current versions of the RealAudio Live encoder do not support broadcast-quality capture with dual ISDN speeds.

Presentation

In theory, audiocasts may be produced and delivered independently of the web. This approach is evident in the design of some programs, such as the RealPlayer Plus (www.real.com), that contain built-in software tuners for selecting audiocasts. In practice, however, most audiocasts will need an associated web site. The design for such sites will differ significantly from a site whose primary content is contained in HTML. The following list provides some concepts useful for audiocast-associated web site development:

Internet radio site design. Webcasters following the virtual radio model often develop simple web sites, assuming that all relevant information is encoded directly into the audiocast. However, since audio files cannot be directly indexed by most search engines, it is important to provide a description of the site and its resources on the web page. This description should appear in the page itself and in an invisible *meta tag* statement in the HTML document. Most users will not want to listen to an audiocast merely to hear announcements of upcoming events. Instead, this information should be organized as an HTML-based web calendar and listed on the site's pages. In order to get feedback about audiocast content and configuration, it is important to place addresses, phone numbers, and email on the site. In the case of music, it is likely that industry professionals interested in reviewing albums will access the site, and so developers should consider creating a separate email box for their messages.

Design for web/audiocast mixes. Sites that integrate significant quantities of web-based content with audiocasts must be dynamic (have content that is changed regularly, independent of the audiocast) and interactive (provide feedback for user actions). Audio is the main content on the site, so pages should generally be restricted to text and graphics coded in standard HTML or JavaScript. And because end users already must run two programs (audio program and web browser) to hear the audiocast, memory-hog page design should be studiously avoided. This includes extensive use of Java, elaborate graphics, animation, plug-ins, and pages with large num-

Case Study: LiveConcerts.com

URL: www.liveconcerts.com
Contact: Eric Magnuson (themanager@liveconcerts.com)

This site, shown in Figure 8.7, provides a highly effective example of integrated web and audiocast information. Acting as an audiocast events calendar, the home page of LiveConcerts.com lists audiocasts in a hierarchical fashion, with a few featured events listed above the main search box. A special page, shown in Figure 8.8, provides links to the necessary media players. On the left side, a vertical menu bar provides access to a large number of

Figure 8.7 LiveConcerts.com.

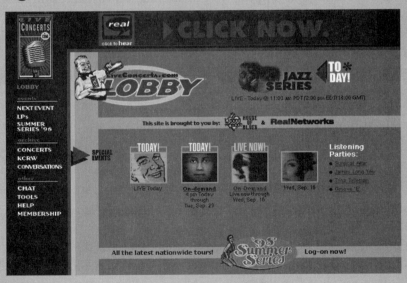

bers (and/or sizes) of images. An exception to this rule is if the audio stream itself is played with a multimedia-aware plug-in such as Macromedia Shockwave. The player automatically provides support for additional multimedia, therefore it is not necessary to launch a

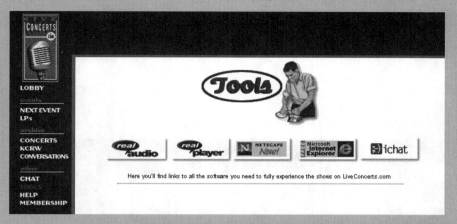

Figure 8.8 The media player "toolkit" page on LiveConcerts.com.

archived events. The menu options are set in a fixed frame and do not require scrolling the page for viewing; this is important for new users more comfortable with television than word processors.

To help develop a dedicated audience for its events, LiveConcerts.com offers extensive community-building services. Visitors may register for membership and join chat rooms running in either HTML, Java, or Ichat (www.ichat.com) versions. A user survey is prominently listed on the home page to encourage additional feedback from the audience. The registration form itself, shown in Figure 8.9, takes into account that many users may forget their usernames/passwords, and provides a way to recover them. Users access the media database by selecting an option from pop-up menus. In addition to archiving audiocasts, the site archives non-

second program. Continuity between the web content and the audiocast may be further enhanced by using the <embed> HTML tag to put audio player controls into the page body, as illustrated on a page from Musicnet, shown in Figure 8.10.

streaming-related material relevant to the streaming performances (including artist/musician interviews), making it useful to visitors who cannot receive the audiocast. With a well-thought-out design, LiveConcerts.com is an appealing place to select and hear webcasts.

Figure 8.9 The LiveConcerts.com registration form.

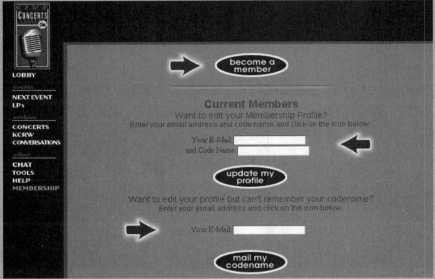

Providing audience support. Due to the strong entertainment appeal of audiocasts, many new and inexperienced users are likely to visit the site in large numbers. This means that the audiocast content, as well as the design of the hosting web site, must support individuals just learning how to use the web. Pages describing the audiocast should contain clear links to the necessary player software and provide a test page that analyzes the user's equipment for compatibility. Several sites, including Macromedia's Shockrave (www.shockrave .com), have web pages written in JavaScript that interactively inform users of installed and missing components on their systems.

Figure 8.10 Musicnet.

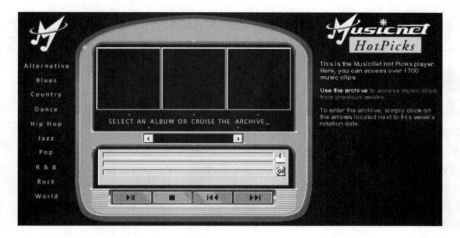

Audiocasts designed for student access should generally run with as low bandwidth as possible (e.g., 14.4K modem speeds) because many students use older 486 and pre-PowerMac systems that do not run fast enough to decode 28.8K audio streams. Inexperienced audience members frequently have problems with Java; even if they have a Java-compatible browser, the slow loading time of many Java applets may cause them to conclude that their computer has crashed. This problem is particularly acute on older Macintosh (e.g., 7100) systems at the low end of Java support.

Community-building features. Pages describing the audiocast should contain clear links to chats, contests, opinion polls, discussion groups, and registration forms available on the site. Webcasters interested in featuring regular audiocasts should consider implementing mailing lists for fans on their sites. These lists may be used to notify members of live events and/or promote discussion among members. Community building is also enabled by providing interaction between the audiocast performers and their audience via email or online chat.

Credits. In developing an audio program, the webcasters should remember to give credit where credit is due. It may also be a good idea to provide copyright information on audiocast pages where it will be clearly seen by users, and explain that making unauthorized copies of the audiocast is illegal. Within the webcast, announcers should periodically identify themselves and the show for individuals who have just tuned in.

TIP   **CALENDARS**

Calendars are essential components of audiocast web sites. A good example of an audiocast calendar may be found on the Timecast site, shown in Figure 8.11. Each listing is sorted by the date and time of the live event, and ongoing events are highlighted relative to past and future events. Another useful feature of the calendar is a Remind Me button, which allows users to set up notification email when the event is about to occur. Another calendar possibility is a "countdown," which lists days/hours/minutes until the event. The web maintainer should make sure that calendar schedules are kept up to date, since obsolete event information will cause visitors to assume the site is no longer active.

Figure 8.11 The Timecast (www.timecast.com) event calendar.

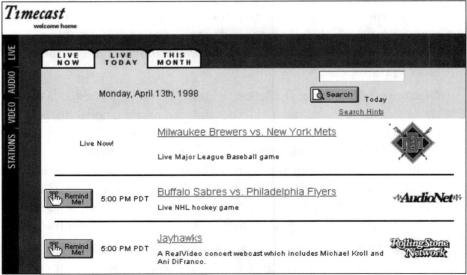

Case Study: Broadcast.com (formerly AudioNet)

URL: www.broadcast.com
Contact: David Burrows (bizservices@broadcast.com)

Broadcast.com is a pioneer of Internet-based streaming audio. Founded in 1995 by Mark Cuban, it quickly established itself as the leading content aggregator for audiocasts on the Internet. In March 1998, the service provided access to live continuous audiocasts of more than 260 radio and television stations and networks, along with thousands of college and professional sporting events, concerts, and club performances. During the 1998 Super Bowl, the site delivered audiocasts to a total of 500,000 listeners. Virtually all streaming media formats are supported, including RealAudio, RealVideo, Flash, Shockwave, streaming wordcasts, VDO, and NetShow. Broadcast.com offers production services to its clients that include analog/digital conversion, a production studio for webcasts, and support for live webcasts, which combine to create a one-stop audiocast solution.

The steps necessary to deliver Broadcast.com's content are shown diagramatically in Figure 8.12. Live audio is recorded using Electro-Voice (www.electrovoice.com) analog microphones interfaced to Shure (www.shure.com) mixing boards. Recorded audio comes from analog output from radio, television, CD, or VHS players. The signal is sent directly to a PC sound card and is converted by the appropriate encoder software. The sound engineer captures audio at 16-bit for NetShow and 8-bit for RealAudio. According to Broadcast.com, the requirements for good webcast audio processing are virtually identical to those in standard broadcast. Broadcast.com developers use Macromedia's DECK II/Pro Tools (www.macromedia.com) for editing. Once captured, content is passed to the ISP's media server using ISDN or 56K modems. In some cases, Broadcast.com has installed its own ISDN lines to support live audiocasts. A mixture of

Case Study: Broadcast.com (formerly AudioNet) *(Continued)*

UNIX and Windows NT hardware is used for media serving. Typical server configurations use a 300MHz processor, a 3-gigabyte hard drive, and at least 128 megabytes of RAM. The servers are connected to the Internet via multihomed T3 connections to national ISPs. Broadcast.com's network is capable of serving up to 25,000 simultaneous connections to its service. Broadcast.com also multicasts through networks provided by Uunet (www.uu.net), MCI (www.mci.com), and Sprint (www.sprint.com). The effectiveness of each webcast is checked via a mix of access software tools such as WebTrends (www.webtrends.com) combined with human testers. Traffic spikes and slowdowns are detected automatically by administrative programs. Broadcast.com reports that the majority of problems during webcasts are caused by packet loss between source and destination, with a smaller percentage coming from users with slow modems.

Broadcast.com's model for webcast production is similar to a cable company. This strategy ensures fast response and effective use of team talent. Performers and industry professionals are recruited from local talent, either directly or through agencies.

Figure 8.12 Broadcast.com (www.broadcast.com) capture and delivery system.

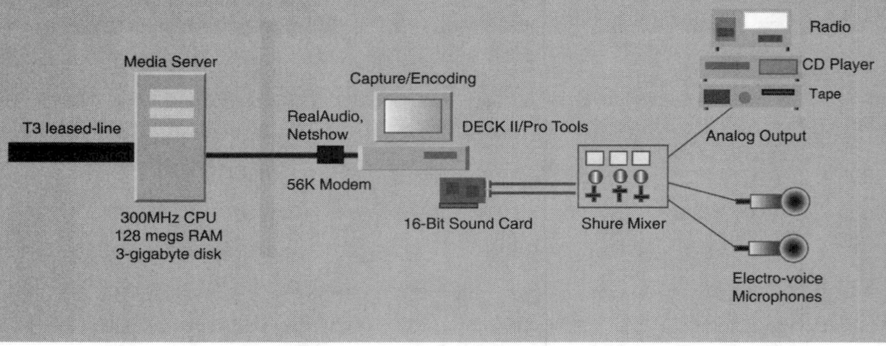

Effective presentation will make the difference between a successful and an unsuccessful webcast. Internet users must feel it is worth their while to download the audio and possibly player software as well. Content aggregators such as Broadcast.com serve a valuable function in this respect. Prior to Broadcast.com, most Internet users were either unaware of audiocasts or did not know where to find them. This points to a strong future role of branding on the Internet as a key aspect of webcast presentation.

Publicity and Promotion

Entertainment audiocasts, particularly those involving music or celebrities, may be promoted effectively in offline media such as trade newspapers and magazines. Online promotion possibilities include listings in media-specific event sites such as Timecast (www.timecast.com) and RealPlanet (www.realplanet) for RealAudio, and the NetShow Features column (www.microsoft.com/netshow) for NetShow. Since high-quality audio is available to consumers from many sources, publicity for Internet-based audiocasts should emphasize the unique nature of the audiocast. For example, a live audiocast from an exclusive club might be promoted by listing the famous individuals who have performed there, and emphasizing that the information was not available via traditional broadcast channels. Publicity for educational and news sites has the additional challenge of helping its intended audience to understand the webcast concept. Despite widespread interest in distance learning at colleges and universities, many students do not realize that courses may be conducted entirely online. Instructors either may not understand the Internet or feel that the medium is not appropriate for their course material. Web-based promotion for online education designed to entice students and instructors to use the service should include detailed tutorials and Frequently Asked Questions (FAQs).

Archiving Strategies

Sites providing on-demand audio will need to develop a strategy for storing and indexing content that takes into account the invisibility of audio files to most search tools. In many cases, this may be accomplished simply by storing a web page along with each audio clip. In moving a page to the archive, the developer should add text that clearly distinguishes prerecorded information and truly live events. Since it is difficult to browse through long audiocast clips, additional text should be provided that describes the contents of each clip as is practical. To increase space, the developers may elect to remove <embed> commands that put player controls on the page. Programs such as RealPlayer 5.0 allow the user to start at arbitrary points in the streaming audio clip, so that extensive text annotations might list key events in the clip along with the time of their occurrence. While programs like Magnifi (Chapter 6, "Webcast Promotion, Commerce, and Analysis") allow automated indexing of video, comparable software has yet to be developed for audio content. Typical audiocast archives providing clips from 14.4, 28.8, and ISDN-quality webcasts will take up to 100 megabytes an hour to store.

Estimating Costs

Due to the widespread availability of commercial streaming audio platforms, developers will not need to budget for custom hardware and software programming. Beyond the basic expense of installing encoding and delivery systems (see Chapters 3 and 4), the main costs are for recording equipment and/or studio development. Home recording studios may be created for a few thousand dollars, while high-end professional studios may cost several times as much. Renting a studio for a few days of recording will add several thousand dollars to the production budget. This brings the cost for setting up a medium-level audiocast service with significant marketing and promotion to at least $20,000—not including the server or Internet connection. If live on-site events are planned, it will be necessary to purchase audiocast equipment specifically designed for travel—adding more expense. Depending on the audience, monthly charges for audiocast bandwidth may range from about $1,500 (20 listeners) to $20,000 (1,000 listeners). Educational and corporate intranet sites may be able to use their preexisting campus network, saving this expense. An estimate of the costs in these circumstances may be found at Real Education (www.realeducation.com). This online course development company charges $4,000 to $5,000 for setup of individual classes, including conversion of audio and video content. To recoup ongoing costs, the service charges approximately $100 per virtual student.

Next . . .

In many ways, audiocasts mark the cutting edge of webcast development. The demand for production values that match the relatively high quality of webcast sound has made design and production closer to broadcast. With costs for developing a production running into the tens of thousands, the field is rapidly professionalizing and developing its own suite of companies, traditions, and programming. In contrast, Internet video is still largely experimental. The features of current videocasts, along with trends that may turn it into a major webcast medium, are covered in the next chapter.

VIDEOCASTS AND ANIMACASTS

9

When most people think of webcasting, they think streaming video. Due to its superficial resemblance to television, streaming video is often portrayed as the cutting edge of Internet-based broadcast, if not the future of the Internet itself. Major media companies and news organizations regularly provide webcast video from their Internet sites, and independent sites such as No Label Music Video (www.nolabel.com), shown in Figure 9.1, archive hundreds of music videos for on-demand play. Equally important is the rapidly developing area of streaming Internet animation, or animacasts. This exciting form of webcasting combines animation with streaming audio to create a high-quality visual experience capable of delivery within current Internet bandwidth restrictions. Outstanding sites such as Smashing Ideas (www.smashingideas.com), shown in Figure 9.2, and Legendary Productions' GeoSync (www.dextech.com/legendary/geosync/index2.htm) are using this new technology to create the first generation of animated storytelling on the Internet.

Traditionally, video and animation have been considered distinct fields requiring separate discussion. However, webcast technology is driving a convergence between these two formerly distinct media. Both are considered in this chapter for the following reasons:

- The quality of streaming animation and video is severely limited by the available bandwidth on the Internet.

Figure 9.1 No Label Music Video (www.nolabel.com).

- Streaming animation authoring platforms, including Macromedia Flash (www.macromedia.com) and GEO Emblaze (www.emblaze.com), allow video to be inserted as a component of the webcast stream.

- New streaming video standards, such as QuickTime 3.0 (quicktime.apple.com), provide support for animation-style vector drawings as well as traditional bitmap-style video.

- The Internet audience for videocasts and animacasts is largely the same, unlike traditional broadcast where the animation audience is distinct from the live-action audience.

The fusion of video and animation may help realize the promise of a new communication medium expected for the Internet. Without the read-only limitations of the CD-ROM world, streaming animation and video can provide the most compelling interactive experience possible. The dynamic features being built into Internet video and animation allow it to go beyond the broadcast par-

Figure 9.2 Smashing Ideas (www.smashingideas.com).

adigm and create a unique environment, which mixes professional high-quality broadcast with an unprecedented degree of user control.

Unique Features

While videocast and animacast technologies have the potential to revolutionize communication, it is important for webcasters to realize that the revolution will be long in coming. Currently, the main features of Internet video and animation are limitations rather than strengths. The following is a list of reality checks, which stand between the long-term potential for videocasts and animacasts and their present-day realization. These limitations should be understood by any webcaster planning to use videocast or animacast technology:

Image quality. Video on the Internet is definitely not for prime time. The default windows (approximately 160 × 120 pixels) suitable for modem bandwidth are simply too small for extended viewing, and slow frame rates and blurred images combine to make watching a videocast (see Chapter 3, "Webcast Equipment and Authoring Environments") less than satisfying. Low image quality makes it impossible to present certain types of demanding content involving rapid motion or complex scenes. An exception to this general rule is found in ambient video, which uses slow frame rates (hours to days) to send higher-quality images. Animacasts run at higher quality (typically 10 to 20 frames/second with 320×240 pixel screens) than videocasts, but still fall short of the visual experience of television and film.

Content. There have been few original programs developed for videocast. Some shows, such as Byte Media's *Byte Me* (www.bytemedia.com) and InterneTV's *Austin* (www.internetv.com/austin/index.htm), are currently on the Internet, but their impact is relatively limited and is not competitive with traditional broadcasts. By contrast, animacasts have achieved high enough quality to warrant original content development. Web 'toons are being developed at a breakneck pace, and the emergence of Internet-based storytelling for a mass audience is likely to occur in the animacast medium.

Audio. The information required to transmit a moving image takes up most of a 28.8 modem's bandwidth; therefore, webcasters frequently compromise on audio tracks—making them far lower in quality than audio-only webcasts. Videocast audio seldom rises above telephone quality (approximately 8-bit, 11Kbps sampling), except in special cases where the video portion runs as a slow-frame slide show.

Production values. Despite low quality, videocasts and animacasts demand high production values. Webcasters planning to provide original streaming video must understand stage design and direction, lighting, camera operation, and sound design. The inevitable comparison to television necessitates duplicating the fast-paced programming features of that mature medium. Streaming animacasts must acknowledge a similar historical precedent comprising more than 80 years of classic animation. The audience for live action and animation expects strong, one-way storytelling—unlike the interactive, information-gathering paradigm of the web.

Hardware and software. In order to decrease bandwidth, most video compression algorithms require high-speed signal encoding and decoding on the production equipment and end-user's computer. This makes videocasting an expensive development option and limits the audience for the finished product to the subset of power users with the latest hardware. Videocasts and animacasts reach a subset of the small audience that has successfully downloaded, installed, and configured the necessary media players. Hardware and software issues ensure that videocasts and animicasts will remain a niche market for some time to come.

Incompatible formats. The videocast market is fragmented by incompatible formats developed by Microsoft (www.microsoft.com/netshow), RealNetworks (www.real.com), and VDO (www.vdo.net). A similar competition may develop for animacasts between Macromedia's Flash (www.macromedia.com), Microsoft's Liquid Motion animacast format (www.microsoft.com/liquidmotion/default1.html), and Adobe's (www.adobe.com) *Precision Graphics Markup Language (PGML)*. Unless a single cross-platform standard is developed, webcasters will have to create multiple copies of their productions, each optimized for a particular player and format.

With these problems, some webcasters may wonder whether developing video and animation-based webcasts is worth the trouble. The answer is a qualified yes, partly because streaming animation has achieved acceptable quality for distribution and partly in the hope that future bandwidth increases will lead to high-quality videocasting. Webcasters developing streaming video and animation should be ready to dig in and patiently develop their product in anticipation of future success. Webcasters developing for intranets and educational networks have a definite advantage due to the higher bandwidth of their users.

Applications

The audience for videocast and animacast content is not as well defined as that for audiocasts. This is because installed software is still the chief determinant of whether a user will join a videocast—rather than content provided by the webcasters. Within the general class of videocast-ready users, a few subgroups have begun to distinguish themselves. The following provides a breakdown of these groups, listed in terms of the likelihood that they will be interested in receiving a videocast:

Education. Videocasts, particularly those following a videoconference-style *distance learning* approach, have a natural audience in the educational market. Many colleges and universities have been experimenting with non-Internet distance learning, and regard videocasts as a continuation of this trend. Webcasters working with educational groups may need to educate members about the primitive character of current Internet video, as well as the additional interactive features on the web not supported in videoconferencing or closed-circuit television.

Corporate training. In some companies, an internal audience for on-demand access to training videos creates a market for videocasts. With their generally higher connection speeds, many corporate networks support partial or even full-screen videocasts, allowing training to be effectively conveyed.

Music. The search term used more than any other entertainment-related word on the Internet is music, so webcasters creating music video have a significant potential market for their efforts. Depending on the popularity of the group or performer, an audience may be willing to tune in, regardless of problems associated with replicating video on the web.

Animation fans. This relatively untested group may be very important to webcasting's future. Many animation fans and developers have complained of limited options in traditional broadcast media, particularly for screening unusual or controversial 'toons. The Internet holds a natural appeal for this group, and enables easy formation of the tight creator/fan communities necessary for their success.

Infomercial. A somewhat surprising but very real audience segment for webcasts consists of people willing to watch on-demand video promotions. In the past, the chief complaint against the infomercial was targeting: Most people watching broadcast are unlikely to be interested in the particular product and service. On the Internet, surfers may access on-demand archives and select only those pitches that interest them.

Certain market segments that receive Internet audio effectively are less attractive candidates for videocasts and animacasts. For example, it is better to use an audio-only webcast stream for news reporting, despite the similarity of television newscasts to the talking head format used in webcasting. The market outside the United States is also underdeveloped, due to slow Internet connections and the difficulty of installing and configuring the necessary software. Pay-per-view videocasts are virtually nonexistent, since most audience members are unwilling to pay for low-quality video. Animacasts may also find it difficult to gain an audience, not because users aren't interested, but because many don't realize that high-quality animation is available. Animacast developers may elect to expend their marketing budgets for general site promotion rather than targeting a specific audience.

Videocast and Animacast Formats

Videocasts have such severe bandwidth limitations that webcasters are forced to choose from a very limited number of formats, including the slide show and talking heads discussed at length in Chapter 3, "Webcast Equipment and Authoring Environments." Animacasts suffer less from bandwidth, but developers must use authoring tools that are still in their first generation. With these limitations, there are a only few content types that may be delivered effectively using videocasts and animacast formats.

Repurposed Film/Television

While possibly the easiest form of visual webcast to generate, repurposed excerpts from film and television generally leave much to be desired. The dramatic size difference between a television monitor and a webcast video window make the latter valuable only as promotion for the real show. Without a well-known name or face, this content is unlikely to attract an audience. For adequate resolution, repurposed content generally requires a minimum of 56K

Working with Videocast Clients

Webcasters working with a client interested in developing original videocast content should ask themselves the following questions before beginning:

Does the client understand the technology? Developers should make sure that the content provider understands the major limitations imposed by current Internet technology.

Is the client comfortable with Internet distribution? Due to widespread negative publicity, many content providers view the Internet as inherently dangerous. Unless these fears are quieted, the project is unlikely to proceed.

Does the content already have an audience? It is much easier to attract fans to experiment with video than to promote it to new users.

Is the content interesting for what it is or for how it looks? Video with unique or novel content preserves its value at low resolution, while video depending on special effects will translate poorly to the Internet.

Does the video consist of short promotional clips or full broadcasts? In general, short promotional clips will attract greater interest, since they are easier to download.

If the video is recorded, is high-quality composite or Super-VHS (S-VHS) format available? Low-quality VHS video produces even lower-quality webcasts.

Does the video feature close-ups or panoramas? Videocasts of distant objects may be unable to display sufficient detail of the subject.

modem connections, with dual ISDN speeds being more realistic. Some video-cast sites provide 28.8 options, but the quality is generally so low that the webcast is often unwatchable.

Examples of repurposed television content may be seen at UltimateTV's Promo Lounge (www.ultimatetv.com) and Mediadome (www.mediadome.com). Alternative content not accessible through television is available at sites such as Freespeech.org Internet Television (www.freespeech.org). One area where repurposed content is gaining ground is in *infotainment,* which mixes entertainment and information. Currently the most common form of repurposed infotainment is used to sell products and services. In this case, the low quality of the webcast is partly compensated for by the hard sell implicit in the content. Archived infomercials indexed by product and service are potentially a far more attractive marketing system than random viewing on television.

Music Video

Currently, music video is the most common kind of videocast on the Internet. While webcast video falls far short of those seen on television, many music fans seem willing to tolerate low quality to catch their favorite group online. Aggregation sites such as SonicNet's Streamland (www.streamland.com), InterneTV (www.internetv.com), and OnlineTV (www.onlinetv.com) provide access to celebrity musicians as well as unsigned independents. Other sites providing streaming music video include No Label Music Video (www.nolabel. com) and AltVideos (www.altvideo.com). OnlineTV, shown in Figure 9.3, uses a 160 × 120-pixel screen common in most music videocasts. In order to leave sufficient bandwidth for the music track; frame rates are decreased to slide show speed (1-2/second). If individual frames of the slide show are chosen carefully, some of the visual impact of the music video may be maintained. Audio tracks are generally set in the 8-bit, 11Kbps range, which provides quality somewhat better than telephones but less than 28.8 audiocasts. A few streaming video developers have tried to optimize for action, but the resulting blurry scenes are often less appealing than the slide show format.

The convergence between videocast and animacast information is clearly seen on webcast sites featuring music video. In their desire to make the web pages emulate the movements and scene transitions of a television broadcast,

Figure 9.3 OnlineTV (www.onlinetv.com).

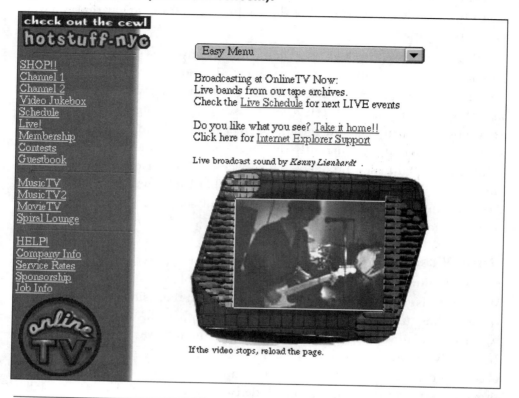

many developers cram their pages with Shockwave, Java, and Flash animation programs (supposedly) making up for the deficiencies of the video product. Interestingly, the MTV site (www.mtv.com) avoids streaming video entirely in favor of animation, wordcasts, and online chat. In contrast, the Box (www .thebox.com), while providing access to video online, has taken a step toward convergence by making every word in its titles a flickering mini-animacast.

Lectures and Speeches

Common in education and corporate videoconferencing, lectures and speeches feature individual personalities presented through the talking head webcast format (Chapter 3, "Webcast Equipment and Authoring Environments").

Since spoken words require less bandwidth than music, the audio quality may be dropped to 8-bit, 7Kbps sampling without seriously compromising intelligibility (an example is shown in Figure 9.4). This provides slightly more bandwidth for imaging, and the resulting picture may be quite sharp if the speaker keeps head movements to a minimum.

Companies such as RealEducation (www.realeducation.com) provide talking head video development as part of their standard course design. Some news organizations have used talking heads to convey information, but they continue to include text-based wordcasts or basic web pages as a supplement. Since significant motion leads to blurring of the image, it is difficult to communicate anything other than facial expressions. This eliminates videocast forms where, for example, an instructor demonstrates the use of handheld equipment. Animacasts using cartoon-style characters may fill this niche in the near future.

Spycams

Forsaking any attempt at moving pictures, spycams utilize the ambient video webcast format (Chapter 3, "Webcast Equipment and Authoring Environments") to

Figure 9.4 Talking head featured on the RealNetworks (www.real.com) web site.

stream single frames to the user on a time scale of minutes to hours. Though audio tracks could potentially be supplied with ambient videocasts, most provide a silent window to interesting or unusual places scattered throughout the world. In January 1998, there were more than 5,000 ambient videocasts available through aggregator sites including Ambit (www.ambitweb.com/nasacams/nasacams.html), Spacezone (www.spacezone.com/nasavid/85vid.htm), ConnecTV (contactv.2nd.net), and the DCN World Webcam Index (www.dcn.com) shown in Figure 9.5. Dozens of sites operated by NASA include a web spycam that allows visitors to watch the assembly of spacecraft. Ambient videos are also used to report wave height, snow conditions at ski resorts, the atmosphere in nightclubs, and the appearance of famous objects such as the Hollywood sign (www.rfx.com/Hollywood/).

An emerging use for ambient webcasts is surveillance. Webcams are already being used for security in large buildings, and teleoperation systems like those offered by Perceptual Robotics (www.perceptualrobotics.com) should increase their value to webcasters. NOVEX Canada (www.novexcanada.com) provides its Video Catcher software/webcam combination, shown in Figure 9.6, specifically for monitoring family property or children. It is likely that spycams will become a major videocast growth area as Internet connections become part of the typical American household.

Show-and-Tell Animation

One of the most interesting near-term uses of video and animation on the Internet involves show-and-tell animation. Drawing from animated instruction strategies used in broadcasting and computer software, this format uses movement to demonstrate principles not obvious in still images or the spoken word. For example, a physics demonstration might illustrate the laws of hydraulics by animating fluid movement through tubes of different sizes. Animation may also be used for clarity, as in a graphic where objects in a scene are denoted in sequence by a moving arrow. Since the purpose of the format is instructional, audio tracks with narration typically accompany show-and-tell animation.

The relatively modest requirements for show-and-tell animacasts allow the user to interact with full-screen, high-resolution images with a quality that

Figure 9.5 DCN World Webcam Index (www.dcn.com).

exceeds that of television. Options for creating this type of animation include Macromedia's Flash Generator or Adobe's Precision Graphics Markup Language (PGML). A good example may be seen with the Breathing Earth animacast (www.sensorium.org) shown in Figure 9.7. Although not connected to a streaming source of data, this Shockwave-based animation uses seis-mometer values from a two-week period to produce an exaggerated graphical representation of the globe's distortion by earthquakes.

Web 'Toons

One of the newest and most innovative forms of webcast, web 'toons exploit the advanced streaming animation features of Macromedia Flash and similar

Figure 9.6 NOVEX Canada's Video Catcher (www.novexcanada.com).

programs to create original stories designed exclusively for the Internet. These web-based cartoons vary from short promotional sketches showcasing the work of design shops to full-length narratives featuring Internet-specific characters. By using authoring techniques analogous to traditional animation, it is possible to design characters that move and act naturally within the bandwidth limits of consumer modems. Pioneering examples of web-based 'toons and developer studios have been collected in Macromedia's Shockrave (www.shockrave.com) web site shown in Figure 9.8. Launched early in 1998, this site showcases Flash storytelling from dozens of Internet cartoonists. Other sites featuring Flash 'toons include Spumco (www.spumco.com) and Jig Interactive (www.jigint.com). Web cartoonists already have an online community at the Internet Cartoons Forum (www.cartoonsforum.com). A listing of design shops that develop web 'toons is found in Table 9.1. With even a modest jump in consumer modem speeds (e.g., single-channel ISDN at 64K), web 'toons will be fully comparable to their broadcast television equivalents in quality and perhaps superior in diversity of content. It is likely that the first

Figure 9.7 Breathing Earth animacast at The Sensorium (www.sensorium.org).

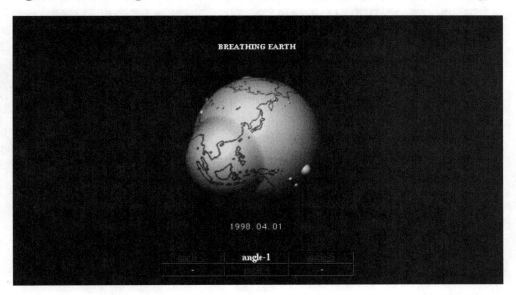

real test of the web as a mass-market broadcast will occur using web 'toons—possibly as pay-per-view content.

Table 9.1 Companies Providing Animacast Production Services

Company Name	URL
156 Productions	www.156.com
Fusionary Media	www.fusionary.com
Gabocorp Imaging	www.gabocorp.com
MK-Ultra	www.mk-ultra.com
Smashing Ideas	www.smashingideas.com
Spumco	www.spumco.com
Webtrips	www.webtrips.com
InterVU	www.intervu.net

Figure 9.8 Macromedia's Shockrave (www.shockrave.com).

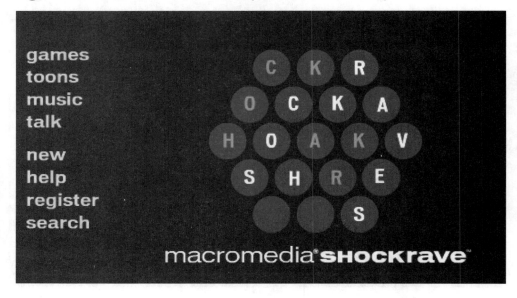

Teleoperation

One of the most exciting variations of the standard videocast is provided by systems that allow end-user control of camera operation. Both educational sites such as the University of Iowa's Automated Telescope Facility (inferno.physics.uiowa .edu/REMOTE_OBS/remote_index.shtml) and commercial products from companies such as Perceptual Robotics, Inc. (www.perceptualrobotics.com) offer user-controlled cameras. Perceptual Robotics' iCam is an integrated solution that includes software, a server computer, and a video subsystem for the delivery of photographic-quality images via the Internet. The iCam system supports from one to several simultaneous users who may independently control the pan, tilt, and zoom of the camera. Currently, most teleoperated cameras run in spycam mode, but the iDirector product also supports streaming video. The Jason Project (www.jason .org), developed by Perceptual Robotics, allows students to drive an automated submarine via Internet connections. Other examples of teleoperated cameras include the Tiger Cam at the Lincoln Park Zoo (www.perceptualrobotics.com/live/livezoo .htm) and the Channel 5 News camera in Palm Beach, Florida (www.tcpalm.com/

nc5/index.html), shown in Figure 9.9. Specialty teleoperated webcams include The City of Night Live Camera (www.citynight.com/camera) and The Mt. Fuji Server (www.flab.mag.keio.ac.jp/fuji/). User control of a different type is provided by the Wearable Webcam (www.wearcam.org), which integrates a webcast camcorder directly into an individual's clothing.

| NOTE | ### TELEOPERATED WEBCAM USE

An outstanding use of Perceptual Robotics' teleoperated webcams is found at the Jason Project, an educational program designed to let students interact with the underwater world via webcasts. During special shows, students use web-based controls coupled with streaming video to drive remotely operated underwater cameras at sites such as the Monterey Bay Aquarium (www.mbayaq.org) from their computers. The remote driving system consists of two cameras mounted in underwater enclosures in Monterey Bay, which are connected by long cables to computers located on shore. There are two computers for each camera: one to control where the camera is pointed and periodically take still pictures, and one to take the video and stream it to the mechanism that actually moves the camera.

Advertising

With standard videocasting limited by low bandwidth—and with animacasts just beginning to have an impact—streaming video's most practical application may be in advertising. Extending the animation loops seen in many banner ads, companies such as InterVU (www.intervu.net) are actively developing ads combining streaming video and animation. While implementation of streaming advertising is problematic (most consumers resent the intrusion of advertising they cannot control), the short sequences found in streaming advertising are similar to television commercial sound bytes and are a better fit to current videocast technology than longer narrative storytelling.

Certain types of video-based content are not suitable for the Internet. A good example of this is sports broadcasting, where players move quickly and camera positions change frequently. With less than a dual ISDN connection, videocasts

Figure 9.9 Channel 5 News camera in Palm Beach, Florida (www.tcpalm.com/nc5/index.html).

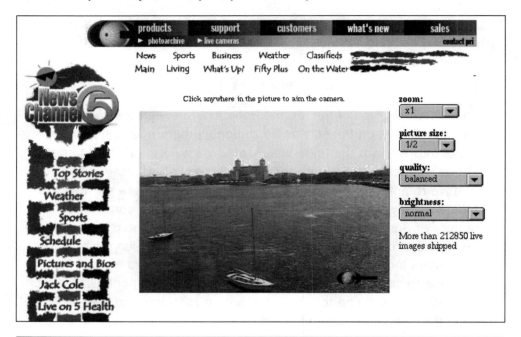

simply cannot convey enough of the ambience of the event to be convincing. Displaying text within a video window is generally impractical, since any word more than a few letters long will be unreadable on screen. Video with complex shifting patterns and/or colors will also produce webcasts of unacceptable quality. Animacasts have limitations related to the degree that on-screen objects change their appearance. For example, scenes in which the same object moves across the screen work better than those in which the object rotates or changes shape. This means that animacasts work well with 2D scenes but have problems displaying the 3D environments characteristic of much computer animation.

Videocast Production Principles

Videocast production requires expertise in analog recording and digital webcast conversion. On the analog side, it is necessary to manage cameras, lighting, and performers—or analog tape recordings. On the digital side, it is important to find acceptable compression standards for delivering video at Internet speeds. Integrating productions of this complexity needs careful planning and may also require the services of an outsourced video production company. The following subsections describe the main features of videocast production likely to affect typical webcasts using live and recorded material.

Team Design

The formation of videocast production teams closely parallels strategies used in traditional live and recorded broadcast. As a real-world example, Broadcast.com's videocast service in April 1998 employed the following personnel:

- Two producers
- Four content developers/scriptwriters
- Three writers
- Two sound engineers
- One video engineer
- One camera/microphone operator
- Four marketing/promotion reps
- Three obsolete site content removers
- Six web site administrators

Webcasters looking to outsource their primary video production may check the extensive listings in Yahoo! (www.yahoo.com/Business_and_Economy/Companies/Entertainment/Video/Production/) for video production. In many cases, smaller firms specializing in corporate or commercial video production may be better suited for webcasting than those providing services for national broadcast—and may provide an end-to-end solution including transportation and primary editing. The developers should check to see that the company has some experience with computer technology and digital video authoring environments.

Recording Format

If the video will be recorded for later encoding, webcasters will need to determine the tape format. Material destined for traditional broadcast is typically shot using Beta SP or similar quality formats. For a webcast, this level of quality is overkill. Instead, most groups should shoot the video using the cheaper Hi-8 format for transfer to VHS or Super-VHS (Chapter 3, "Webcast Equipment and Authoring Environments"). It is possible to shoot webcast video for small-screen (160 × 120) productions using standard VHS, but it will not be possible to re-record or edit the video with analog equipment due to rapid loss of image fidelity. Computer-heavy webcasters who shoot in VHS may use all-digital nonlinear editing software, such as Adobe Premiere, to circumvent this problem. Since digital copies retain the same quality as the original, multiple edits and duplications are acceptable. The Hi-8 format requires a special VCR recorder supporting this video standard for playback, but most computer video cards support Hi-8 input by default.

| NOTE | **LOW-COST VIDEO CAPTURE**

In April 1998, Broadcast.com (www.broadcast.com) began offering videocast services in addition to the hundreds of audiocasts it supports. To capture live videocasts, Broadcast.com uses Panasonic analog camcorders recording in VHS and Super-VHS. Using SuperVHS is easier for the team and provides quality that is close to beta without the additional expense. Beta is used for some situations, such as broadcast television, demanding the highest video quality. Due to the diversity of content, Broadcast.com does not use standard capture formats, and it varies frame rate, colors, and screen size on an event-specific basis. Synchronized multimedia that combines video and animation are created using NetShow, Flash, and Shockwave. Recent Broadcast.com videocasts have featured repurposed television shows from the Dallas area. Broadcast.com has specifically avoided webcasting network programming because of legal uncertainties over who owns the rights to the programming.

On-Screen Movement

A defining feature of webcast video production is suppression of unnecessary bandwidth by reducing movement on screen. Performers and on-screen objects or shifts in the camera's location may produce movement. Common videocast compression algorithms accommodate this movement by reducing the resolution of the entire screen. This effect may rapidly turn a videocast scene into a pulsing object of abstract art. Some algorithms skimp on the number of bits used to convey motion, causing moving objects to degrade to a semitransparent blur flying across the scene. To compensate for small scene shifts caused by unsteady mounts, the webcaster should use cameras with image stabilization technologies such as *Electronic Image Stabilization (EIS)*, *Optical Image Stabilization (OIS)*, and *Digital Image Stabilization (DIS)*. All these systems react to small camera moves and automatically adjust the image so it remains stationary. Movement within the scene may be reduced further by instructing performers not to gesture unnecessarily and by filming performers seated rather than standing or walking.

Point of View

Traditional video production frequently changes the audience's view of a scene by moving the camera. Properly used, camera moves may signal the beginning or end of a scene, create a feeling of anticipation, or explore different aspects of objects and characters in the videocast. Film and television use one or more of the basic camera moves listed below:

Tilt. By moving the camera up and down, scenes move vertically.

Pans. Back-and-forth movement on a horizontal axis.

Truck and dolly. Trucking moves the camera assembly parallel to the scene being shot; dolly moves the camera closer to or farther away from the scene.

Handheld. The camera is carried by the operator, who follows the action.

Using any of these techniques to create a webcast video will greatly increase the required bandwidth. To avoid this problem, webcast developers should consider using *jump cuts,* or abrupt transitions between one stationary point of view and another. To reduce the jarring effect of jump cuts, a *cutaway shot* may be added. An example of a cutaway shot is shown in Figure 9.10. In the first case, two scenes of the same performer taken at different distances have been stitched together to create an abrupt transition. In the second case,

Figure 9.10 Using cutaway shots to reduce camera movement.

No Cutaway

Cutaway

an intermediary shot of the audience has been placed between the two cuts. This hides the transition and provides better context for the overall scene. In designing for these limitations, producers would do well to study very old film techniques (pre-1920) when the existing technology had limitations comparable to current videocasts.

Scene Composition

Scene design for the videocast's tiny screen requires considerable planning and effort. Unlike film and television, small objects in a videocast are not merely small, they're nondescript blurs. For this reason the paramount requirement for scene composition is to keep things big. For example, a face in a talking head videocast should fill at least half of the screen to remain recognizable. Any remaining area should be used carefully to introduce context, scale, or perspective to the scene. To create these images, webcasters need to work at close range to their subject more frequently than in other media. This subsection discusses the impact of these production requirements for the common videocast formats, which are also illustrated in Figure 9.11.

TIP · MUSIC VIDEO PRODUCTION

Almost by definition, music videos contain everything that is problematic for webcasts: fast camera movements, rapidly moving characters, and a demand for broadcast-quality audio. Changing any of these features deprives the video of the things that make it interesting to the audience. Taking this into account, webcasters have little option other than trying to reduce bandwidth. Some videos compress well using codecs that retain motion and compromise clarity. This may be most appropriate for music videos of live performances. The more common alternative is to use a slide show approach with only an occasional frame change run over the soundtrack. To implement this strategy, the developer should capture video with a larger screen size than that which will be used in the final webcast. After selecting particular frames, each image should be reduced using a graphics program such as Adobe Photoshop. This approach greatly increases the quality of each frame in the slide show. Since music videos are typically watched end to end, the developer should also consider inserting titles and credits along with the video itself.

Monologue

Scenes with monologues should be shot as straight-on close-ups of the performer—including the talking head, along with some of the neck and body. If the body is not visible, the viewer tends to see the head as an isolated object—an undesirable effect that makes the image appear more artificial. Head movements and gestures should be avoided, but changing facial expressions may be encouraged. Performers should be instructed to look at the camera, since off-camera gazes aimed at nothing are distracting to the viewer.

Dialogue

Scenes with dialogue should be shot with a single performer's head taking up somewhat less of the screen than for monologue. As shown in Figure 9.11, each

Figure 9.11 Scene composition for common videocast formats.

participant should be facing in the other's direction so it is clear they are speaking to each other. In scenes with more than one person, the director should position the performers very close so that their heads will be large enough to recognize.

Medium Shots

For medium shots, the camera operator should invoke the "rule of thirds," which places the most important element of the scene about a third of the way from the top. This is more efficient than simple centering (notice the extra space above the centered head in Figure 9.11), and it provides more room at the bottom of the frame to show the performer's body, background objects, or subtitles and captions. Since medium-distance shots tend to have more objects in them than monologues or dialogues, it is especially important to restrict movement. If movement must occur, only objects contributing to exposition or story development should change position. The jerky, handheld camera format often used in film and television should be avoided.

Distance Shots

Since webcast video does not contain enough resolution to adequately indicate faraway objects, the chief reason for using distance shots is to display a large object in the background. For example, a shot of a foreground object might include distant mountains to give an aura of spaciousness. In contrast, shots of many small distant objects (e.g., faces in a crowd) will be unrecognizable and distracting.

Camera Focus and Contrast

In general, webcasters will want to produce the sharpest, high-contrast image possible. Precise focusing is necessary to achieve this effect. Since it is difficult to keep very close objects in focus, the camera operator should maintain a moderate distance of a few feet from the subject. If the action moves rapidly between close and distant points, the camcorder should have a macro lens that allows rapid flips between preset close-up and distance focus positions. If scenes are shot outdoors, contrast may be improved by putting a large shade over the lens to reduce glare.

 MANUAL FOCUS

To manually focus using a zoom lens, set the camcorder to maximum zoom, get the best focus possible, and zoom out to the desired setting. This ensures that shots will stay in focus as you zoom in and out. If this is not done, the camera will go out of focus when zoomed in.

Lighting

Correct illumination of a videocast is a major contributor to the professional look and feel of the production. Within the scene being filmed, light comes from objects and background; and the mix of lit and shadowed areas depends strongly on the angle and orientation of the light source. Correct lighting and background selection is an art in itself, which often requires help from experienced professionals. However, due to the relatively simple nature of most webcast videos, there are a small number of rules that act as guides for appropriate lighting in most situations. Figure 9.12 shows an example of a basic lighting pattern that might be used during a webcast.

Webcasters new to videocasting work may benefit greatly from studying independent video production. Resources on the web include Elite Video:

Figure 9.12 General-purpose videocast lighting setup.

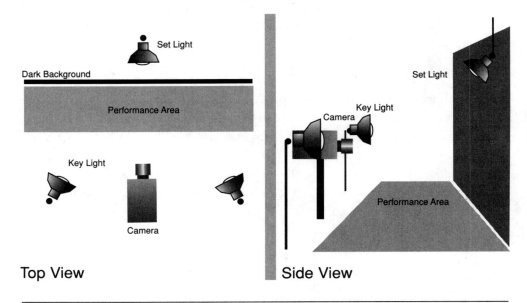

A Videographer's Resource Center (www.elitevideo.com) and Vidpro (www .vidpro.org). The latter runs online discussion groups and forums, and includes articles on lighting, product reviews, on-location production, and guides for writers/directors. An excellent series of books on independent video production have been authored by Dr. Peter Utz, whose web site (home.att.net/~peterutz/index.htm) features additional useful information. His "10 things to know" list for cameras, lenses, batteries, and tripods should be especially valuable to new videocasters.

Animacast Production Principles

While many videocast principles may be applied equally well to animacasts, there are some important differences that will affect the overall strategy used by the producers. Unlike video, animacast production typically does not have an analog component. Instead, each aspect of performance is developed directly in an all-digital authoring environment. In addition, animacast performers are

LIGHTING

The simplest lighting arrangement uses a single key light positioned either on the camera itself or side of the scene. This approach is simple to set up but tends to flatten the scene by removing shadows.

More sophisticated shoots use two lights placed on either side of the camera. The key light provides most of the total illumination, and an opposing fill light prevents shadows from being too dark.

Depth is created by adding a third set light positioned above and behind the scene. This light creates an illuminated edge around foreground objects that helps to separate them from the background.

Bright backgrounds or too much light streaming from behind the subject will cause the camera to compensate by darkening the overall scene, making foreground objects too dark to see.

Colored lights may be used for special effects, but webcasters should stay away from elaborate color schemes that are likely to reduce contrast or visibility in the small videocast screen. For this reason, it is also a good idea to avoid artistic shooting styles using color filters, contrast-reducing filters, or star filters that add patterns to the image.

created and controlled by the designers, leading to great simplification of many aspects of production. On the Smashing Ideas site (www.smashingideas.com), character costumes are critical, but colors and styles can be altered with a click of a mouse. This section considers the unique features of animacasts that webcasters are likely to encounter during development.

Team Design

Animacast teams usually recruit individuals experienced in traditional animation, CD-ROM, or game design. In general, these individuals have little trouble adapting their skills to webcast authoring tools such as Macromedia Flash. Since web-based animation is currently the only practical area for original storytelling, the webcasters should specifically look for writers experi-

Case Study: Smashing Ideas

URL: www.smashingideas.com
Contact: Glenn Thomas (glennt@smashingideas.com)

Smashing Ideas develops original web 'toons, including *Say Uncle* (also available on Shockrave at www.shockrave.com), *Louís Deli Dayze*, and *Bad Luck Boy* (shown in Figure 9.2). The company also develops web animation for other entertainment companies, advertising agencies, and web studios, including cartoons based on Dilbert, Peanuts, and South Park. Their avowed goal is simple: "to make people laugh."

Although parts of the production team resemble a traditional animation studio, other positions are completely new. For example, Smashing Ideas has a "bit rate checker" who looks at every frame of the animation and decides whether it can stream. In general, the team makeup includes more technical people than would be needed in a traditional animation studio. Animators come from traditional 2D character animation backgrounds and are trained to create animation for the web. According to Smashing Ideas, this involves some shifts in work patterns for traditional animators.

The production team works entirely in Macromedia Flash. If a client wants final output in Java, it is generated from a Flash movie. Currently, Java-based output runs slower than the Flash plug-in and has lower sound quality. Visuals for each 'toon are developed using a standard PC workstation with Wacom Technology (www.wacom.com) drawing tablets, Adobe Photoshop/Illustrator (www.adobe.com), and Macromedia FreeHand (www.macromedia.com). Sound is edited using

enced in plotting cartoon-style action. Traditional animators frequently originate from a nondigital background and often need computer training to adapt to the new medium.

Macromedia SoundEdit 16 and Sonic Foundry's Sound Forge (www.sfoundry.com). Standard animation storyboarding techniques are used in both paper and electronic format. If done in electronic format, they are created directly in Flash.

The company uses several methods to optimize animation for the web, relative to broadcast or CD-ROM platforms. Keeping bit rates low requires special attention to designing the characters and backgrounds, keeping lines clean throughout the animation and being extremely efficient with creating reusable characters and other symbols. The methods are similar to but much more rigorous than those used in traditional cel animation and CD-ROM; consequently, they took many months of ongoing work to develop. Without these efficient procedures, web animation is not economically feasible. As connection speeds improve, Smashing Ideas plans to increase sound quality and import bitmap graphics for areas that vector graphics have difficulty creating. Smashing Ideas does not try to integrate video and animation because the current version of Flash does not support streaming video, which would result in long user delays during file downloads.

Currently Smashing Ideas does not try to make money directly from its original works. Cartoons are offered online in order to create a fan base while the company waits for business models to develop. Since the commercial potential for streaming animation is still undefined, the company charges lower rates for web animation than for traditional media or CD-ROM.

Software Platforms

Macromedia's Flash program has become the de facto standard for streaming animation on the Internet, and the recent proposal of Flash as a standard to the World Wide Web Consortium (W3C) is likely to cement its position. Animators will want to design for the Flash 3 standard, which includes transparent overlay of animation on video, automatic calculation ("tweening") of frames intermediate between one scene and the next, and tools optimizing for low bandwidth. Macromedia has also integrated Flash with its FreeHand development tool, allowing users to export FreeHand files directly to the web.

With the rise of Flash, other solutions are becoming less popular for animacasts, though they continue to be used in special cases. Custom Java animation is often used for small streaming images, particularly in advertising banners. Headspace's Beatnik (www.headspace.com) has found a niche in providing interactive animated controls and background music on some sites. VRML remains more hope than reality, though recent moves in the forthcoming VRML '98 spec (see Chapter 2, "Developing a Webcast Strategy") shows that it has the potential to become a viable animacast medium.

Authoring Strategy

Despite the use of digital software tools, the strategy for producing animacasts follows the pattern laid down in traditional animation and continued in multimedia authoring platforms such as Director. To begin a project, developers will want to create a storyboard. Visual artists and character animators develop the look and feel of the project and plug it into the storyboard concept. Instead of bitmaps, the animators should explore a gradient fill technique, which creates smooth color transitions by storing formulas rather than bytes using the color model enabled by Flash. Not only do these download quickly, but the clear, luminous color of gradients imparts a unique style to animacasts. Unlike videocasts, low production values are not acceptable. Animacasts should try to meet or exceed the quality of animation carried by broadcast outlets, which means that equal attention will need to be paid to what the animation is saying as well as how it says it.

Movement in Animacasts

Animacasts (like videocasts) should not introduce more movement into the scene than necessary. In this case, bandwidth is less the issue than computing power. Since motion in animation is calculated rather than sent as a succession of images (bitmapped), fast movement may degrade the quality of a scene if it exceeds the software's calculating capacity. Large numbers of moving objects increase requirements for memory and processing power and may cause the user's computer to crash.

Scene Design and Transitions

Videocast transition constraints do not apply to animacasts. In these environments, the developer may apply scene transitions with only a modest increase in bandwidth. Animated virtual cameras are not restricted by the physics of mountings and easily produce complex, three-dimensional shifts in point of view. To increase interest in content, the animacast designer should explore various movements and scene transitions, and determine which of these can be supplied without overloading the user's connection.

Appropriate Internet Design

Streaming animators who migrated from broadcast may need to unlearn certain habits. In particular, developers should recognize the importance of interactivity and provide the user with some degree of control over the animacast. For example, many Flash-based web sites include high-volume soundtracks that play automatically upon page loading and cannot be turned off. This is a serious problem for the huge numbers of surfers who use the Internet at work. As attention-getting noises bleep from their systems, visitors quickly back out of the site and thereafter avoid it like the plague. A few companies such as Gabocorp Imaging (www.gabocorp.com) have recognized the need for interactivity and provide "sound off" buttons on their streaming animation demos. This makes them far more likely to attract the interest of business users exploring animation options. On the content side, animators should remember that the majority of their potential audience consists of adults for whom kid-oriented 'toons are interesting only as nostalgia or camp. The exploratory nature of the Internet should encourage animators to try out new ideas at both the design and content level.

In the traditional broadcast industry, there is little overlap between animation and video production. Current animacast studios have inherited this schism, but the Internet is likely to drive increasing convergence between the two kinds of

Advice to Animators from John Kricfalusi

John Kricfalusi of *Ren & Stimpy* fame recently began developing original animacasts for the web. Characters from *The Goddam George Liquor Program* shown in Figure 9.13 are currently being showcased on the web through a series of narrative web 'toons.

Figure 9.13 Spumco's George Liquor animacast character (www.spumco.com) begins his day.

production. As webcasting matures, it is likely that a new kind of production studio will emerge that treats live and animated webcasts as points on a continuum.

Advanced Production

Videocasters and animacasters who master the basics of creating and delivering their programming through the Internet are ready to consider additional aspects of production that will become increasingly important as Internet

Based on his experience on and off the web, Kricfalusi offered the following tips for young animators:

- Draw all the time to improve your skills. Don't use stylistic shortcuts such as wiggly lines, deliberately bad construction, and perspective to hide underdeveloped drawing skills.

- Check outstanding examples of good solid cartoon drawing such as the Warner Brothers cartoons of Bob Clampett (www.cartoon-factory.com/wb_bc.html). Try to draw the characters exactly the way they appear in these cartoons, and compare your drawings with the ones in the film to try spotting the differences. Then draw the same pose again, trying to get it even closer to the original. As you struggle to draw exactly like the old guys, you'll learn their tricks.

- Analyze the work of animators from the golden age of animation. When you see animation that you like, study it, still-frame through it on video, and try to figure out what it is that makes it great. By studying older cartoons, you'll discover drawing techniques, timing, and ways of depicting convincing motion that you can apply to your own work.

- The best book on animation is also one of the least expensive: Preston Blair's *Cartoon Animation* (Walter Foster, 1995). Everything an animator needs to know is in that book.

speed improves. Since increased bandwidth will encourage longer video with larger screen sizes, production principles that would pass unnoticed in a small-screen, 30-second clip will be critical to the webcast's success. This section considers some of these advanced production principles. While they may have less applicability to the current generation of streaming video and animation, developers who begin working with them will have a competitive advantage as the Internet increases in speed.

Continuity and Anticipation

In order to retain audience interest, the elements of an animacast or videocast must have logically consistent behaviors and appearance from one scene to the next. This means that lighting, camera shots, storyboards, and scene composition must always be checked for continuity. This is particularly important for videocasts, which are frequently assembled from several scenes shot at different times. For example, consider a video following the actions of a person at a workbench. Unless the positions of tools on the bench are carefully noted and adjusted, scenes shot at different times may show them jumping around in a highly unrealistic manner. Other continuity mistakes include shooting parts of the same scene at different times of the day, instant clothing changes, and background objects that magically appear and disappear. To ensure continuity, the producer and/or director of the videocast should determine in advance where potential problems could arise and plan accordingly. Large productions may require a dedicated continuity editor who checks recorded material.

One useful production method to augment scene continuity is anticipation. In this strategy, the end of the each scene is laid out in a way that prepares the audience for the next one. As an example, a video production team could easily apply anticipation to a scene that has a performer enter a crowded room. In the first scene, the director would show the crowd to the audience. As the scene ends, heads would turn to look at the door. The point of view would then cut to the performer opening the door. This strategy is especially prominent in animation. Classic animators deliberately distort characters and objects to create anticipation, as when a cartoon character elastically stretches in a direction it is about to walk.

Presentation

Videocasts and animacasts (like audiocasts) may run independently of the web, but they are usually integrated within a larger site. While character generators and closed captions may be applied directly to video, the developers will probably want to supply this information via the associated web pages. By using the <embed> extension to standard HTML, it is possible to create informational pages with integrated audio/player controls. Web pages may also provide a graphic border that helps to distract the user from the size of the videocast window. An example of this technique is shown in Figure 9.14 for SonicNet's Streamland. In this case, the page design improves the user's experience of the video.

Animacasts do a better job of providing stand-alone experiences independent of the web. Unlike video, animation authoring software provides direct support for integrating high-resolution text into the production. Instead of creating HTML pages, developers may elect to use Macromedia Flash and/or Java to create pseudo-web pages containing virtually no HTML at all. In this case, the web browser simply provides a player window for the animation, which alternates between a static page and animated narrative. Flash and other animation platforms have support for standard hyperlinking, so the developer may elect to construct some parts of their animation to appear as web pages. An example of this approach is found on the Smashing Ideas site. As shown in Figure 9.15, star-shaped and rectangular hyperlink buttons, generated using Flash, connect the user to other parts of the web site. The larger size of animacast windows also makes it practical to use standard video titling techniques such as character crawls down the screen.

Figure 9.14 SonicNet's Streamland (www.streamland.com).

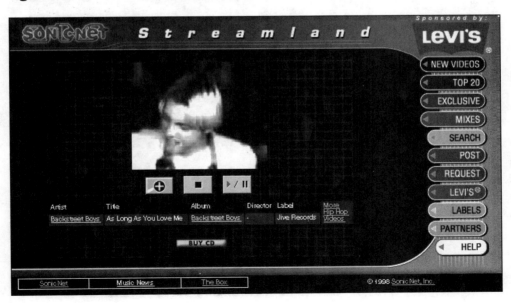

Interactivity

Current generations of Internet video and animation authoring software allow individual frames or scenes to be hyperlinked to other video or web pages. This may greatly increase the educational value of a videocast. For example, a videocast featuring celebrities in a talk show format might link each performer to official and fan web sites or connect directly to a commerce site featuring entertainment products. Educators might create running commentary on a historical film, complete with links to the director, studio, and performers. To make this strategy effective, the developers should focus on a few web sites whose information provides context to broad areas of the video or animation. Since loading a web site may take several seconds, the developers might insert a pause into the broadcast or create the link in a relatively monotonous area of

Figure 9.15 Smashing Ideas (www.smashingideas.com).

© *Copyright Smashing Ideas Animation 1998.*

the webcast. This will give the viewer time to examine the web content without missing crucial information in the video and/or animation.

The next level of interactivity puts the audience in contact with the webcasters. Following the precedent set by talk radio, the producers should consider allowing "backtalk." It is not necessary to support upstream audio and video signals from viewers to accomplish this. For example, an educational videocast featuring a panel discussion might include an email link that forwards questions directly to the instructors. During later portions of the webcast, the performers can read and answer individual messages. This form of webcast puts a face on the current featureless world of Internet chat and discussion groups.

As webcasting becomes a recognized medium in its own right, special production techniques specific to the Internet are likely to become widespread. It is easy to see that unique Internet features such as interactivity and multimedia will have an impact on production, but it is difficult to predict its future course. In one scenario, the fast jumps users make between web sites may push production to shorter and shorter program formats, and scene transitions within a performance might come to resemble web surfing. Future discussions of continuity should consider the audience's ability to control point of view within the story. Interactivity may blur the boundary between performance and authoring. For example, future animacasts may include software-controlled characters (*avatars*) for live performers.

Providing Audience Support

Videocasts and animacasts require more customer support than any other type of webcast because the required media players must be downloaded by the user and often require additional configuration in order to function properly. The complexity of many videocast sites—combining Java, Flash, RealVideo, and other programs—makes it essential that users test their computer's toolkit prior to entering the site. An excellent test page for streaming multimedia has been created by Macromedia on its Shockrave site. As shown in Figure 9.16, complex JavaScript programming on the page displays a set of red or green lights indicating browser compatibility and whether any players or plug-ins need to be installed. While helpful, this approach does not always eliminate user problems. To accommodate audience queries, the videocast or animacast web site should have a hot button leading to a Frequently Asked Questions (FAQ) page, as well as email for direct customer support. Support of this kind is particularly important for pay-per-view webcasts.

Publicity and Promotion

Videocasts are good candidates for promotion when they provide unique and intimate access to content that is unavailable in broadcast. While a netpublicist might have trouble publicizing a repurposed television program, the guest appearance of a TV celebrity in a webcast is likely to generate interest. Animacasts have even greater promotion potential, since they provide a new experience for most Internet users. Even audience members familiar with the Internet are likely to be astonished at the quality of animacasts. For this reason, online promotion should include a hyperlink to a sample of animacast con-

Figure 9.16 Macromedia's Shockrave test site (shockrave.macromedia .com/plugins_test.html).

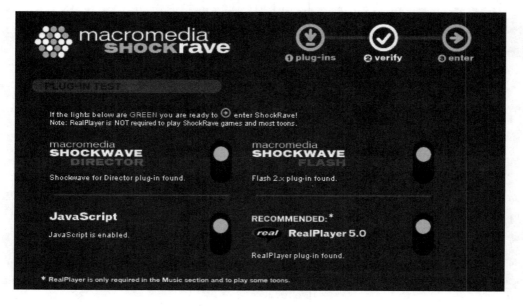

tent, along with detailed instructions for downloading and installing any required software. The storytelling quality possible with animacasts may also appeal to audiences more familiar with television and film programming, and may be suitable for offline publicity efforts. Sites that list and promote videocasts and animacasts are similar to those for audiocasts (Chapter 8, "Audiocasts"). In addition, many webcast ISPs will showcase their clients' videos to promote their own services.

Archiving Strategies

Unlike audiocasts, videocasts lend themselves to archiving and indexing via software available from Magnifi (www.magnifi.com). In general, these and other comparable programs are much too expensive ($50,000) to be implemented by independent webcasters. In addition, some archiving programs are unable to read streaming animation formats. In the absence of software-level indexing, webcasters will need to develop a manual archiving strategy. In most cases, this is accomplished with the use of descriptive text (including the running time for the archived clip) and a thumbnail image from the webcast itself. To avoid graphics-heavy pages with lengthy download times, webcasters should spread links to large archives over multiple web pages. Generally, a single page should have no more than 100Kb of graphics associated with it. This is roughly equivalent to ten-160 × 120 images containing 256 or fewer colors. The pages should also have a description of the software necessary to play the webcast and provide links to the players.

Estimating Costs

It is intuitively obvious that creating video or animation is a more complex and expensive process than developing audio or static web pages. In addition to the requirements for precise control of content creation, it is necessary to pay more attention to writing and layout than is necessary for other kinds of webcasts. Development also takes more time—and time is money! Typically, a few hours of webcast video cost several thousand dollars to develop, not including web design and promotion. Webcasters producing animated web 'toons should check current rates for traditional animation production and assume comparable or slightly lower rates. Actual rates may vary widely, largely due to the

Case Study: InterVU

URL: www.intervu.com
Contact: Chuck Apotolas (sales@intervu.net)

According to Chuck Apostolas of the webcast ISP InterVU, videocast production requires participation from multiple sources. In most cases, the actual video shoot should be handled by a local video production company. Typical costs for a small company specializing in corporate or venue-based video and shooting in Hi-8 format (Chapter 3,"Webcast Equipment and Authoring Environments") runs in the $750–$1,000 range for events lasting a few hours. This charge usually includes editing costs. Once the recorded video is ready, companies such as InterVU typically charge rates similar to the following example of a four-hour webcast with 500 server streams:

500 streams (1 hour setup, 5 hours online):	$891.00
Encoding engineer/encoding assistant:	$700.00
Encoding stations:	$300.00
Web site integration:	$375.00
Crew per diem:	$160.00
Total: ~$2,500.00 + video production =	~$3,500.00

If the videocast requires a leased line or satellite connection to deliver the signal from a remote location, additional costs of several hundred dollars should be budgeted.

newness of webcasting and the lack of standards. As the field matures, costs are likely to move closer to (but remain lower than) comparable work in film and television. Since prices for these services are currently in a state of rapid flux, the developers should consider contacting a webcast ISP such as InterVU (www.intervu.com) to get a quote for their particular production.

Next . . .

As videocasts and animacasts improve in quality, the experience provided by Internet webcasting will inevitably begin to challenge other broadcast media. As this time approaches, interested parties from all aspects of telecommunications, entertainment, and performance will wonder where webcasting fits into other digital and interactive ventures on the information superhighway. The final chapter of this book considers trends in webcasting and tries to define the probable course of events relevant to developers planning a long-term presence in this area.

PART FOUR

THE FUTURE OF THE WEBCAST INDUSTRY

THE FUTURE OF THE WEBCASTING INDUSTRY 10

T he art of webcasting is rapidly moving from its experimental era and is well on its way to becoming a true mass medium. Previously dismissed as a technology with little practical application, webcasting is finally being taken seriously by web developers and traditional broadcasters alike. The next few years will be crucial for the medium as hardware and software standardize and connection speeds improve. What can webcasters, particularly those working with original content, expect during the next several years? Thus far, the discussion in this book has emphasized technological and organizational challenges facing webcasters as they seek to develop a viable product or service. This chapter is more speculative and attempts to predict where developers might best concentrate their efforts in order to remain competitive in the field. It is divided into sections considering technology, content, convergence with other broadcast media, and the potential for competition between true webcasting and various data-enabled broadcast strategies such as *interactive television (ITV)*. The chapter continues with an exploration of unique web technologies, such as teleoperated cameras, that continue to define the unique potential of webcasting relative to other broadcast technologies. Legal and political issues relevant to webcasting are also considered. A graphic summary of the trends considered in the chapter is provided in Figure 10.1.

Figure 10.1 Webcasting trends.

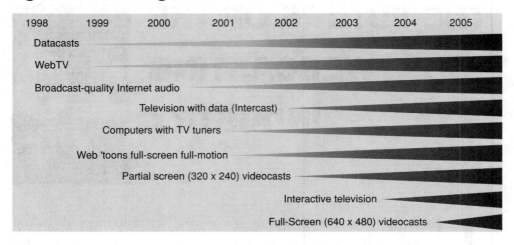

Technological Advances

Bandwidth remains the overriding concern of all webcasters, since delivering real-time content requires the fastest connections available. Widespread use of videocasting will be impractical until audiences have 100Kbps or faster connections. Audio, while able to run with lower bandwidth, benefits greatly from faster connections and suffers less virtual static and dropouts. To support the needed speed increase, advances must be made in end-user computers, Internet connections, and media server hardware. Internet reliability must also be improved to reduce signal dropouts, which are a universal feature of current webcasts. Responding to this need, many groups (often working at cross-purposes by creating incompatible standards and software) continue to develop strategies to push connectivity into the 100Kbps range necessary for broadband webcast. The following is a list of key points necessary to achieve this goal, along with an estimate of their introduction into the Internet community:

> **High-speed consumer connections.** After several years of slow growth, bandwidth is on the rise. Internet Service Providers (ISPs), telecommunications companies, and hardware manufacturers are implementing hardware and software solutions promising 10 to 1,000 times

the speed of existing analog modems. ISDN access is now available in most large cities, and a small but growing number of users have access to DSL (digital subscriber line) or cable modem technologies. Companies such as Ascend Communications (www.ascend.com .au/906.html), and ISPs such as Epoch Internet (www.eni.net/ death2dialup/faq/html), are rapidly making access to high-speed connections a reality. A representative example of the serious push for increased bandwidth is provided by the initiative being developed by GTE Network Services (www.gte.net). The initial version of the service will require a GTE representative to install a small "splitter" to separate voice and data traffic on the local phone lines along with additional wiring. Customers will pay $60 for installation and $140 for complete service. A "splitterless" service following standards developed by the *Universal ADSL Working Group (UAWG)* should be available in 1999.

Recent studies by Kagan Associates (www.kagan.com) and Kinetic Strategies (www.cabledatacomnews.com) predict that cable Internet will be in more than a million homes in the United States by 1999, in comparison to various DSL and other phone line-based technologies, which will reach only 100,000 homes. By 2006, the reports predict 39 million cable data connections versus 25 million DSL lines, with the latter concentrated among business users. Widespread adoption of cable will be supported by the *Data Over Cable Service Interface Specification (DOCSIS)* (www.cablemodem.com), a standard for developing hardware at the end user's and cable operator's locations. Despite these promising advancements, the majority of users will not have access to this technology. In mid-1997, the GUV7 survey found that 64 percent of users have 33.6 or slower modem connections. Jupiter Communications (www.jup.com) recently predicted that in the year 2000 only 20 percent of Internet access would use high-speed technology. In the near future, webcasting will continue to be confined by the 56K download limit imposed by analog modems.

High-speed equipment. Supporting increases in available bandwidth, computer power continues to rise at a steady pace. Consumer equipment selling for under $1,000 in the United States has the

---

capacity to process CD-quality webcast audio and partial screen (e.g., 320×240) videocasts. Typical midrange media servers may support several hundred simultaneous connections, and recent increases in chip speed should drive this figure into the thousands during the next few years.

Compression technology. Codecs that rely on new algorithms may provide modest increases in the quality of low-bit rate (less than 200Kbps) webcast communications. As the power of end-users' computers increases, it becomes more practical to use bandwidth-reducing algorithms, which require extremely high levels of computer power to be effective. Examples of such technology include fractal-based compression, already supported in RealNetworks RealVideo, and wavelet technology planned for the MPEG-4 multimedia standard (drogo.cselt .stet.it/mpeg). Use of more powerful coding and decoding will result in a significant reduction in the bandwidth required to deliver webcasts.

Based on industry trends, webcasters should continue to design for the low-end of Internet connectivity if they plan to attract a general audience. For the next few years, the majority of computer users will continue to have modem-level access. In some cases, webcasters may decide to develop high- and low-bandwidth versions of their products. After 2005, the percentage of high-bandwidth users will constitute a mass audience, and many webcasters will concentrate exclusively in that area. Well before that time, developers will be able to use high-bandwidth Internet connections while developing webcast content in geographically dispersed production studios. For example, Liquid Audio (www.liquidaudio.com) recently announced Liquid Express, a system that uses the Internet for preview, delivery, and archiving of broadcast-quality audio. Both DreamWorksSKG (www.dreamworksgames.com) and Warner Bros. Feature Animation (www.wbanimation.com) are using this technology.

Advances in Webcast Content

A second area of rapid growth and change within the webcast industry is content. To date, content has been dramatically limited by the bandwidth available to the typical Internet user. This appears likely to change with new initiatives by traditional media companies as well as web-based startups such as Broadcast.com (www.broadcast.com), the Alternative Entertainment Network (www.aentv.com), and LA Live (www.lalive.com). Webcasters are also moving beyond the traditional broadcast model for content delivery and exploring on-demand viewing, animacasts, datacasts, and integration between Internet and broadcast programming. As the content area grows, individuals interested in original content are finding a broadening audience for their efforts. The following lists the major areas of webcast content development that are likely to be important during the next few years:

On-demand broadcast media archives. In April 1998, NBC announced its VideoSeeker service (www.videoseeker.com), which was specifically created as an on-demand streaming video archive. The site, shown in Figure 10.2, provides access to short articles, news reports, and clips from well-known NBC programs including *The Tonight Show*. Formed with a partnership with webcast ISP InterVU (www.intervu.com), the site began serving 12,000 simultaneous video

Figure 10.2 NBC's VideoSeeker service (www.videoseeker.com).

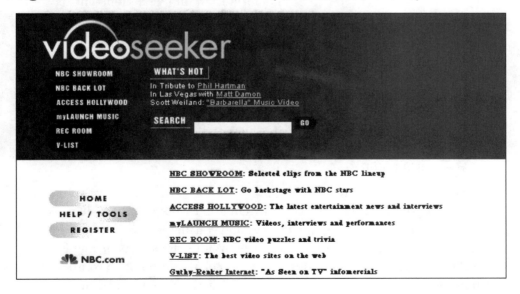

streams in April 1998. CNN (www.cnn.com) is developing a web site with a huge on-demand archive featuring clips from its *Headline News* service called CNN VideoSelect. Joining companies such as Videodome (www.videodome.com), Guthy-Renker (www.guthy-renker.com) offers on-demand access to thousands of infomercials.

Original webcast content. As webcasting becomes more widely accepted, more original content will be developed. Companies including American Interactive Media (www.aime-inc.com) are developing proprietary original content that supplement repurposed broadcasts. Its ComedyNet service, shown in Figure 10.3, is not expected to make money for at least three years, but it will allow webcasters to develop sufficient experience with the medium to become leaders.

Narrative storytelling using webcasts. For the near future, video-cast storytelling is likely to be little more than a curiosity or, in some cases, a poor alternative for traditional broadcast. Webcast animation, particularly real-time streaming solutions such as Macromedia Flash, is a far more likely area for Internet storytelling familiar from film and television. As a medium, animation has concentrated to a greater extent on shorts than on live action. This is valuable because shorter narratives are more compatible with fast-paced Internet surfing habits. As full-motion, full-screen video begins to appear through the Internet, some expect a television-like experience to be the norm. However, it is dangerous to predict the easy triumph of television-style narratives in the new medium, especially considering the rapid changes in content, consumer interests, and technology itself. It is possible that the move to Internet broadcast will increase the trend away from one-way storytelling to interactive world-building.

Live webcast. With technology and connectivity in a primitive state, live webcasts remain more difficult than other webcasts to produce. A recent example of the rapid advances and concurrent problems with live webcasts was illustrated by the 1998 White House Easter Egg Roll webcast, which was provided through the collaboration of 35 companies including EarthLink Networks (www.earthlink.net) and Sun

Figure 10.3 American Interactive Media's ComedyNet (www.comedynet.com).

Microsystems (www.sun.com). The live event collected feeds from 10 cameras and passed them through four T1 lines running from the White House to EarthLink's home in Pasadena, California. Additional mirror sites were provided by the Teleport Communications Group (www.tcg.com). The total capacity was 300,000 streams—double the available capacity of the Mars Pathfinder (mpfwww.jpl.nasa.gov/default.html) web site in July 1997. To reduce problems with installing webcast player software, the Vosaic server and Java-based client were used. The technology was impressive, but many users reported extremely low webcast quality—sometimes consisting of little more than occasional snippets of audio. In the near term, live webcasts are more likely to be effective when staged for smaller audiences.

Advertising. Some groups expect substantial growth in streaming media advertising, and companies such as InterVU (www.intervu .com) already specialize in this area. Development of webcast advertising is being driven by marketers who are attracted to the potential to deliver their messages television-style, rather than competing with information on a web page. In reality, the future of passive webcast advertising is in doubt. VDO (www.vdo.net) conducted a series of experiments in 1996 with streaming advertising, which were largely considered a failure. Some groups have predicted that this attitude will change as a more general audience comes onto the Internet; but it seems equally likely that this group will also adopt the behavior of current surfers and take exception to webcast ads. Advertisers may have better luck with on-demand advertising archives provided by Mediadome (www.mediadome.com) and others pioneering on-demand infomercial archive. Audience members using these services are much more likely to follow-up on the promotion; and, by giving users control, their opinion of advertising is likely to undergo a change for the better.

Webcasting has sometimes been criticized for its preoccupation with retrofitting content developed for other media. Instead of trying to reinvent the virtual wheel, webcasters interested in developing original broadcast for the Internet should take a long look at Internet-specific technologies such as animacasts and datacasts. Unlike audiocasts and videocasts, these formats offer an experience impossible to duplicate in other media. Animacasting also deserves particular attention. As more animators discover that they may webcast their work without a large media distributor, they are likely to move to the Internet. It is possible that animacasts may become the primary area of creative animation development in the near future. Datacasts are even more unique and have virtually no parallel in other media. If the response to recent datacasts from NASA space probes is any indication, significant potential exists for a mass audience. In business applications, real-time datacasts and wordcasts of stock prices, discussions, and ongoing activity within the organization promise to be major areas of growth for the webcast industry.

Convergence

Throughout the discussions in this book, it has been impossible to consider one form of webcast without making mention of others. This is due to the Internet's capacity for integrating various media under a common digital standard. This form of convergence, particularly with respect to telephone and television technologies, has been widely discussed in the press. As developers of streaming audio, video, animation, and datacast services, webcasters are at the cutting edge of convergence. This section discusses several areas where convergence issues are particularly relevant to webcasters. It also identifies areas where convergence is less likely, and where webcasting will have less of an impact in the near term.

Media Standards

A welcome trend in the infrastructure of webcasting is the reduction of dozens of incompatible media formats to a single standard. Due to a combination of software giveaways and marketing muscle, Microsoft NetShow (www.microsoft.com/netshow) and RealNetworks RealPlayer (www.real.com) are likely to become the sole surviving webcast standards for audio and video; and Macromedia Flash (www.macromedia.com) will probably form the basis for most web-based animation. Formats for multimedia are further away from convergence, with Java-based authoring systems such as GEO Emblaze (www.emblaze.com) competing with Shockwave Flash. Until recently, all these standards were proprietary, which made it impossible to write third-party tools capable of manipulating their media files. With the recent appearance of W3C's (www.w3.org) Synchronized Multimedia Integration Language (SMIL) streaming multimedia standard and Macromedia's proposal to make Flash .swf files a public format, it is likely that the future holds a single open standard for streaming media comparable to HTML for the web. This unified format could drastically decrease the complexity of current webcast production, which typically supports several incompatible media formats.

Cross-Promotion

According to Showtime Networks (www.showtimeonline.com), 40 percent of online subscribers have their TVs in the same room as their computers. This makes cross-promotion between the webcast and broadcast one of the hottest areas driving convergence. Interactive Internet services, such as chat and discussion groups, have long been part of broadcast-associated shows, and webcasts are showing up on these sites in increasing frequency. Many broadcasters who created web sites for television programs have begun reserving a subset of unique content exclusively for the Internet. As an example of this trend, in early 1998, the TBS Superstation (www.tbssuperstation.com) ran a marathon of classic James Bond films. During the marathon, the associated web site featured wordcasts providing a running commentary on each movie.

Web-television hybrids such as WebTV (www.webtv.net) provide additional avenues for cross-promotion. With its ability to split the screen between television and the Internet, WebTV provides a major opportunity to compare the merits of broadcast and webcast. Certain broadcast-associated web sites such as E! Entertainment Television Network (www.eonline.com) get almost all their traffic from WebTV, indicating that the platform may play a major role in the future of the Internet. In order for this kind of cross-promotion to grow, current incompatible web-television standards will have to consolidate. In support of this goal, Intel is promoting its Open Digital Broadcast Initiative (www.intel.com/pressroom), and both Intel and Microsoft have developed agreements designed to integrate WebTV with Intel's Intercast system.

Television Content Development

Webcasts are frequently serving as a proving ground for developing traditional broadcast content. In a striking example from January 1998, NBC (www.nbc.com) moved a character from the online series *Homicide: Second Shift* (www.homicide.com) into the parent television show, *Homicide: Life on the Street*. The web site uses streaming audio and an ambient video slide show to tell its story. In its short period of operation, the online version has proven a valuable and low-cost method for developing new characters and scenarios. The webcast forms part of a major effort by NBC Digital Productions to develop custom online content based on broadcast—rather than simply repurposing existing shows for the computer screen.

Independent developers may take advantage of broadcast/Internet synergy by creating shows for public-access cable television. While commercial products and services cannot be sold through public access, the system provides a way to mix webcasting and broadcasting within the reach of virtually any developer. Webcast integration, particularly with calendars and on-demand archives of old shows, will make content developed for public access more accessible and useful to its audience. More about the unique potential of public access television may be found at the Public Access Awareness Association site (www.publicaccess.org).

Webcast/Radio Integration

Web-radio integration is proceeding much more rapidly than television, largely because the smaller production demands of audio webcasts make it practical for independents to develop and/or repurpose their own programming. Larger web sites such as Broadcast.com (www.broadcast.com) and Virtual Radio (www .microserve.net/vradio) also provide a means for radio to immediately distribute information to the worldwide Internet audience. In addition to traditional radio, web-only radio systems such as Better Living through Radio (www.bltradio.com) and DiskJockey.com (www.discjockey.com) are carrying the model even further. Webcast radio will likely provide the chief growing point of original music and other audio content in the next few years. The deregulation instigated by the Telecommunications Act of 1996 (thomas.loc.gov/cgi-bin/bdquery/z?d104:s.652) has resulted in buyouts of thousands of independent radio stations by larger companies. Once stations are part of a single network, the diversity of programming usually drops. Coupled with a 20-year decline in listener audiences, broadcast radio is likely to suffer serious competition from Internet-based alternatives. A sign of this trend is that some radio stations are abandoning their traditional broadcast systems to concentrate solely on the Internet.

Webcast/Film Integration

The prospects for early integration of webcasting with film are much dimmer than those for radio and television. Despite the early appearance of studio and movie-specific URLs, film content on the Internet has remained largely promotional and informational rather than providing aspects of the film experience itself. There is an enormous gap in the experience of a wide-screen feature and tiny jerky video that is characteristic of today's Internet. Bandwidth increases expected in the next five years will not address the quality level (10Mbps/second) needed to deliver on-demand film content through the Internet. What little integration occurs is likely to proceed in the independent film market. Promotional teasers for independent films, provided as on-demand archives, offer the potential for filmmakers to make audience contact and direct sales independent of traditional distributors. In the future, webcasting and film may combine in an unusual way. To bypass the bandwidth problems inherent in creating the moviehouse experience, webcast content might be provided as an adjunct to DVD (digital videodisc) data. In this hybrid system, the videocast might consist of streaming multimedia running in parallel with DVD data—providing captions, commentary, context, backdrops, or "filler" between scenes stored on the videodisc. DVD also allows several soundtracks to be recorded with the video. It is possible that new alternate DVD soundtracks might be delivered to consumers as streaming on-demand wordcasts.

Convergence, while a real event, should not be viewed as the single goal of webcast development. It is far from certain that other media will simply disappear as computers acquire the power to provide digital emulation of their formats. Television did not completely replace radio, and 150-year-old telegraphic signals are still used in specialized situations. Rather than swallowing other media whole, it is more likely that webcasting will develop a unique style and content suite—possibly oriented to broadcast information that gains value when combined with data. In this environment, certain forms of broadcast (e.g., "pure" entertainment) may remain unaffected by webcasts while others merge with the medium.

Alternatives to Webcasting

Throughout this book, attention has been paid to streaming media technology specific to the Internet as opposed to the various interactive TV (ITV) strategies that embed Internet and other data forms within a traditional broadcast signal. This has been done because most developers work independently of the current broadcast industry, and because alternatives to webcasting take a substantially different approach to content, audience, and delivery. Despite repeated failures, some groups remain convinced that ITV technologies are the wave of the future for data and broadcast content. This section considers

ITV in terms of its likely future interaction with the webcast world, as well as its potential for long-term viability alongside a broadband Internet.

Video-on-demand. Originally introduced by phone and cable companies in the early 1990s, video-on-demand strategies have been reactivated by the promise of high-speed connectivity using cable modems and DSL-equipped phone lines. Scientific Atlanta's Explorer 2000 (www.sciatl.com), shown in Figure 10.4, provides a typical example of this service. Offering more power than many personal computers, the set-top box uses a 54MIPS (millions of instructions per second) Sun Microsparc processor running PersonalJava software (java.sun.com/products/personaljava/index.html). In addition to video, the set-top box supports email, web browsing, electronic commerce Internet telephony, and video-on-demand.

The Echostar Communications Corp (www.echostar.com) initiative demonstrates another approach to video-on-demand. This system uses satellite transmissions to push 20 to 30 one-way Internet channels of topic-specific content to end users. Following the model developed for Internet push technology, data is delivered at 400Kbps and is intercepted by a set-top box, which filters a subset of data requested by the user. The resulting video quality is lower than broadcast but higher than that typically sent through the Internet. Either a $400 set-top box or a custom PC card may be used to receive the signal. Content is being provided by SimplyTV (www.simplytv.net), a web-based service with a library of 1,000 programs. A few companies, such as Wink Communications (www.wink.com), have continued to develop strategies that supply limited amounts of non-Internet data within the vertical blanking interval (VBI) of a standard television broadcast. Requiring little additional equipment or expense, the Wink system creates simple push-button options linked to broadcast shows and commercials. It currently provides infrastructure to CBS and NBC to broadcast interactive information.

Web-TV hybrids and initiatives. In direct opposition to data-enabled television, computer manufacturers and software developers are trying to bring TV into the computer. On the hardware side, this

Figure 10.4 The Explorer 2000 set-top box.

requires the use of plug-in cards to receive television signals, or developing computers that masquerade as set-top boxes. These systems provide access to traditional computer software and technology while offering varying degrees of compatibility with data-enabled television. The result of current efforts is that many computers will have TV tuners installed by 1999, and these systems will be able to show webcast and broadcast side by side on the same monitor. Integration will depend on including additional components that allow the television and Internet signal to influence each other, such as those provided by Intel's Intercast (www.intercast.com) system.

Despite millions of dollars being spent by broadcasters, the success of ITV-style content is not assured—even when measured against the decidedly more primitive output of standard Internet webcasts. Several factors make it difficult for these systems to compete in an Internet-aware world. Price constitutes one barrier to acceptance. With price tags of $400 or more, set-top boxes will face heavy competition from low-cost computers whose entire motherboards have been reduced to a single chip. Systems such as that provided by Wink Technologies are cheap but are so limited that they will not draw users already experienced with the Internet. Standards problems also are inhibiting growth. Currently, the industry is split between systems running Sun's Java language (www.sun.com) and those using Microsoft's Windows CE operating system. Some vendors such as TCI (www.tci.com) have announced set-top support for both platforms, but incompatibility and competition are sure to limit growth in this market. The fundamental problem with these projects remains the same: the definition of true user interactivity. ITV models assume consumers are willing to follow a narrow channel of selections predigested by the provider. This approach is attractive to marketers but may be rejected by the consumer, particularly when contrasted with the enormous content diversity of the Internet. The failure of push technologies to remake the web in 1997 should serve as a caution to groups ignoring webcast in favor of alternate solutions.

Legal and Political Issues

A final but very important area of interest to webcasting's future concerns the various legal and political consequences of streaming media production. Currently the Internet is almost completely unregulated, leaving webcasters relatively free to experiment with the medium independent of constraints found in traditional broadcasting. As the Internet becomes part of everyday life, interest in various forms of licensing and regulation will increase. Key areas include updated licensing and performance rights applied specifically to webcast content, access to the Internet by the public, access by persons with disabilities, and bandwidth allocation for the public versus established broadcasters.

Licensing and performance rights. A key issue for audiocast developers is how traditional performance rights enjoyed by copyright owners will be applied to the Internet. Currently, traditional performance rights organizations such as ASCAP, shown in Figure 10.5, and BMI

Figure 10.5 The American Society of Composers and Performers (ASCAP) (www.ascap.com).

(www.bmi.com) have signed a variety of agreements with Internet radio providers. In some cases, sites simply report web play and pay performance royalties. In other cases, the agencies have tied payment to a fixed percentage of advertising revenue generated to the site—without regard to the particular playlist. With such divergent approaches, the final state of webcast licensing is in doubt. As audience numbers rise, other groups such as copyright and artist organizations are likely to seek payment from webcasters as well. Currently, some webcasters do not consider performance rights, while others have signed licensing agreements and report their webcasts as performances. A few groups are even considering paying performers directly and bypassing rights agencies altogether. Differences between webcasts and traditional performance media are likely to result in novel approaches to the issue by webcasters and copyright agencies alike.

Content accessibility. An emerging area that webcasters will need to address in the future is content accessibility. Educational sites may be limited in their ability to deploy audiocast and videocasts because these media are inaccessible to individuals with certain disabilities. In these cases, developers may eventually be required to provide an equivalent presentation via text pages or a streaming wordcast. Vision-impaired students may also have difficulty navigating through web sites employing the latest streaming technology. Complex page designs making heavy use of Flash animation frustrate screen reader programs such as JAWs (www.hj.com), which is designed for the visually impaired. Developers interested in making their sites accessible to all visitors should check the guidelines available at the W3C Web Accessibility Initiative (www.w3 .org/WAI/). Certain HTML editors such as SoftQuad's HotMetal Pro (www.softquad.com) provide built-in accessibility checking. Microsoft also provides a comprehensive list of accessibility programs on its main site (www.microsoft.com/enable/catalog.htm).

Hardware accessibility. As increasing amounts of content are delivered by webcast systems, the issue of access will become more important. In the educational arena, many students do not have equipment capable of delivering webcast content. If content is provided via webcasts, these students may be forced to work on campus to complete courses. In the near term, webcasters should be prepared to create alternate presentations of their content that do not require streaming media. Long-term, the issue of access will affect everyone. Currently, telephone service in remote areas is maintained by taxing telecommunications. The Internet is currently tax-free, but this could change if it is perceived as endangering subsidies for universal access.

Bandwidth allocation for webcasting. As the demand for audio and video delivered over the Internet increases, bottlenecks will begin to form that inhibit traffic flow. To anticipate this change, many network hardware groups are developing bandwidth allocation protocols for the next generation of gigabit network hardware destined for the Internet. These strategies, including Reservation Protocol (RSVP) implemented by Cisco Systems (www.cisco.com) and TCP Shaping implemented by Packeteer (www.packeteer.com), all prioritize individual data packets according to their type and destination. This initiative is being touted as a way to improve the quality of online communication, but it risks splitting the current democratic world of Internet access into people who can afford to reserve bandwidth and those who cannot. This may pose a serious threat to the long-term success of independent webcasting. For this reason, webcast content developers should stay informed of current developments in bandwidth allocation and be ready to oppose exclusive deals that appropriate the public Internet for use by a few major broadcasters.

Conclusion

Trends in industry and society leave little doubt that webcasting is destined to play a major role in the future growth of the Internet. Hardware and software are at an early stage of development, but developers have already used existing technology to lay the groundwork for an exciting new medium. As Internet use grows, webcasting will become more common and will produce a variety of services ranging from classic broadcasting to fully interactive, teleoperated webcasts. As the medium grows and adapts, it is important that developers find ways to integrate their own production strategies with changes in the larger arena. They must avoid treating the Internet as an unusual radio or television, while selecting the features of these media that may enhance the digital world. Most important, webcasters must develop an appropriate vision of their content goals and apply these to make webcasting a useful and exciting experience.

WHAT'S ON THE
WEB SITE?

The web site associated with this book (www.wiley.com/compbooks/novak) provides access to key webcast locations on the Internet, as well as links to the media players and plug-ins required to receive webcast content. All of the hyperlinks listed in the text of this book may be found on the web site. These links contain a wide range of webcast-related information including hardware, software, webcast production companies, webcast ISPs, e-commerce systems, standards organizations, and sites dealing with copyright/licensing issues. Links to the case studies are also provided on the site and are detailed below.

Freeware, Shareware, and Trial Versions

Freeware is free software that is distributed by disk, through BBS systems, and the Internet. There is no charge for using it, and it can be distributed freely as long as it is used according to the license agreement included with it. Many webcast media players are distributed as freeware.

Shareware (also known as user supported software) is a method of distributing software created by individuals or companies too small to make inroads into the more conventional retail distribution networks. The authors of shareware retain all rights to the software under the copyright laws while still allowing free distribution. This gives users the chance to freely obtain and try out software to see if it fits their needs. Shareware should not be confused with *public domain* software, even though both types of software are often obtained from the same sources.

If you continue to use shareware after trying it out, you are expected to register your use with the author and pay a registration fee. What you get in return depends on the author, but it may include a printed manual, free updates, telephone support, etc.

Many commercial web sites provide *trial versions* of their software. Unlike shareware, the trial software is usually limited in functionality, or has a built-in "timeout" after which it will no longer function. Trial versions allow you to test expensive commercial products on your system before committing to a purchase.

In order to access webcast content from the sites listed in this book, visit the following resource areas on the web to collect media player software (these sites are also listed on the web site):

Liquid Audio (player/server)	www.liquidaudio.com
Macromedia (sound and image editors/Flash animation)	www.macromedia.com
Microsoft NetShow (media player/server)	www.microsoft.com/netshow
QuickTime (Macintosh/Windows video player)	quicktime.apple.com
Real Networks (RealPlayer/RealServer)	www.real.com
VDO (player/server)	www.vdo.net
Vivo (player)	www.vivo.com
Vosaic (player/server)	ww.vosaic.com

Hardware Requirements

Any Macintosh or Windows computer running a graphics-enabled web browser will be able to access the companion web site and follow the links listed on its pages. Since webcasting puts high demands on hardware and software, users planning to access webcast audio, video, and multimedia will require a relatively fast computer for best results. Macintosh users will need a PowerPC system with at least 32 MB of RAM and a 500 MB hard disk. Older 68040 Macs may access some forms of webcast audio, but they will not be able to reproduce high-quality sound or video. Windows users will need a Pentium-level system running at 133 MHz or faster, at least 16 MB of RAM, and a 1 GB hard drive. Windows 3 systems cannot support webcasting, but all recent Windows versions should work. Performance will increase substantially if faster (e.g., 400 MHz Pentium II) systems are used to receive webcasts. Playback of full-screen, full-motion video may require installing a separate hardware card. Check the webcast software vendor's site for more information.

Installing the Software

Recent versions of Netscape Communicator and Microsoft Internet Explorer 4 will automatically prompt you and provide the option of downloading the required Installer program for the media player. Upon receiving this prompt, save the Installer file to an easily found disk location. After downloading is complete, start the Installer by double-clicking on its icon, and follow the instructions. Users with older browsers will not be prompted to install the required software and may need to modify the browser's configuration files according to instructions provided by the software vendor. For the best webcast experience, these users should consider upgrading to Netscape Communicator (www.netscape.com) or Microsoft Internet Explorer 4 (www.microsoft.com/ie). Both browsers are available for free download from their respective web sites.

Many webcasts require that Java and JavaScript run on the user's system. These options are normally enabled by default. If they have been deactivated, they may be turned on again by selecting options in the "Preferences" menu of both browsers.

Using the Software

Most webcast audio and video players provide the following set of user controls:

- Buttons for starting and stopping the webcast
- Sliding controls for adjusting the sound intensity

- A graphic display indicating the connection speed
- A sliding graphic indicating how much of the webcast has already played
- Channel buttons leading to popular webcast content
- A "Save as…" option for copying the webcast media file to disk

By default, most webcast media players automatically determine the speed of the user's connection to the Internet and adjust their playback accordingly. If the Internet connection is of poor quality, it is often possible to manually reduce the connection speed. For example, a 28.8 modem user experiencing static or dropouts in webcast audio can change their connection speed to 14.4 to smooth playback. Note that audio/video quality decreases with slower connections. Changing to 14.4 modem speed may also improve playback on slower hardware (e.g., 68040 Macintosh or 486 Windows systems).

GLOSSARY

Active Server Pages (ASP) Programming standard developed by Microsoft to supply interactive features to web sites running on Windows computers.

Active Streaming Format (ASF) A replacement for Video for Windows (AVI), ASF provides a framework for delivering webcasts from Microsoft media servers. It also integrates and synchronizes sound and images into multimedia presentations.

Advanced Technology Attachment/Enhanced Integrated Drive Electronics (ATA/EIDE) Also known simply as Integrated Drive Electronics (IDE); a relatively inexpensive hard disk connector used by many computers. ATA/EIDE is generally slower than SCSI disks and more limited in the number of devices that may be connected to a single computer.

Ambient A form of webcast in which the recording device is left on to transmit real-world events without an attempt at scripting or storytelling. Examples of ambient webcasts include live video of famous traffic intersections, fish tanks, and bedrooms.

Analog Electronic equipment that directly records the features of audio or video signals instead of representing them digitally. All webcasts feature at least one analog-to-digital conversion.

Animacast Also known as a web 'toon, an animacast consists of moving pictures with drawn or rendered scenes, objects, and characters. Animacasts may be transmitted as video or with the use of web-friendly vector graphics.

Antialiasing A set of graphic techniques that blends the colors at the boundaries of two objects, creating a less jagged and more natural appearance on screen.

Application Programming Interface (API) Specialized set of programming standards and software tools designed to allow easy integration and data exchange among different programs. APIs are frequently used to integrate web and media servers with databases.

Asymmetric Digital Subscriber Line *See* Digital Subscriber Line.

Audiocast A webcast that consists of sound, spoken word, or music. Currently, the most common form of Internet webcast, an audiocast is relatively easy to produce and deliver. Unlike videocasts, relatively high-quality audiocasts may be received through standard consumer modems.

Authoring computers Specialized workstations that have the necessary hardware and software to edit audio, video, and multimedia for a webcast.

Bandwidth The amount of data transmitted over a network in a given time, usually measured in bits per second (bps).

Betacam video format A professional, high-definition 3/4" videotape format, betacam is commonly used in postproduction of film and video and has much higher quality than VHS or Hi-8 formats.

Bidirectional response Audio pickup mode characteristic of some microphones (such as ribbon microphones) in which maximum sensitivity occurs at 180-degree positions around the microphone head. For this reason, a bidirectional microphone mounted to pick up sound from a stage would also collect audience noise.

Bits per second (bps) A measure of bandwidth commonly used for Internet connections. Larger units are expressed as kilobits per second (kbps) and megabits per second (Mbps).

Bridge Short musical interlude used to connect two sections of a performance, such as instrumental music played between acts of a play.

Broadcast A strategy for information delivery in which a single identical message is sent to large numbers of end users at the same time. Broadcast is characteristic of traditional media such as radio or television, and Internet-based webcasts are a variant of this strategy.

Camcorder Compact video recording system consisting of a transducer that converts light into electrical signals and a device that copies the signal to tape.

Captioning Technology that overlays text onto an analog video signal. Captioning is generally not used in webcasting, since text may be provided on web pages or in associated multimedia applications.

Capture area The number of pixels used to convert an analog video signal into video format. For maximum resolution, the capture area should be two times the square of the number of scan lines in the video image.

Cardioid Highly directional microphone that picks up sound in a narrow space; useful in noisy environments and for recording individual performers.

CD-R Write-once computer data format compatible with CD-ROMs; frequently used to create CD-ROM and audio CD masters for duplication.

CD-RW Read-write computer data format compatible with CD-ROMs; often used to record webcast music for later offline performance.

Chaperone Member of the production team for live webcasts that allow online audience participation. A chaperone acts as a moderator, discussion leader, and crowd controller during the webcast.

Charge-Coupled Device (CCD) Specialized integrated circuit similar to RAM memory. Each storage unit on the chip is light sensitive and converts the local light intensity value to a number suitable for digital storage.

Chrominance Term used in video production that measures the relative intensities and saturation of primary colors (e.g., red, green, and blue).

Clearance The process of obtaining the right to showcase, broadcast, or otherwise use copyrighted material.

Click-through A measure of the number of users who select a banner ad on a web page, usually connected directly to the advertiser's site. A click-through is generally considered a more accurate measure of consumer interest than page loading or impressions.

Color The range of hues or light frequencies available on the computer or video screen. Electronic equipment typically builds color from a few primary colors (e.g., red, green, and blue). Digital systems and image files typically have a fixed number of colors, while analog systems such as videotape have continuous color variation.

Common Gateway Interface (CGI) Generic method for linking external programs with web servers. Commonly used to implement database connections and programs processing web-based fill-out forms.

Condenser Microphone that captures sound by measuring the electrical potential between a vibrating membrane and a charged backplate. Sound vibrations alter the voltage on the backplate, resulting in a small current.

Content developer A member of the webcast production team, this individual acquires and/or creates webcast programming and manages other individuals involved in content development. Duties may include scriptwriting, content selection, and choosing webcast software and formats used in the production.

Continuity A measure of how effectively all elements of a story or program are logically consistent with the original script or storyboard. Examples of continuity control include keeping clothes and hairstyles consistent from one scene to the next, even if they are shot out of sequence.

Contrast Also known as luminance, this parameter specifies the number of greys that exist between black and white within a video image. High-contrast images appear sharp with clearly defined edges, while low-contrast images have indistinct, fuzzy outlines.

Copyright The right of the owner and/or creator of content to control its use and distribution. Control includes regulating who makes copies, how many copies are made, and whether parts of the work may be used to create new works.

Cue card A piece of paper or screen (invisible to the audience) that lists the performers' spoken lines.

Cue sheet Used by the webcast recording engineer, this list details the entries and exits from the performance space by actors. Knowledge of these events allows the engineer to control lighting and sound and make smooth transitions between different phases of the performance.

Cutaway shot Film and video production technique in which the soundtrack continues while the video changes. A cutaway of a man speaking about baseball might start with a close-up of the narrator and then cut to scenes from individual games while the spoken track continues in the background.

Datacast A stream of numerical or symbolic information broadcast to the Internet. Depending on the implementation, a datacast may contain text, numbers, audio, video, or animation.

Data Over Cable Service Interface Specification (DOCSIS) Available at www.cablemodem.com, this emerging standard ensures compatibility among cable modems developed for end users and Internet access hardware used by cable operators.

Decibel (db) A logarithmic unit based on the minimum sound the human ear can hear. Sounds become painful above 90db.

Demographics Statistics tabulating external features of individuals and groups within a population, including age, height, gender, and income.

Diaphragm A component of a microphone consisting of a thin membrane vibrating in response to sound waves.

Digital Audio Tape (DAT) Audio recording system that uses 4mm tapes and drive mechanisms similar to those used by computer backup systems.

Digital Image Stabilization (DIS) Technology used by camcorders to automatically adjust for small camera movements, keeping the recorded image stationary.

Digital Subscriber Line (DSL) Technology that enables medium-speed Internet connections (0.1–10Mbps) over ordinary phone lines. Unlike modems and ISDN, DSL technologies bypass the older Public Switched Telephone Network (PSTN).

Digital Video (DV) A set of standards that implement direct digital encoding of video signals to tape or other storage devices. The professional version is called DVCpro, and the consumer version is called DVCcam. DV is likely to replace analog videotape formats such as VHS and Hi-8.

Digital Video Disc (DVD) Video storage technology using a disc similar in appearance to an audio CD or CD-ROM but with much higher storage capacity. Video signals are encoded using MPEG-2 compression. The DVD standard also incorporates interactive features and is directly compatible with current computer technology.

Digital Video Disc-Read Only Memory (DVD-ROM) A drive capable of reading data from a DVD videodisc. DVD-ROM may also read and display video directly from DVD video encoded with MPEG-2.

Director Individual responsible for scheduling and managing performances used in a webcast production. Responsibilities include making sure the necessary performers and props are available to shoot a scene, working with performers, and adjusting the script/screenplay as necessary.

Distance learning Remote education technology that beams televised classroom instruction directly to students. It contrasts with more recent online education initiatives that use interactive multimedia and that may not necessarily have a "live" instructor present.

Dithering Method used by digital computers to approximate color by interleaving individual pixels of two colors in a pattern. At a sufficient distance, the eye converts the dithered pattern to a third intermediate color.

DS1 *See* T1.

DS3 *See* T3.

Dynamic Microphone that collects sound through a diaphragm, connected to an electric coil surrounding a permanent magnet. Sound vibrations move the coil relative to the magnet and generate an alternating electric current. Dynamic microphones are often used to record large musical instruments such as drums.

Dynamic HyperText Markup Language (DHTML) Blanket name for a variety of software and programming techniques used to introduce interactivity into web pages. Common technologies used in DHTML include JavaScript and the <layers> HTML tag.

Electret A type of small condenser microphone containing a permanent charge on its backplate that eliminates the need for an external power supply. Electrets are often used in clip-on or lapel microphones.

Electronic Image Stabilization (EIS) Technology used by camcorders to automatically adjust for small camera movements, keeping the recorded image stationary.

Equalizer A sound processor that increases or decreases the volume of different frequencies within the audio signal. Equalizers can partly compensate for improperly recorded sound by enhancing a subset of high-, middle-, or low-frequency sounds.

Error rate On the Internet, a measurement of the percentage of data packets that reach their destinations. Some transmission protocols such as Transmission Control Protocol (TCP) enforce zero error rates, while others such as User Datagram Protocol (UDP) tolerate some loss of packets.

Fair use Exception to a copyright, which allows limited use of certain works without contacting the copyright owner. Examples of fair use may include short quotes in magazine reviews and educational events.

Feedback Self-amplification of a signal resulting in a very rapid, uncontrolled increase in intensity. Feedback often occurs between a microphone/loudspeaker pair, which reflect increasing volumes of sound between themselves.

Focal length Feature of camera lenses that measures the distance at which light is brought to a point. Focal length is determined by the curvature of the lens surface. Short focal lengths are useful for close-ups, while long focal lengths are used for imaging distant objects.

Format Summary of the specific physical parameters that make a particular information-bearing media unique. In a webcast, a format is defined by sampling rate, Internet bandwidth, data compression protocol, and required image or sound quality. Formats may also dictate a restricted set of content that is compatible with the physical parameters (e.g., "talking head" performances in low-bandwidth Internet video).

Gain Measurement of the range between the loudest and softest sound in an audio signal. High-gain audio sounds realistic, while low-gain audio may sound fuzzy or tinny.

Hand held Medium-sized microphone, often using ribbon technology, held by performers during a webcast or other broadcast event.

Harmonic frequency An audio frequency related by a standard mathematical formula to a primary tone. Acoustic instruments and the human voice have characteristic harmonics that act as "fingerprints" identifying them to a listener.

Hertz The measure of the frequency of an audio, video, or other signal expressed in cycles per second, abbreviated as Hz.

Hi-8 A medium-resolution analog video format that provides higher quality than VHS but lower than professional Beta. Hi-8 is popular for independent and multimedia film production.

HyperText Transfer Protocol (HTTP) The standard method used to send and receive signals over the web. HTTP streaming is a webcast that relies on the web server for delivering data streams. A separate media server is not used. HTTP streaming is simple to set up, but the webcast is generally of lower quality than one provided by a media server.

Hue A measure of the frequencies of light comprising part of a video image, usually expressed in fractions of a few primary colors used by the video display.

Infotainment Hybrid media form that blends entertainment and information. Examples of infotainment include films with extensive product placement, and infomercials, which promote products through a television talk show format.

Integrated Services Digital Network (ISDN) Digital data protocol running over phone lines and offering up to 128Kbps of bandwidth. ISDN is commonly used for Internet connections but may be supplanted by faster Digital Subscriber Line (DSL) and cable modem technologies.

Interactive Television (ITV) A series of strategies developed between 1980 and 1998 for converting broadcast television into a two-way, non-Internet medium. Generally designed as a proprietary system offering a smaller degree of user choice than the web.

Interactivity The degree to which a computer program or web site immediately responds to user activity. Examples of interactive features include an on-screen control that makes a noise when clicked upon with a mouse and web pages that automatically adjust displayed fonts when the user increases the size of the browser window.

Interlaced A video technology designed to reduce on-screen jerkiness. Each image frame sent forms a series of lines separated by dark areas. The next frame's lines fall within these dark areas, and the eye fuses both frames into a single image. The technique results in less screen flicker at low frame rates.

Internet Protocol (IP) Multicast Strategy for delivering webcasts over the Internet to a large number of users. In a multicast, a single media server sends its signals to a series of other media servers, which in turn relay signals to other media servers accessible to thousands or millions of Internet users. Multicast technology overcomes the bandwidth bottleneck that would occur if this data were streamed from a single location.

Internet Protocol Multicast Backbone (MBONE) An early, experimental implementation of IP multicast strategy, used to carry the first Internet webcasts in 1994 and 1995.

Internet radio A specialized form of Internet audiocast that delivers a constant stream of talk, news, or music in a manner similar to a radio station. Some Internet radio sites simply repurpose existing radio signals, while others have developed their own Internet-specific content.

Internet service provider (ISP) A company that offers Internet access and value-added services such as web hosting. ISPs frequently use portions of cable, phone, and satellite networks to implement their service, but they are distinct from these organizations.

Internet/web coordinator Sometimes referred to as the "webmaster," this individual's role in the webcast production team is to create and maintain any associated web sites. The Internet/web coordinator is also responsible for archiving webcast files for on-demand viewing.

Java Programming language developed by Sun Microsystems (www.sun.com). Individual programs are downloaded from a web site and are executed by the end-user's browser. Java brings increased interactivity to the web, allowing a simple, cross-platform technology for implementing new programs and linking legacy applications such as databases.

Jump cut A technique used in filmmaking that features abrupt transitions from one scene to another. The effect may be jarring and add suspense or danger to the story.

Lapel A small microphone, often using condenser technology, that is attached to clothing and usually hidden from view, allowing more natural conversations.

Laserdisc Sometimes referred to as a videodisc, a high-quality, read-only analog video format. Videodiscs provide higher image quality than conventional consumer videotape players, but they are likely to be replaced by DVD video in the near future.

Latency The time elapsed between a data request and actual receipt of data. Due to the nature of Internet communication, latency values may change during a webcast, requiring constant compensation by the media server and the end-user's player software.

Lavalier Medium-sized microphone hung around the neck of a performer. Not commonly used, since smaller lapel microphones can provide the same sound capture without the bulk.

Leased line Dedicated circuit rented from the phone company and left on at all times; often used to carry Internet traffic. Examples of leased lines include T1 (DS1) and T3 (DS3) connections.

Line conditioner Analog or digital equipment used by broadcasters to deliver high-quality audio over phone lines via non-Internet protocols. To condition the line, two devices similar to modems are installed at each end of a phone line, compensating for bad connections. Conditioned lines generally deliver higher audio quality than comparable Internet connections over the same connection.

Line-of-sight A form of wireless radio data transmission in which the sending and receiving antennas must lie in a straight line without intervening obstacles. Commonly used to send data for short distances (e.g., between building rooftops in metropolitan areas).

Load balancing A strategy for distributing a large number of Internet data requests over several media servers, routers, or other network hardware. Load balancing protocols also route data requests to the least-occupied server, thereby increasing efficiency. Generally more efficient and flexible than a single extremely fast media server.

Local Area Network (LAN) Network linking groups of computers, usually within several hundred feet of each other. Most networks use Ethernet protocol to implement a LAN. It may be interconnected to form a Wide Area Network (WAN), of which the Internet is the largest example.

Luminance Parameter, also known as contrast, that defines the overall amount of light delivered from a video image, and the range between the brightest and darkest areas of the image.

Many-to-many Mode for Internet communication in which any member of a group may forward a message that automatically echoes to everyone else in the group. Common examples of many-to-many include chat rooms and email-based discussion groups.

Marketing director Member of the webcast production team responsible for promoting the webcast in the online and offline worlds. Duties include posting to search engines, securing an audience of reviewers, and creating press releases for traditional media. The marketing director may also analyze statistics of visitor traffic for a webcast and correlate them with demographics or purchasing patterns.

Media server Specialized software and/or hardware that implements an efficient system for delivering webcast content streams. Media servers usually consist of fast, high-end computer hardware coupled with webcast software optimized to support multiple simultaneous data streams.

Metafile Used by some streaming media servers, this file points to several audio or video files holding the same content at different resolutions. The media server uses the metafile to find the individual media files and then chooses the best file for the available bandwidth and quality of Internet connection.

Meta tag HTML code written invisibly to a web page that may be accessed by search engines.

Microphone A broad class of transducing devices that convert sound energy into electrical current and/or digital data.

Mixing board Component of an audiocast production studio that accepts input from multiple microphones and sound processors, combining them into one or two output streams. Mixing boards are necessary for complex webcasts involving several microphones.

Motion Pictures Expert Group (MPEG) Set of protocols developed for delivering digital video over the Internet on CD-ROM/DVD discs and through satellite broadcast. CD-ROMs generally use MPEG-1, while DVD and satellite systems implement MPEG-2. MPEG-4 is an integrated video/multimedia format based on Apple Computer's QuickTime software.

Multicast *See* IP multicast.

Multipurpose Internet Mail Extension (MIME) A code that tells a web browser, email program, or other Internet software application how to handle a downloaded file; typically specifies which program should be used to open it.

Musical Instrument Digital Interface (MIDI) A digital signaling format used to control synthesizers. MIDI also defines a specialized Local Area Network (LAN) so that several electronic instruments may be controlled at the same time by the composer/performer.

Narrowcast Specialized type of broadcast that is delivered to a highly targeted, small audience, rather than to a large, general audience. Narrowcasts are typically used to address focused niche interest groups.

National Television Systems Committee (NTSC) Standard U.S. format for television signals used in video, containing 525 scan lines (480 visible) and running at a rate of 30 frames per second.

Netpublicity Set of methods used to promote content, goods, and services through the Internet, including registration in search engines, banner advertising, and email.

Network Access Point (NAP) Public center where Internet traffic is exchanged among Internet ISPs. Most public NAPs are crowded, so many ISPs make private peering arrangements with a subset of their peers to speed traffic.

Normalize An audio, video, or data processing strategy that sets the maximum value of the signal to an arbitrary value. Useful for making sure that a signal does not exceed the range of a software program or analog device.

Omnidirectional Microphone designed to have equal sensitivity to sound in all directions.

On-demand Webcast strategy that makes individual programs available for play at any time rather than confining them to a specific broadcast schedule.

One-to-many Strategy for exchanging information over the Internet in which a single sender supplies information to a large number of receivers. A common webcast form, it has many similarities to traditional radio and television broadcast.

Optical Carrier (OC) 3 Specialized high-speed data line used for the fastest Internet connections. It uses optical fiber instead of copper wire, and is generally restricted to metropolitan areas.

Optical Image Stabilization (OIS) Technology used by camcorders to automatically adjust for small camera movements, keeping the recorded image stationary.

Parabolic Highly directional microphone using a curved dish as an acoustic lens that focuses sound waves from a distant source.

Patch bay Switchboard module for plugging in the numerous input and output cables required to support complex audiocasts and videocasts.

Patch cords Short cables used to connect different pieces of audio or video equipment.

Performance rights A set of laws designed to compensate musicians when their work is performed or mechanically reproduced by others. The copyright owner receives royalties each time the work is performed.

Peripheral Component Interconnect (PCI) Bus Part of the underlying architecture of many computers, it connects memory, processors, and disk storage devices, and defines methods for exchanging information between them.

Phase Alternate Line (PAL) A European television broadcast format used in video, containing 625 horizontal scan lines (585 visible) and running at 25 frames per second.

Phasing Audio artifact in which sound waves bouncing off different areas of a performance space interfere with or reinforce each other, causing sudden increases and decreases in volume. The conflict of signals reduces overall sound quality.

Pick-up mechanism A mechanical device that converts sound into electrical energy (e.g., a microphone).

Plain Old Telephone Service (POTS) The standard phone circuits created within the Public Switched Telephone Network (PTSN) to route calls. Internet traffic may run as an overlay to POTS.

Player Generic term for end-user software that converts a webcast data stream into the appropriate audio, video, animation, or multimedia format.

Point-of-view The apparent location of the viewer within a videocast scene. Point-of-view is determined by the location of the camera during the performance.

Proc amp A signal processor used with analog video that increases contrast and improves color balance.

Producer Leader of the webcast production team who is responsible for developing and approving all aspects of the team's content, hardware, software, and management strategies.

Production team Group responsible for conceiving, developing, and implementing a webcast.

Psychographics Statistics recorded for individuals and populations that detail their interests, lifestyles, and desires rather than external demographic information such as age and income.

Public Switched Telephone Network (PSTN) Refers to the traditional telephone system in which the sender and receiver are connected through a dedicated circuit. This strategy is distinctly different from networks such as the Internet, in which multiple messages may move through a single circuit at the same time.

Push Generic term for the automated Internet delivery of filtered content to the user's computer. Push technology is similar to webcasting but does not require a continuous, real-time data stream for its operation. Push is useful for delivering some kinds of data, but it has yet to attain widespread acceptance for Internet content delivery.

Real Time Streaming Protocol (RTSP) A high-level webcast streaming format running on top of the lower-level RTP data transmission protocol. RSTP supports prioritizing transmission, typically giving webcast streams preferred access to the available bandwidth. This reduces latencies and sudden losses of the webcast data stream.

Real Time Transport Protocol (RTP) A variant of the UDP data transmission protocol used on the Internet. Like UDP, RTP allows occasional loss of individual data packets in order to avoid disrupting the flow of information. RTP is not useful for delivering software or files, but it is ideal for audio and video webcasting.

Reduced Instruction Set Computing (RISC) The central processing unit (CPU) found in Unix and Macintosh systems.

Redundant Array of Independent Disks (RAID) Specialized collections of hard disks that function together as a single, extremely fast hard disk. Data is written in parallel across the disk array. RAIDs are used to increase access speed and reliability.

Referrer log A record kept by many web servers that indicates the last site a surfer visited prior to loading a given web page. Useful for developers interested in discovering which web sites direct traffic to them.

Release A form provided by program developers and signed by an actor or other performer that gives producers the right to use the performer's likeness and performance in a production. Releases are commonly used to allow unlimited use of minor performances without paying royalties to an actor.

Repurposed Content originally developed for one medium that is modified for delivery via another medium (e.g., webcasts of standard radio and television programming).

Ribbon Microphone that uses a thin metal strip vibrating in response to sound. As the ribbon moves, it cuts across magnetic lines of force and generates a small electric field, which in turn induces an output current.

Saturation A measure of the percent of color relative to the maximum displayed in a video image. Images with low saturation appear pastel-like or gray, and highly saturated images may have unrealistic colors.

Scan lines A series of horizontal paths traced by the electron gun of a picture tube as it constructs a video image. The image quality of analog video signals is directly dependent on the number of scan lines used to construct the image.

Segue Transition from one scene to another. In webcasts, segues are typically used to link distinct scenes in a video or tie opening and closing credits to the main content.

Sequential Color and Memory (SECAM) A French broadcast television format used in video that is very similar to PAL.

Shooting script Specialized action plan developed from an original program script. The shooting script breaks up individual scenes into an order most convenient for the production. For example, the shooting script may specify that several unrelated scenes be shot at the same time to take advantage of equipment or weather conditions.

Shotgun Ultra-directional microphone placed in a long tube that limits sound collection to a narrow area of performance space. Useful in noisy environments, such as an interview conducted in a crowd.

Simulcast Generic term for live webcasts that collect and repurpose an existing broadcast signal. Simulcasts rely on the broadcasters for all aspects of production and attempt to duplicate them as closely as possible.

Small Computer Systems Interface (SCSI) High-speed standard for connecting hard drives and other data-intensive peripherals to computers, with throughputs ranging from 5 to 80Mbps. Faster and more robust than ATA/EIDE systems, SCSI also allows chaining of several peripherals to a single computer.

Society of Motion Picture and Television Engineers (SMPTE) Standards group that created a timecode system widely used to synchronize analog sound and video in the broadcasting world.

Spider A specialized Internet program that automatically visits web sites and collects information without the intervention of the site operators. Major search engines such as AltaVista (www.altavista.com) use spiders to locate and index pages on the web.

Storyboard Graphical technique for story/program development in which individual scenes are drawn and placed next to each other. This allows the screenwriter, producer, and director to examine the storyline for continuity and make adjustments in the script. Very commonly used for developing animated programming.

Streaming Term for Internet data that is delivered from server to end user in a steady flow, requiring a continuous Internet connection. This is distinct from web data transmission, in which individual page elements are requested and independently downloaded.

Synchronized Multimedia Integration Language (SMIL) A subset of the eXtensible Markup Language (XML) that allows simple creation of streaming multimedia files using an ordinary text editor. Competitive with proprietary streaming multimedia formats such as Microsoft's ASF.

T1 Also known as DS1, shorthand term for a leased-line providing 1.44Mbps of data in both directions. T1s are widely used to connect Local Area Networks (LANs) to the Internet. A single T1 can supply about 25 webcast data streams at consumer modem speeds (28.8–56Kbps).

T3 Also known as DS3, a very high-speed (45Mbps/sec) Internet connection running over multiple leased phone lines. Since costs increase rapidly with distance, DS3 lines are generally restricted to downtown metropolitan areas.

Technical engineer The member of the webcast production team responsible for ensuring that all the complex hardware and software needed to support the webcast operates correctly. The technical engineer supports lights, cameras, and microphones, computers, interface boards, and network connections.

Teleprompter An electronic cue card consisting of a television screen with scrolling text, visible to performers but invisible to the audience.

Time base corrector Analog video processing unit that fixes synchronization problems between the audio and video track of an analog video recording, usually using the SMPTE (Society of Motion Picture and Television Engineers) standard. Digital video editing software may also be used for this purpose.

Timecode Numerical markers written within analog audio and video storage formats that make it possible to precisely synchronize soundtracks with moving images. The SMPTE (Society of Motion Picture and Television Engineers) timecode standard is used for most video. High-end video editing software usually includes the capability to read and write timecodes to videotape.

Transducer A system that converts light into electrical signals, such as the charge-coupled devices (CCDs) found in camcorders.

Transmission Control Protocol (TCP) A very widely used Internet data transmission protocol. TCP enforces perfect data transmission and will rerequest individual data packets lost in transmission. Due to this feature, TCP transmissions on noisy data lines frequently experience long gaps or latencies within the transmission. For this reason, many webcast systems use more fault-tolerant protocols such as UDP.

Unicast Strategy for delivering webcast data streams in which a single media server supplies all connections. Since all users share a single server, this method suffers rapid losses in performance as the webcast audience grows large.

Unidirectional A type of microphone that receives sound equally well from all directions. No microphone is completely unidirectional, but many dynamic microphone systems come close.

Universal ADSL Working Group (UAWG) Standards organization developing a common framework for implementing high-speed Internet data transmission over ordinary phone lines.

Universal Power Supply (UPS) Hardware containing batteries and electronic circuits that protects computer hardware against momentary power surges and temporary power loss.

Universal Serial Bus (USB) Standard for implementing connections between Windows-based computers and peripheral devices including keyboards and microphones. USB devices are expected to be simpler to install than comparable products using the serial or parallel port of the computer.

User Datagram Protocol (UDP) An Internet data transmission protocol that tolerates some loss of data packets while keeping the overall flow of information smooth. UDP cannot be used to transmit files or software, but it is ideal for delivering audio and video information in a webcast data stream.

Vertical Blanking Interval (VBI) A short gap inserted between successive frames of programming in a television broadcast that is necessary for the eye to blend the frames into a moving image. It is possible to embed data in the broadcast signal during the VBI that may be used for one-way Internet connections or Interactive Television (ITV).

VHS A low-quality video format storing information using 1/2" inch tapes. A somewhat higher-quality form called Super-VHS (S-VHS) is also available. Supported by virtually all consumer videotape players.

Videocast A form of webcast that delivers video, often with synchronized sound. Videocasts superficially resemble television programming and have generated great interest within the traditional broadcast community.

Video Compact Disc (VCD) An older digital video format using CD-ROM disc technology and MPEG-1 compression. VCD quality is significantly lower than broadcast television and DVD.

Videodisc *See* laserdisc.

Video for Windows (AVI) Older video format specific to the Windows platform. Currently being replaced by the new Active Streaming Format (ASF) developed by Microsoft.

Virtual Reality Modeling Language (VRML) Standard for creating three-dimensional models and environments developed for the Internet. VRML offers a potential method for embedding webcasts in a virtual world-style multimedia interface.

Voice-over Technique used in audio and video broadcasting in which a spoken word track overlays a background track, often used to segue to a new scene or describe a scene's content.

Vosaic Datagram Protocol (VDP) Proprietary network transmission protocol developed by Vosaic (www.vosaic.com) for transmitting webcast data using its videocast products.

Watermarking Method used to uniquely tag documents, images, and other data so that unauthorized copies may be detected and tracked.

Wavelet An encoding and compression strategy well suited to the low bit-rate data transmissions characteristic of consumer modems. Wavelet technology may be used to deliver some types of webcast data more effectively than other standards such as MPEG.

Webcast Type of Internet data transmission delivered using a steady data stream, closely resembling traditional broadcast via radio and television.

Wide Area Network (WAN) A collection of Local Area Networks (LANs) forming a larger network (e.g., the Internet).

Wireless Group of related technologies that deliver Internet and other data via radio transmitters and receivers.

Wordcast Webcast consisting of a real-time stream of text, usually transcribed from a live speech or conversation. Hardware and software requirements are modest relative to other forms of webcast.

INDEX

X